7—

7— 12 99

—WILL—

More than a Pilot

More than a Pilot

Don McVicar

Illustrated by L. R. Williams

Airlife
ENGLAND

ISBN 0 906393 67 1

First published 1986
by Airlife Publishing Ltd.

Printed in England by Livesey Ltd., Shrewsbury.

Airlife Publishing Ltd.

7 St. John's Hill, Shrewsbury, England.

Contents

Preface

My books have covered a long span of aviation history. Sometimes I have wondered if the effort was all worthwhile. But Colonel Charles Lindbergh reassured me in his foreword to Anne Morrow Lindbergh's book *Listen! the Wind*, published in 1938. He said:

'This book is about a period in aviation which is now gone, but which was probably more interesting than any the future will bring. As time passes, the perfection of machinery tends to insulate man from contact with the elements in which he lives. The "stratosphere" planes of the future will cross the ocean without any sense of the water below. Like a train tunneling through a mountain, they will be aloof from both the problems and the beauty of the earth's surface. Only the vibration of the engines will impress the senses of the traveller with his movement through the air. Wind and heat and moonlight takeoffs will be of no concern to the transatlantic passenger. His only contact with these elements will lie in accounts such as this book contains.'

And, I hope, mine too.

D. McVicar

Chapter 1
Roamin' in the Gloamin'

I smiled with satisfaction as I replaced my circular slide rule in my shirt pocket. It had told me that our sleek Beech Bonanza was making an impressive three miles per minute as it streaked across the plains of Indiana far below. We were about to run off the western edge of our navigational chart, so I looked across at my cockpit companion who had the next multi-coloured sheet ready. Loretta's face was solemn as she exchanged the maps because she took her duties as assistant navigator very seriously. In addition I had taught her to hold an altitude and course as well as any automatic pilot. On the ground she performed other functions with equal skill, making her an invaluable companion.

Just 91 minutes ago we had left the noise, the dust, the surging crowds and the bone-chilling excitement of the 1948 National Air Races at Cleveland, Ohio. There we had watched formation flying, parachute jumpers and daring pilots shaving pylons during the closed-course speed races. It was a bitter-sweet visit for me as we watched the contestants flash across the finish line in the cross-country Bendix Trophy race, because I was not one of them. A blown engine near Wichita, Kansas had forced my de Havilland Mosquito out of contention.

While serving with Royal Air Force Ferry Command in World War II, I had flown the swift agile Mosquito bomber for many hours. It had been designed without armament, relying solely on its outstanding speed to evade Luftwaffe fighters, and the novel idea had been a success. As the first foreign entrant in the race I had been sure it would defeat the North American Mustangs which were cleaning up in the gruelling race. Lacking a wealthy sponsor I had used my own company,

World-Wide Aviation, to carry our green maple leaf.

I had bought two Mosquitoes from Canada's War Assets, then sold one to an American, Jesse Stallings, to help finance the conversion of the other one. Jesse had raced under American colours, of course, and had been able to start the race from Long Beach, California, and although he wasn't in the early finishers, at least he *had* finished. I certainly didn't begrudge him his victory, but I still wondered why fate had made me sell him the Mosquito which had stayed the course while the one I had kept for myself had let me down.

Lacking hangar space we worked outside on the ramp at Dorval airport that summer. We had overcome many problems while changing the wooden aircraft from a bomber to a racer. Military bomb shackles, armour plate and radio had to be stripped out to save weight. Just one oxygen tank instead of four, and so on. I calculated the Rolls-Royce Merlins would last at power settings of full throttle and 2,850 rpm, far above the wartime maximum allowable for a long cruise. This would allow me to average better than 400 mph true airspeed at altitude from the shores of the Pacific to the shores of Lake Erie. And 400 mph was the minimum necessary to beat Paul Mantz and the other Mustang entries. Extra gas tanks to feed the thirsty Merlins filled the bomb bay and the nose, with the cockpit in between as sort of meat in a gas sandwich. We sprayed her with a coat of 'Diana Cream' trimmed with bright 'Stinson Green' and now, without her drab wartime camouflage, her truly beautiful lines were enhanced.

Our conversion problems seemed major, but they turned out to be minor compared to those encountered with the Department of Transport, Canada's aviation regulatory body. Numerous bureaucrats thought that military aircraft, so essential and well-proven in war, should be allowed to rot on the ground in times of peace. Defeated at the local Montreal DOT level, I flew to Ottawa and tramped through the maze of the corridors of power in search of some kind of a flight permit. A variety of excuses which I considered to be weak and weasely finally made me blow my stack. I knew Stallings had *his* permit, so I told them that if they didn't let me race under Canadian colours, why, damn it, I'd race under American ones; and, furthermore, when I won the Bendix I wouldn't be shy about telling the world why I'd flown under the stars and bars instead of the maple leaf. The threat worked. Registration

CF-FZG and a racing permit were granted, but in the process I may have accumulated more than my share of powerful enemies.

The paper-work having been disposed of, it was time to check the Mossie out. With my Rolls-Royce expert engineer Tommy Colahan on board I made a control-tower condoned pass at 'nought' feet at Dorval at a red-hot 465 mph on the clock. The noise and the vibration were beyond anything we'd ever experienced before, but the Mossie took it and checked out perfectly when we landed to some loyal fans' applause. Bendix, here we come! Yanks watch out!

But all the delays made it impossible to arrive 48 hours before the start, for the usual impounding of the contestant's aircraft. Paul Mantz, head of the race committee, put it to the boys — and Jacqueline Cochrane. They all said, hell, don't worry, just get here for the start. Good sports indeed. Still, the pressure was really on as I set out for Buffalo to clear US Customs. After we landed, Colahan immediately proved his worth by working all night, aided by local volunteers, to fix carburettor, exhaust stack and sundry other defects which almost grounded us. The take-off from Buffalo the next afternoon seemed to take forever and when we landed at Wichita in Kansas we found a large piece of the exhaust manifold had burned off with the high power I was pulling. With the aid of some friends from Beechcraft and an ace welder who worked all night, refusing any payment, we got that all glued back together again.

Even in the cool air of the dawn the take-off from Wichita, 1,370 feet above sea-level, made the Buffalo take-off look like a breeze. But as I got the landing gear up and the Mossie started to climb away strongly it looked as if all our troubles were behind us. Fools! This feeling of euphoria soon vanished as the starboard engine began to run so roughly that I was sure it would jump out of its mount. At the same time an ominous streak of black oil appeared on the cowling. Black shows up vividly against cream. It was time for corrective action. But I knew that if I feathered the propeller all my dreams would be finished. So it was with great reluctance, and perhaps too slowly, that I reached up and punched the red button. The blades turned sideways on and the engine stopped vibrating as I cranked on rudder trim; but with our massive overload and no way of jettisoning the gas the sensitive aircraft felt as if it was on the razor's edge of a stall — a stall which could turn into a fatal spin. The Mosquito's single-engined safety speed was the highest of any warplane at 200 mph, so it took a lot of luck, and maybe some skill, before we made it back to Wichita's long runway. We had both decided to ride the stricken racer down, rather than hitting the silk. Intent on getting onto the airport and then staying there, I came in a bit too fast and made the worst bounce in my whole flying career. But I managed an almost miraculous recovery to a perfect three-pointer, and in that attitude the Mossie was a perfect lady.

After I had shut down and climbed out I looked at her and wondered if it was possible that an aircraft could be schizophrenic, like some people I knew.

Together, Colahan and I unfastened the Zues fasteners holding the bottom panel of the failed engine. It was strangely heavy. When we set it on the ground we could see why. It was loaded with fragments of metal. A connecting rod had failed and the broken end had been flailing around inside the case, intent on destroying the engine. We stared at one another, speechless, both realizing that just a few more seconds' delay in feathering would likely have resulted in the nose case separating. Then the prop turning at almost 3,000 revolutions like a mad banshee would have smashed through the thin plywood of the cockpit. We both could well have been sliced up like pieces of bologna under a butcher's carving knife.

As the realization of total defeat hit me with stunning force the fact that we had both survived took some of the sting out of our situation. Some of the sting, that is. Not a lot, but even a little helps. I rented a Bonanza that night so that we could get to the Cleveland races in time, as no airline could help. There we met a Dak full of rooters, including Loretta, who had come from Montreal to see their hero zip across the finish line, in first place, of course. We were all bitterly disappointed, and the Dak, the faithful fans and Colahan went back home after assuring me it had been a good effort, and, famous last words, 'wait 'til next year.'

So now I was returning the rented Bonanza to Wichita, where a brand-new Canadian-registered one was waiting to be delivered to an anxious buyer at the Westinghouse factory at Hamilton, Ontario. As we made our way westward in the late afternoon, Mother Nature did her best to sooth my wounded pride with a spectacular display of heavenly fireworks.

Every pilot is privileged to see many memorable sunsets, but this one was especially glorious. I looked over at my copilot/navigator/stewardess to make sure she wasn't missing the display. I needn't have worried. Her eyes were fixed and her mouth was open just a bit, in awe. As the sun slid below the distant purple horizon it lighted up some stratus clouds to an ethereal coppery-yellow glow. Suddenly, random shafts of yellow light erupted like the heavenly spokes of some giant wheel and illuminated the darkening sky for a few brief seconds. Then, with dramatic suddenness the display was over and the darkness of night began to encompass us. A mile or so below, previously invisible automobiles revealed themselves by two tiny 'V' beams of whiteness as home-bound drivers turned on their headlights. A wildly waving bright white searchlight called urgent attention to a hurtling locomotive, warning drivers that instant demolition awaited their cars at level crossings. At the same time another powerful fixed beam illuminated the twin ribbons of steel for the engineer, although it was probably wishful thinking to believe that a heavy train could stop within the half-mile tunnel thrown by the headlight. Across the wide prairie, scattered pinpoints of light appeared as farmers and others relaxed after their labours. It somehow was all very reassuring although I suspected that if the ground people ever bothered to look up they probably thought aviators were crazy. Perhaps so.

A gentle turn avoided a towering cumulus with vestiges of a high-altitude anvil top. The Bonanza was sweetly sensitive on its flight controls and suddenly the memory returned of how the Mosquito performed in exactly the same way. Once again the bitter memory of my recent defeat flooded back, and it was with some effort that I tried to put the past out of my mind. But I suppose the fact that I had sold to my Bendix competitor, Jesse Stallings, an American Airlines pilot, the Mosquito which had run perfectly to the finish line, while I kept its mate, would never be forgotten. Loretta was watching me, probably reading my mind, which she had a disconcerting habit of doing. She snapped me out of my gloomy thoughts by pointing a slim, red-nailed finger at the altimeter which I had allowed to drift down from our chosen altitude. As I corrected with a gentle pull on the control wheel the sun, in a final futile effort to hold back the night, illuminated the top of the towering cu.nim. The ice-cream-shaped cone with its sharply defined temporary whiteness contrasted dramatically with the jet-black pillar below.

We were in that period of the day called twilight, which the Scots call 'the gloaming.' The words of the old ballad which Sir Harry Lauder used to sing with so much gusto drifted through my mind.

'Roamin' in the gloamin' on the bonny banks o' Clyde,
Roamin' in the gloamin' wi' my lassie by my side.
When the sun has gone to rest,
That's the time that I love best.
Oh, it's lovely roamin' in the gloamin'.'

The 'bonny banks o' Clyde' were now a half a world away. They were where I had delivered three Catalina flying boats for Royal Air Force Ferry Command, during a war which now seemed more than half a lifetime distant.

More to the point, 'roamin' in the gloamin' ' isn't very romantic without 'my lassie by my side.' Just as flying solo is pretty lonely. But I had *my* lassie by my side as Loretta and I flew together into the sunset, like in the movies. She was completely relaxed with her chin cupped in her hand and her elbow resting on the Bonanza's convenient arm rest. Her sexy legs were encased in a pair of well-cut slacks, which helped me to concentrate on my flying. Her jet-black hair was bound by a white silk scarf, making a striking contrast. She had removed the amber-coloured 'Ray-Ban' glasses which she, in common with a lot of other copilots, thought added to the costume of authentic aviators. Now I could see her green-blue eyes were thoughtful. They could change colour with her moods, I was certain. Now they were dark green, at peace. I motioned as if I were going to flip over the control column, which meant it was her turn to fly. Her full scarlet lips curved in a charming smile as she shook her head. Obviously not in the mood. There was no point in arguing as this was no ordinary copilot subject to the Captain's orders. No sir! So I slouched down, totally relaxed, with both feet flat on the floor. One finger and a thumb on the control wheel gave me perfect control even without the rudder. Only the Bonanza was like that.

As the immense dome comprising outer space changed from blue to black a few stars which the ancients had called 'heavenly bodies' began to twinkle cheerfully. Loretta murmured the old incantation:

'Star light, star bright, the first star I see tonight,
I wish I may, I wish I might
Have the wish I wish tonight.'

She turned to me with a question: 'What is that really bright star on the horizon I'm wishing on? And no, I won't tell you my wish, it's bad luck.'

Knowing her, I believed her wish would have something to do with my happiness so I replied with appropriate gravity, almost like a college professor. 'It's not a star at all, although most people call it the 'Evening star'.' It's also called the 'Morning star' when it reappears on the other side of the Earth. Many an airman over the North Atlantic has mistaken its bright light for a beacon.'

She pouted a little as she replied, 'Well, what is it then, Mr Ace Navigator?'

I suddenly realized that maybe my little lecture had been a tad heavy, so I tried to make amends. 'It's the planet Venus. The one the Romans called the Goddess of Love. So you wishing on it is really appropriate for us, eh?'

'Oh my, yes,' she replied, at the same time giving my bare forearm a fond pat which did my blood pressure no good at all. To return my mind to the business at hand I reached for the electric propeller control switch and set the revolutions a tiny bit lower, so now the wooden prop was in perfect harmony with the engine, the airframe and my heart's left ventricle. Or possibly it was my left testicle.

Then, a few thousand feet higher, an occulting red light drifted across our course with deceptive slowness. It was probably a scheduled airliner carrying some passengers paired in love as we were. I was certain that none of the girls aboard could compare with the heavenly body close by my side. Even as I had the thought her warm flank seemed to respond, promising pleasure when we got to the privacy of our hotel room.

To continue the pleasant mood I switched the Motorola transceiver from the aviation communications band to the broadcast band and selected a station which was featuring a romantic ballad. There were dozens available at our altitude. The loudspeaker in the cabin roof wafted the melody to us without the uncomfortable headphones necessary in other more noisy aircraft. The announcer switched to the popular 'I Don't Want a Ricochet Romance', which made me reflect it had not been easy to convince Loretta I was really the man she should have. A female with her attributes could flick her finger and any red-blooded pilot would come a-running. I remembered Captain George Evans from St. Louis, Missouri, where we would soon be landing for fuel, a sort of odd coincidence. He had appreciated her good looks and pleasant personality a long time ago, just as I had. But she had chosen him, which unfortunately put her right off limits for me, because Evans was my friend and flying buddy in Ferry Command. After Evans had been killed while flying a Consolidated RY3 over the North Atlantic she had taken it very badly and gone into seclusion. I had done what I could to convince her that life must go on, and she'd granted me the pleasure of her company occasionally. She also had taken a liking to Captain Jacques Charmoz, who was really tough competition. He was a former champion Olympic skier nicknamed 'the Blue Devil.' What woman could resist a man described like that? He had flashing Gallic eyes and perfect manners that no Canadian oaf like me could hope to rival. Eventually he had gone away; forever, I hoped. But he had been replaced by one of the Norwegians who had escaped when the Nazis took over his country. This blond menace had been called overseas finally, so it was through sheer patience and perseverance that I had finally knocked off my opposition.

While admitting it really was none of my business, I tried to inquire into how I stacked up with her previous lovers. I never did find out, as her nimble brain and quick tongue was too much for any mere man.

There was one time when I really goofed. We had gone to the 'Tic Toc' with Clyde Pangborn, a fellow Ferry Command pilot who was also world famous for his many pioneering flights. I'd had a few drinks and somehow Pank talked me into thinking the night club singer had eyes only for me. He was a smoothy in the air and on the ground, that man.

But by the time her act was over the singer had changed her mind, if indeed she had ever considered me. As usual, it was dawn when the club closed and somehow or other Loretta and the pioneering airman had disappeared, and I was left looking at an empty table. When I questioned Loretta closely later she reported that Pangborn had acted at all times like a perfect gentleman, with the implication that I had not always acted as such. On the defensive in the first moment of the argument! I decided, not for the last time, to drop the subject and accept defeat.

With Loretta, the world seemed a little brighter for me. I considered myself a pragmatic, cautious airman who figured the odds carefully before each flight. I had to be, in order to survive. In an aircraft an unexpected noise could mean a possible fatal emergency, and the smell of burning oil or insulation made me, like most airmen, rigid with apprehension. Maybe even break into a cold sweat. So having a slightly flaky, carefree person on board relieved my tension. After a tough flight her company on the ground was greatly to be desired. A truly dual-purpose person!

We refuelled at St. Louis and pressed on directly to Wichita, flying over some black and desolate country, the Ozark mountains, as we did so. In the hotel room at the end of a long, long day my reward was all I had dreamed of.

The next morning I turned in the Bonanza, just like a Hertz Rent-a-car, and made sure my Mosquito was being well looked after. In the grey dawn the feathered starboard propeller, stark, black and ominous, reminded me of a grave marker, which it well could have been for Colahan and me. It was hard to realize my forced landing had occurred only four days ago. So much had happened that it seemed more like four weeks. I opened the belly hatch, installed the metal ladder and climbed in, letting Loretta sit beside me. The cramped, rough English interior of the warplane made her shudder. So I retrieved my mike, earphones and parachute and we both climbed out. I

made sure the little hatch was locked and said to Loretta,
'Maybe next year.'

She replied tersely, 'Maybe *not* next year.'

I shrugged my shoulders. There didn't seem to be a good
answer for that one.

The fixed-base operator who would look after the Mosquito
had his company car drive us over to the Beechcraft factory.
There we signed for a brand-new Bonanza CF-FZH — and
had a hard time tearing ourselves away from the friendly Beech
people, who were most sympathetic about my failure. So it was
late in the afternoon when we got away to cash in on the urgent
invitation of my Bendix rival, Jesse Stallings. He had painted
the Mosquito I'd sold him a sparkling white with maroon trim.
He'd named it 'Miss Marta' after his recently acquired baby
girl and it carried American CAA registration N66313. Both
Loretta and I thought that our Mosquito's paint job was
superior, but then, maybe we were a little biased. I still thought
Stallings should have won, but he hadn't installed as much
extra gas as I'd done, and had throttled back when he was in
the lead over Denver when he realized his enormous
consumption. So he had at least finished and I . . . I put that
thought out of my mind once again.

The new Bonanza had all those new-aircraft smells, just like
an automobile's new-car smells. Once inhaled, never
forgotten. The engine and prop were in perfect tune as we flew
along, but, of course, the sun had set when we landed at
Springfield, Missouri, for gas. The cabin crew had to be
refuelled too, and we had a pair of Cokes and hamburgers,
pretty well staple diet for any aviators on cross-country flights.
Away again, with landing lights piercing the darkness, we
roared down the long runway and climbed to a cool altitude.
Then the broad Mississippi passed below with just tiny moving
pinpoints of light on the black water to indicate the tug boats
which were pushing barges full of the nation's goods. Mark
Twain's *Tom Sawyer* and *Huckleberry Finn* had given me a
good understanding of life on the muddy river. No doubt the
sons of the picturesque pilots he had described so well were
even now relying on their memories to negotiate the twist and
turns of 'Old Man River', its ever-changing channels and
dangerous sandbanks.

It was a comfortable feeling to be safe in the air.

After we crossed the wide river I realized we were in

Tennessee airspace, with Kentucky to the north and Mississippi, Alabama and Georgia to the south. I had studied the war between the States and now, at last, I was going to visit a genuine Southern family. But how would they receive a Canadian? Would I be classed as a 'Damnyankee'? Always spoken with venom and as one word, of course. Or would Canada's British connection make me a friend? One who had run the Union blockade, sort of? I was just a little nervous at being invited into a Southerner's home. Loretta did not appear to be in the least worried, however, as she had met Stallings at the Air Races and had been completely charmed by his courtly manner.

As we entered the landing pattern at Nashville's Berry Field a friendly voice gave us landing clearance. Once on the ground the tower controller wished us welcome and directed us to a hangar at the east side of the field where Stallings' Capitol Airways was based. This was reassuring because it meant that someone wanted to roll out the welcome mat. As I taxied along with the aid of the Bonanza's powerful landing lights I remembered that Stallings had been a senior American Airlines Captain with experience going back to before the war. Then, during the war, he had flown with American Airlines' Military Division under the USAAF's Air Transport Command. He had logged many ocean crossings to Prestwick and Africa, and I remembered he had told me that he loved the Douglas C54 but hated to fly the heavy Consolidated C87 with its insensitive flight controls. The C87 was the passenger version of the Liberator B24. I had to agree with him.

Ahead, two flashlights wielded by a line boy were making welcoming white tracings in the darkness, and soon we were parked. I tried to remember what I knew about Stallings' new venture, away from the cockpit of a scheduled airline protected by a powerful union, into a venturesome project much like mine in Montreal. He had told me he had bought out the local fixed-base operator and his hangar, then set to work getting more charters for his twin-engined Beech 18s. A lot of his work was shuttling around the bands for which Nashville's Grand Ole Opry was famous. Most Country and Western music performers called Nashville home base. One sidelight he mentioned was that a jug of corn whiskey accompanied many of his charter flights. The musicians had to have something to mix with their Branch water, he said with a grin. Also he had told me that American Airlines were selling fully equipped Douglas DC3s for $10,000 each, which we both agreed was a real bargain. The airline didn't see it that way, however, and took full-page ads in many magazines telling their customers that the age of the stage-coach was over and that the new Convair 240s with pressurized cabins were the only way to fly. Undoubtedly they were right, but a DC3 at ten grand could still compete against a 240 at half a million or so. Anyway, Stallings had bought two of the reliable DC3s and was going to start not only a bigger charter operation but also a scheduled set-up between the large cities of Tennessee. Under the laws of the USA the Civil Aeronautics Board did not have the authority to force him to apply for a licence which would be fought vigorously by the established 'Big Four' scheduled airlines of United, TWA, Eastern, and his old employer, American. This was because his flight route was 'intrastate', all within the boundaries of Tennessee. I felt a pang of jealousy as I thought of World-Wide's two DC3s lying idle because of the Canadian Air Transport Board's policy. That government body would never, ever, license an air carrier based at Montreal which would compete with the Crown Corporation called Trans-Canada Air Lines. It reeked of Communism, or maybe Socialism, and it sure wasn't free enterprise.

But now, as the engine chattered to a stop and the flashing wooden disc of the prop disappeared, I leaned over and opened the cabin door on Loretta's side. It was a feature of the little aircraft I didn't like. The handle was very difficult to turn as it forced two steel rods into the outer doorframe to secure the somewhat flimsy door. After it swung open Stallings' face sporting his lopsided grin instantly appeared and he helped my copilot out and down the sloping wing, not forgetting to guide her foot onto the retractable step. As she touched the tarmac she interrupted his speech of welcome by throwing her arms around his neck and planting an enthusiastic kiss on his cheek. For a moment he seemed embarrassed, then he gave her a hearty hug which made her cry out and she laughingly said he was breaking her ribs. He released her and I joined them, whereupon he gave me a bone-crushing handshake. We stood in the circle of light shed by a spot on his hangar and it was very apparent that if Captain Stallings had anything to do with it our visit to his city would be a very pleasant one.

Chapter 2
Southern Comfort

As we drove along the rather narrow winding roads of the hilly city both Loretta and I began to relax after our hectic week. Stallings was a careful driver who pointed out the sights to us just as he would have to any friends of his whom he had invited to his home. But we were sure that we were among a lucky few to be introduced to the rather closed society typical of a Southern city. Stallings had been quiet for several minutes and I sensed he had something on his mind. He turned towards me to make his message more impressive and said, his voice low, 'You know, Don, there's one thing that bothers me, and I apologize for mentioning it because it's really none of my business.'

I was a little startled but answered quickly, 'Hell, Jesse, you know you can say anything you want before Loretta and me.'

'She has something to do with it too. What I'm really trying to say is that you've been flying that Bonanza of yours a lot on instruments, and at night too. Am I right?'

I scratched my cheek, for a moment at a loss for words, then said, 'You're right, of course, but if you think the engine is going to quit, you've gotta admit the odds are pretty long against a total failure.' At the same time I could sense Loretta tensing up. She had faith in my judgement until now. And here was a good friend warning me. But she didn't say anything.

'Well, Don, I guess flying on instruments is all right if you have the skill, but,' he slowed again to emphasize his message, 'night goes clear to the ground.'

'True enough,' I replied, but not making any promises to stop what he thought was a dangerous practice. But as a sort of token agreement with myself I decided that if the sun had set I wouldn't take off, because, yes indeed, night *did* go clear to the ground, with total blackout during a forced landing, But, I decided, if the sun set while we were *in the air,* well, we'd just continue to our destination. That would come under the heading of an act of God over which I had no control. Talk about mixed-up thinking!

Then there was one of those unexpected pauses in the conversation, and I thought that if I wanted to break the awkward silence I could ask Stallings about Cyndy Lee, the beautiful redheaded American Airlines stewardess I'd met during the war when I'd done a Communications Squad Hudson flight to Berry Field. Surely Stallings would have met her if they were both based at Nashville. I opened my mouth and started to say, 'Jesse, do you happen to remember . . .' Suddenly I realized that this would be a very insane subject to bring up with Loretta sitting beside me, so I gulped and again there was an awkward pause in the conversation.

'What were you saying, dear?' Loretta said sweetly, but I could sense an undercurrent of antagonism there. Damn all women and their extra-sensory perception anyway!

'I wanted to know if Jesse remembered that the USAAF had a big heavy-bomber training base at Sewart Field during the war. It's near Smyrna about 30 miles east of here and they flew Liberators.' This remarkable bit of improvisation seemed to satisfy Loretta, although what hold she had over me for a romance long before we met would have confused any good psychiatrist, just as it confused me.

'Yes, indeed,' Stallings came back quickly and the moment passed. 'I certainly do remember. They turned out four-engined pilots hot and heavy. We were always careful around Smyrna when we flew the airline. There were droves of the beasts in the air night and day.' He slowed down and then turned up a long driveway to his home, which was a two-storey brick and wood house painted shining white with blue trim. There was a faint aromatic smell of burning leaves in the air and the porch lights were ablaze to welcome us, and then his wife Anne appeared to wave us in. It was all we had dreamed of Southern hospitality, and somehow right then and there I was determined that the McVicars and the Stallings would be friends for life. And so it came to be.

We carried our luggage up to a plainly furnished spotless bedroom and admired the big four-poster bed with a soft eiderdown quilt. After we had washed up we went downstairs and ate the snack Anne had thoughtfully prepared, then sat around the living room in front of a bright blaze in the stone fireplace. Soon the ladies started to exchange confidences and Stallings and I reverted to type. Which is to say we started to talk about aviation. I told him about my hairy forced landing at Wichita on one engine and he nodded, obviously impressed.

Then, possibly urged on by the healthy shot of Jack Daniels finest Bourbon he had poured for each of us, he said: 'Don, do you remember in Dorval when I said I didn't need to do a landing with an instructor, and that the Mossie was just another airplane?'

'Sure do. I was pretty impressed.'

'Well, my friend, that Mossie taught me a lesson. It isn't just another airplane, because it got away from me on my first landing in Ohio.'

I sat up, shocked. 'Did you wreck it?'

'No, but I did a pretty good ground loop. Those hand operated air-brakes are real tricky.' He paused, then said: 'And seeing as I'm levelling with you, the damn thing almost got away from me on take-off in the race.'

I wanted to soothe his feelings so I said: 'Well, to tell you the truth she snapped at me a couple of times. Anyone who tells you he's never had a close one with a Mossie is a damn liar.'

He grinned at me. Obviously just a few words from another veteran had had the desired effect. 'You know, I was winning that race, well ahead of Paul Mantz and the rest of the Mustangs until I was just near Denver. Then I checked my gas and realized I'd run out unless I throttled back. So I pulled the power back to about plus 4 and 2400 rpm and coasted in, so that at least I finished in the money. I sure wish I'd had a set of those external wing tanks. That might have made the difference, because we didn't have as much gas in the bomb bay as you did.'

'Well, we just couldn't get those slipper tanks, Jesse. And besides, an RAF Group Captain who flew a Photo Mossie to a speed record from London to South Africa told us that they slow you down a good 20 miles.'

He swirled his drink around in his glass as he worked out the arithmetic, then smiled and said, 'Well, it's over now and I'm glad I did it. What do you think, Anne?'

Anne took a long time to answer, then said: 'I think anyone who flies a Mossie is crazy.' She pronounced Mossie as

'Mausie' in her deep Alabama accent, and I caught Loretta nodding her head. So now the magic of the evening was shattered. We drained our drinks and climbed the polished hardwood stairs to our respective beds, wishing each other a pleasant sleep and promising more stories tomorrow.

The next morning I was lying in bed, wondering why love under an eiderdown quilt was so satisfying, when I heard a strange voice. 'How yo want yo' aigs this mornin' Mistah Stallins?' it softly cried from downstairs.

'Sunny side up, please, Laurell,' he answered, then called through to me, 'What about you, Don' I assured him that sunny side up was fine with me, and he passed the message to his housekeeper in the kitchen.

After washing and dressing I joined my host in the dining room, where a silver pot of aromatic coffee invited an immediate cure for a slight hangover. I had just poured the first cup when Laurell came bustling in with a generous helping of eggs and back bacon. We were introduced and she sort of curtsied, and in return I sort of bowed.

When I first saw her I was instantly reminded of Scarlett O'Hara's 'Mammy', as described in *Gone with the Wind,* the famous Southern plantation and Civil War novel by Margaret Mitchell. She wore a grey uniform with a white apron and a maid's cap and her figure was plump and sturdy. Her skin was purest African, shining black, and glistening white teeth split her round face in a friendly smile. Although slavery had been abolished many generations ago I felt that she and the Stallings were equally loyal to each other. She obviously was proud to be the housekeeper and cook for the Stallings and he was equally proud to be able to introduce me to her.

Soon we were joined at the table by tiny brown-haired 'Miss Marta', who was just learning how to navigate the steep stairs. It was gravely explained to me that the Mosquito named 'Miss Marta' was so called because the cute little girl had yet to master the pronunciation of 'Martha'. Of Anne and my bedmate there was no sign. It was apparent that they weren't in the least interested in visiting the airport with us. This decision on their part failed to elicit any opposition from us, and so we talked about the Air Races as we drove along. We both agreed that possibly the most thrilling part of the Thompson closed-course unlimited power race was when Cook Cleland's Goodyear F2G Corsair with the monster 4,000 horsepower Pratt and Whitney engine had begun to shed cowling and exhaust manifold parts. Or maybe it was when Charles Brown had to force-land on the nineteenth lap of the twenty-lap race when the Allison engine in his Bell P39 faltered. We both agreed that the addition of the midget racers was interesting, and that the Kendall AT6 race for women only was a good thing. But we differed on whether the presence of the military was proper. Stallings said that overall they did a lot for the meet, but I thought that the Government-sponsored contestants took away a lot of the glory from the men who made it on their own.

I admitted that the jet-powered aircraft were faster, but on the other hand the loud high-pitched whine and the stink of the turbines were damned annoying. Not as enjoyable as the powerful bellow of a big piston engine at full bore, turning the prop at more than 3,000 rpm. When he didn't answer I said that the comparison was a lot like that of a diesel train engine, which was just a big stinking hunk of noise, versus a fire-breathing steam locomotive, which emitted the tangy smell of live steam as it panted and wheezed in the station with the engineer adding yet another romantic smell as he poked his long oilcan into the innards of the running gear. Stallings admitted I might have a point, although I couldn't decide whether he really agreed with me or was just being his normal polite self.

He parked his car and hopped out to make a quick inspection of his hangar. The office came second, just like it did for me. I noticed his employees all greeted him with a smile, so obviously he was building a loyal organization capable of a lot of expansion. One of his key men was a solidly-built person with a reddish complexion and a lot of those tell-tale aviator's wrinkles around his eyes. His name was Mack Rowe, and when I heard that name I asked if he was related to Gene Rowe, whom I had known quite well in Ferry Command before he had been killed flying a light bomber called the Baltimore.

'I sure am related,' he answered. 'We were brothers.'

'I'm proud to meet you', I said sincerely, because your brother was one hell of a fine man and a hell of a fine pilot. What he did to save his crew's lives is something very few people would do. He should have been given a medal.'

'I'll say he should have. By the way, this is what the local newspaper had to say about it. Heroic death fits, doesn't it?' He hauled out his wallet and handed me a well-creased clipping.

HEROIC DEATH OF NASHVILLE AIRMAN IN BRAZILIAN JUNGLE CRASH RELATED BY R.A.F. FERRY COMMAND.

The heroic — and tragic — story of how a Nashville civilian pilot gave his life to save two Royal Air Force transport command officers from death in a snake and crocodile-infested Brazilian jungle early in February was told yesterday by the transport command at Dorval, Quebec, and released by the United Press.

The pilot, Capt. Gene Hamilton Rowe, 22, R.A.F. Ferry Command, son of Mr. and Mrs. L. Mack Rowe, 1131 Sunnymeade Drive, stayed at the controls of his plane while the two officers parachuted to safety. When Captain Rowe left the plane, it was too late to give his chute a chance to open.

Flying over the matted jungle land one engine of the bomber, which was being ferried from Nassau to the Mediterranean, had failed completely and the other was limping. Rowe ordered the two officers to jump.

Flying Officer J. B. Clark, radio operator of the plane, sent out a distress call and released a carrier pigeon with a note giving the plane's position before he and Flying Officer J. G. Doherty carried out Rowe's orders and leaped. Rowe went to his death in the crash which occurred at the mouth of the Amazon River, near Isle Marajo.

Receiving the distress signal and the carrier pigeon note. American and R.A.F. airmen at the Ocean Ferry Base at Belem, Brazil, soon located the position of the two British officers and picked them up in a U.S. Navy blimp, the only type of aircraft that could have attempted a landing in the confined and dangerous terrain.

The land party, designated to find the wreckage and recover Rowe's body, was forced to resort to horses and oxen, which frequently sank to their bellies in quagmire. However, they reached the wreckage and returned the body to Campo Teso Des Coieras on the Amazon, where it was buried.

Captain Rowe first became interested in aviation with his

brother, Capt. Mack Rowe, who is now with the U.S. Ferry Command at a Detroit, Mich, base, when both were students at Isaac Litton High School. They took civilian pilot training at Vanderbilt.

He was married to Miss Pauline Bruce of El Reno, Okla, in May, 1943.

His family here had already been notified of his death.

After I read it through I said: 'That's not a bad story, so damn often the reporter gets it all wrong. One thing for sure, though; if he'd been in the military he undoubtedly would have received a medal. Somehow a lot of heroic deeds were just passed over when they were accomplished by civilians in Ferry Command.'

He scratched his head, 'Too true. But now it's too late, I guess.'

'I'm afraid so. But I do know that Clark and Doherty made special trips to the Ferry Command cemetery in Nassau to place flowers on his grave. *They* knew what a sacrifice he made for them.'

'That's good to know, I must tell my mother.'

'Glad to bring some good news,' I replied, then, as I read the clipping again, I said: 'It says here you were stationed at Detroit with the US Ferry Command. I never even knew there was another Ferry Command.'

He grinned at me and said, 'Oh, yes, there certainly was. It was formed on 29 May 1941, not so long after yours. The United States Army Air Corps woke up to the fact they didn't have nearly enough pilots to ferry the aircraft the factories were beginning to churn out. They were finally getting tooled up, even if the States wasn't in the war.'

I couldn't resist it. 'Thanks to the British orders.'

He glared at me, then relaxed and let me have my little victory. 'Sure, those British orders set up a lot of aircraft factories. Now, if you don't mind I'll continue my little story that you requested.' So I got a shot of sarcasm in return, which I probably deserved.

'Go ahead.'

'So the Army Air Corps scooped up very nearly every guy with a commercial licence and put him to work. It sure was hectic. And there was such an emergency that we were all civilians, just like you and Gene.'

'How long did that civilian bit last? The RAF left *us* alone. I guess they had enough on their plate overseas with the other Commands.'

'They left us alone to do our jobs until some bureaucrats in Washington decided to make us real officers and stapled a couple of brass second lieutenant's bars on our shoulders. That way Uncle Sam had us by the balls. Which is the way the people in Washington thought it should be done.'

'So how long did the US Ferry Command last, then?'

'Just about a year. Also the Army Air Corps became the US Army Air Force on 20 June 1941, but the oldtimers kept calling it the Air Corps for a long time.' He thought for a moment. 'After they wrapped up our Ferry Command into the Air Transport Command they split it into two divisions, one for ferrying and one for general transport.'

'Which one were you in?'

'I stayed in ferrying, especially fighters. I know Gene liked the bombers, but I'll take a peashooter every time. You know, we once met in Khartoum and neither one of us could believe our eyes. What a coincidence! We circled around like a couple of stray dogs and then I said, "You certainly look like my brother from Nashville," and he replied, "You're ugly enough to be *my* brother from Nashville." What a night we had.' His eyes turned sad as he thought of the brother he'd loved and lost.

There was a moment of rather uncomfortable silence before Stallings broke in to change the subject. 'You might not know this, but I visited the Clayton Knight Committee in New York when they were recruiting for the transatlantic ferrying service.'

'No, what happened?' I asked quickly.

'Well they offered me a thousand dollars per delivery provided I could report to St. Hubert the next week.'

I'd heard of the thousand dollar per delivery before, although *I* only got a thousand a month, never mind how many deliveries I made. 'So what happened? What were you getting a month with American?'

'As a scheduled airline captain with good seniority I was getting just about a thousand a month flying nice safe DC2s and 3s, so I suppose they had to offer me more.' He paused, his eyes far away, obviously wondering what would have happened if he'd taken the adventurous ferry pilot's job.

'So what happened?' Rowe asked. He was leaning forward in his chair, face eager.

'American wouldn't let me go. They said my job in the company was just as important as the ferrying job. And furthermore they told me that if I quit they'd raise a stink with the two governments and I'd never fly a scheduled airline aircraft again.' He paused. 'That made me pretty mad. I don't like being threatened like that, but later that night I realized they had me in a real box, so I went back on the line with American.'

There was another short silence and then Rowe said, 'Maybe it was just as well. You're here now and a lot of men who joined Ferry Command are not.'

Stallings wiped his forehead and said 'Too true.' Then he paused and said, 'Enough of this. After work let's drop by the local aviators' club and hoist a few for old time's sake.'

So we were just a little late for the feast of real Southern Fried Chicken, hot rolls and steamed rice Anne and Laurell had cooked up in honour of their Canadian guests.

So for several days we lazed around. The hospitality was terrific and every evening we ate off Spode English bone china with Gorham sterling silver and Waterford crystal glasses as accompaniment. We met several of their close friends, one of whom was a dentist who lived next door. He was a congenial companion and a good drinking buddy. He also had a very attractive wife. Late one afternoon after a few mint juleps I mentioned that my hair needed trimming. She averred she was an expert with the scissors, and the first thing I knew I was sitting on a kitchen chair with a large towel wrapped around my neck. As she trimmed away I happened to mention that she had a lovely touch. This harmless compliment pleased her a lot. But Loretta didn't see it that way. She frowned at me and ran upstairs in a proper sulk. But somehow this didn't really disturb me, because I thought a little of that old devil jealousy flowing the other way was only just. Still, it did take a long time to get her to unthaw that night.

Finally it was time to go. I realized that although real hosts will try to convince their house guests to prolong their stay, yet everything good must end. So when I checked and found the weather all the way to Montreal was good, and furthermore a nasty front was approaching Nashville from the west, I decided it was time to get back to work. But this idea was quite unpopular with Loretta. It was astonishing to me because she had always hopped in our aircraft without any argument up until now. Obviously, Southern hospitality had captivated her, and she refused to get out of bed. Laurell and Anne swore that she had influenza and shouldn't be moved but I saw the so-called patient's eyes peeping over the covers. To me they looked healthy as a cat's. Then Laurell couldn't hold back and giggled, and Anne smiled. Loretta's cover was blown. So I ordered her out of bed and her new friends accused me of being a heartless tyrant. So be it.

The women shed tears as we left, with many promises to return. At the airport Stallings shook my hand warmly and watched as we taxied out. It was a sad parting. After take-off and levelling off at 9,000 where the best tail winds were Loretta turned to me and said: 'I think I'd really like to live there. Could you make a living in Nashville in aviation?'

This was a question I had been asking myself, and I was still reluctant to answer. Finally I took a deep breath and said, 'I'd like to live there too, but it would be a tough grind breaking into the local aviation scene. Even with Jesse's backing I'd probably be regarded as an outsider 20 years from now. Those people are right hospitable to visitors, but they're damn close and clannish in business. I'd have to work for myself in any case, because that's just the way I'm built.'

She sighed before responding. 'I suppose you're right. But I hate the thought of that long winter ahead. How I wish we could have stayed.'

'Well,' I replied a bit impatiently, 'that place with the long winter is where we make our living. After all, you're just as much a Canadian as I am, and don't you go forgetting it.'

I couldn't hear her reply, but could those classic lips I loved so much be mouthing what looked suspiciously like 'Nuts to you?'

The air was smooth and very quickly it was time to land at Akron for gas. Away we went, then stopped at Buffalo for Customs clearance. Lake Ontario fell behind and soon we were following the broad St. Lawrence river, surely the best landmark any aviator could ask for. As the sun began to dip below the horizon in a blaze of gold and scarlet we passed over Lac St. Louis and there was Dorval under our wing, with the welcoming voice of the control tower officer handing us our landing clearance. Once on the ground and a quick Immigration and Customs inspection and we were again Canadians on our own soil. I had often thought as I sweated my way through obstinate, sometimes even hostile immigration officers in strange countries that there was one country they couldn't bar me from . . . Canada.

I hadn't really looked forward to my reception on returning because of my failure to win with my Mosquito. I expected some sneering remarks from some of my acquaintances. But I had misjudged my fellow man. All of them congratulated me for trying and said how sorry they were that I hadn't finished the race.

It seemed that the old philosophical attitude that it is better to have loved and lost than never to have loved at all had another, nicer application.

Chapter 3
Rimouski Airlines

The tower at Dorval granted taxi clearance and I opened the throttles of Douglas DC3C CF-FKY, sorry to be losing such a fine friend. The big twin-engined aircraft had begun life as a C47A, then become an RAF Dakota Mark IV, thanks to World War II's Lend-Lease programme. I had seen it and its sister ship, now CF-FKZ, on the war surplus disposal airfield at Silloth, England, where I was buying 24 volt C47s for Charlie Mathews, a broker in Miami who was supplying them for customers in Cuba and South America. The prices varied from twenty to thirty thousand, flyaway field, the variations depending to a large extent on the engine and airframe hours since manufacture. And be wary of aircraft that had towed gliders. They could be a few inches longer than Donald Douglas had designed them after their heavy work. In the middle of the huge flock I found my two birds at a bargain price of ten thousand each. They had low engine times and were in excellent condition, and the reason they were marked down was that they had 12 volt electrical systems. Most airlines had changed to 24 volts, but we in World-Wide Aviation had no such rules. So I bought them, hoping to get into the Canadian airline business.

I had personally ferried FKY home, over the route through Iceland and Greenland which Louis Bisson, George Evans and myself had pioneered with RAF Ferry Command in 1942, and she had never even burped. Then came the trauma of complying with the Department of Transport regulations to take her from military to civilian configuration, not the least of which was removing the many layers of paint she carried in camouflage. Now, bright, shiny and ready to expand Canada's aviation horizons, the two aircraft stood idle because the

Government had a 'chosen instrument' policy to protect TCA. But the would-be airline based down the St. Lawrence on the south shore had no such restrictions thrust upon it.

Rimouski Airlines had started in 1946 with the dreams of three men. They were Paul LaPointe, an ex-Spitfire pilot, Alphee Gagnon, an active man who believed in aviation, and Albert Dion, who supplied the money. From a strip near the town they had gradually worked up their airline, in spite of having to use rather unsuitable aircraft for their trans-river flights such as an Avro Anson CF-EHU, and a twin Beech 18A CF-BQJ. Their Grumman Goose, CF-FEM, had the additional feature of being usable for charter flights into any of the millions of lakes north of the big river.

I well remembered the night I'd sold them FKY at Rimouski. I had been under the impression they wanted to buy the Beech Bonanza parked outside on the side of the grass strip when the meeting was called. I suppose the French method was sort of diplomatic in that they were a long time in coming to the point. Maybe a Bonanza later, they said, but what about a DC3? I was taken right aback and said my two just weren't for sale. There was a pause while this apparently shocking information was translated. It was directed at a man, sitting in the back of the smoke-filled room, who had said nothing during the long palavering. Now he nodded, then uttered a few guttural words in the old-fashioned French common to the lower St. Lawrence region. The translator, who was also their operations manager, turned to me with a very basic thought. He said, 'Mr Dion says to tell you that *everything* has a price.' He leaned back to observe the result of this missile while I chewed it over.

I had determined to keep my two DC3s because no airline can hope to function and serve the public properly with just one of a type. Any mishap and . . . But on the other hand I'd just blown more than five grand on my Mosquito caper and the overseas deliveries were at one of their periodic low periods. Cash in the bank would be even more welcome than usual for an outfit struggling to expand. But I determined to hang tough, because FKY was exactly what Rimouski needed to climb out of the 'bush' league. It was in excellent condition and had low engine times. That meant a lot of revenue hours before expensive repairs were necessary. The big cargo door made it versatile. Maybe the 26 bucket seats weren't quite up to normal scheduled airline comfort standards, but for the 18 minute flight across the river the lumberjacks wouldn't complain. They could throw their packsacks and equipment on the heavy metal floor, making the baggage handling problem easy. Even the strong quarter-inch cable suspended from the cabin roof was a plus. The previous passengers, parachutists on a one-way trip, had used the cable as a place to clip their release lines. To forget to pull the release ring was not a good idea. Now the line was an aid in climbing the often wet and slippery floor. Maybe the heating didn't turn out many BTUs, but the loggers were dressed for 60 below. The cross-river air fare was $10. The river ferry boat charged $6, but took four or five hours, with a free chance to get sea-sick. It worked out, therefore, that the DC3 could gross out at almost $800 per hour.

While I was figuring out these hard economic facts, and taking my time doing so, it was with some amusement that I noticed the opposition was showing signs of strain. Good. If they were becoming nervous and impatient during our negotiations this was surely a condition much to be desired under the circumstances. Finally I made up my mind. 'Fifty-five thousand,' I said, knowing that was almost twice what the licensed ships were selling for in the United States.

There was a sort of stunned silence, then the executives huddled in the back of the room, the buzz of their argument floating up to me. But I did not care, because they knew my knowledge of the French language was limited to ordering 'Jambon et ouefs.'

The ops manager was sweating. He was on a spot. He sort of stumbled, '*is* that your best price?'

'You bet,' I answered, scenting victory, 'and in cash.'

This caused another confab, with the usual arm-waving, and finally the man in the back nodded, although I could see his lips were a tight line and his brow a bit furrowed. So the deal was made. I actually wondered if they really had the cash, well knowing just how little profit three small aircraft could generate. I could have spared myself the worry, for when I got back to Montreal there was a certified cheque in the full amount waiting for me from the Ford Motor Company, for whom Albert Dion was the distributor for a wide territory on the south shore of the river and the whole of the Gaspe peninsula.

So the lumberjacks could now take their hard-earned money

and get back to civilization from Baie Comeau on the north shore in a comfortable hurry. Civilization for some would mean their little farms along the river, others their girl friends, and still others a big blast with lots of booze.

Baie Comeau was where the Quebec North Shore Paper Company had their huge newsprint mill. It was owned by the *Chicago Tribune,* captained by that well-known American tycoon of Irish descent, Colonel Robert R. McCormick. I thought it a bit strange that Canada should supply him with the material to print his newspaper, which always had something nasty to say about the British. The lumberjacks were mostly employed by a woods contractor, who would contract to log an area of perhaps two square miles of balsam and spruce, up on the River Outard. They got an hourly salary of about two and a half dollars out of which they had to pay their own board at 90 cents a day. They slept in a low bunkhouse in rather spartan discomfort. If they exceeded a certain number of cords of wood, which were measured as four by four by four feet, they got a bonus. That required a really extra effort with their saws. Their cords were made ready to be skidded down to the river where the spring floods would wash the rafts down to the mill to be stored in towering piles. The ultimate results of their efforts were giant rolls of newsprint weighing almost a ton, which were taken by the Colonel's private shipping line to the newspaper in Chicago, via the St. Lawrence and the Great Lakes. So the *bûcherons,* as the loggers were called in French, worked all winter and the ships worked all summer when the ice had left their waterways.

Now it was my opportunity to deliver the aircraft which I was sure would turn Rimouski Airlines into a viable aviation company. As I sat at the end of runway 24 after the Pratt and Whitney engines had run up with not even a small drop when I'd checked the mags, I took a long look around the cockpit. Douglas had built just one DC1 in 1933 at their factory on Clover Field, near Los Angeles. The Pacific coast seemed to inspire aircraft designers. TWA had laid out the basics to make the aircraft viable for an airline. It must have a roomy cabin, two engines, not three, controllable propellers, flaps to reduce landing speed, cruise over 180 mph, have a retractable landing gear and, most importantly, it must fly at a safe altitude over the Rocky Mountains on one engine. The opposition was the

Boeing 247, which was similar but smaller. In Europe no manufacturer was even close to these advanced features. The Germans had their three-engined Junkers JU52, the Dutch were sticking with their three-engined Fokkers and the English were using a stately four-engined Handley-Page biplane which, although comfortable, had trouble cruising at 100 mph.

The DC1 was so successful that TWA ordered 25 of the improved DC2, which could carry 14 passengers and cruise at 196 mph. Anthony Fokker, certainly no dummy, wangled European sales rights for the advanced aircraft. KLM bought a fleet. Other airlines followed. Then the forward-thinking Dutch entered a DC2 in the McRoberts air race from England to Australia in 1934 and were only beaten by an advanced de Havilland Comet, built especially for the race.

On the US domestic scene, United and its 247s were being wiped out of the competitive cross-continent challenge for aviation passengers. Then C. R. Smith, the president of American Airlines, who were also suffering got in the act. He promised to buy 20 of advanced Douglas DC types, sight unseen, in spite of the fact his airline had no funds to complete the purchase. That was the way the pioneers of scheduled airlines operated in those days. One requirement was for 21 passengers and another a landing gear that didn't have to be pumped up and down by hand. So Douglas enlarged the fuselage and a new wing was designed. The result was aerodynamic perfection. It even forgave clumsy pilots, although the flexible wing waved at them from time to time. Soon United and Eastern joined the Douglas customers' list and by 1939 a full 75 percent of American air travellers were being transported by DC3s.

The cockpit showed the influence of practical airline pilots and their engineers. The flap indicator was a movable stiff which was connected directly to the board-like slabs attached to the inner wings. This indicator was easy to see so that a pilot in a tough instrument landing could make his selection without losing his concentration on his flight instruments. There were two full sets of those flight instruments, so the copilot got a good view of what the captain was trying to do. The two fuel selectors were well marked, with five positions so that any of the four wing tanks could be fed to either of the two engines without a hassle, as on some military aircraft I'd flown. The brakes were powerful and smooth, being controlled by the

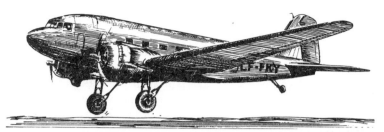

rudder pedals which were easily adjustable. The controls for the props, throttles and mixtures were well laid out and came nicely to hand. I especially liked the tail wheel lock control, which could be easily engaged by a swipe at its knob under the pedestal. On the fault side, the pilot's seat was almost straight up and not too comfortable and the cockpit leaked like a sieve in even the lightest precipitation. There was one story of the airline pilot who made his en-route weather report as 'light rain outside, heavy rain inside.' Believable.

Now the control tower gave us take-off clearance and I swung out on the runway with a flourish as I opened the throttles. At her light weight FKY leaped into the sky. Then it was down the familiar river. I didn't even need a map as I saw the town of Sorel. That was where I'd damned near killed myself, flying close over an uncharted high-tension span with my Stinson float plane when I was returning from a session in the bush in a fur-trading venture. Soon Quebec City and its graceful span across the river was left behind and then typically Quebec names like Trois Pistoles and Riviere du Loup showed up as small groups of buildings adjacent to the many narrow fields of the typical habitant farms. Down river was Matane, where Jerry Burnett and his flying wife were trying to eke out a living doing the same type of work as Rimouski Airlines. They provided a good service but were doomed to remain a small operation because of the lack of sufficient operating capital, like a lot of other people.

Near Father Point I swung over the wreck of the *Empress of Ireland*, which had gone down in 1914 after colliding with a Norwegian collier. Over 1,020 people had drowned, making the big ship a close catastrophic second to the *Titanic*, which had lost 1,517 unfortunate souls. On a clear day the *Empress* could be seen, down only about 70 feet. But today the St. Lawrence waters were uncooperative, with wind riffles shielding the tragedy from my eyes. So I got back to business and slipped into Rimouski's grass field, now firm, but pretty sticky in spring and fall.

The welcome was tumultuous, really coming from their hearts. Now their local company could give the not-too-well-liked Canadian Pacific Airlines run by those 'maudit blokes' in Montreal a real challenge. I was exempted from this insult, maybe because I'd been in the bush or maybe because I never tried to lord it over anyone with a French accent. As a matter of fact I was known as 'Mike Vigar', because what French Canadian could possibly pronounce such an outlandish name as McVicar with its two quick, hard consonants?

Chapter 4
No Island in the Sky

The next morning, as I struggled to the surface with loud pounding in my temples and a light haze of pain across my eyeballs, I blearily wondered if a successful sale of a large aircraft in Rimouski was worth it. My eyes focussed on the off-white ceiling of the King George VI hotel but it failed to produce an answer, just like a reluctant radar screen. After an interval laced with numerous glasses of ice-cold water I thought I might actually qualify as a genuine alcoholic, like some of those legendary bush pilots who allegedly flew through thick and thin aided by a 40 under the seat of their rickety ski or float equipped aircraft.

Then my thoughts naturally turned to Clarence 'Duke' Schiller, who had been a real early bird in this region when he flew for Dr. Cuisinier's optimistically named 'Canadian Transcontinental Airways' away back in the 1920s. Maybe only I with my World-Wide Airways' had been more optimistic! I had met the Duke when we had been fellow Catalina flying boat Captains with RAF Ferry Command. One night in Elizabeth City, North Carolina, when we were both waiting for our Cats to be readied for the long transatlantic flight, he had spun a few gripping tales about his long and fabulous career.

Perhaps the many gallons of booze he'd allowed to slip past his vocal cords had affected his voice, which was as gravelly as that of a circus barker. The liquor certainly hadn't affected his decibel output, which was attention-getting in any bar, as were the deep blue adjectives with which he spiced his speech. He had dismissed his career with the Royal Flying Corps as a fighter pilot in WWI with the cryptic remark that he always felt he had been damn lucky to get out alive. Then in civilian life he'd eked out a sporadic living in the bush and recalled that the old saw about the most dangerous part of flying was starving to death was no exaggeration. Then, just as he'd hoped, he got his big break when Canadian businessman Philip Wood chose him to fly the Atlantic in a Stinson named *City of Windsor*. He would pursue the £25,000 cash prize offered by a brewing company to the sponsors of the first aircraft to fly from London, Ontario, to London, England, with a refuelling stop in Newfoundland, of course.

The generous prize had caught the imagination of the public, because earlier in that epic year of 1927 Lindbergh had made his historic solo flight from New York to Paris, France. There were many people who said they were in contention for the money, but the Duke's main opposition was another Stinson piloted by Terry Tully and Jimmy Metcalf, Canadians who were based right in London and who were sponsored by a suds company, as indicated by the name of their aircraft, *Sir John Carling*.

While Schiller paused and we both replenished our drinks I remembered reading about those hectic months of the summer of 1927. Everyone, it appeared, wanted to emulate Lindbergh. And none was able to succeed. A Fokker named *Sir Raphael* had taken off from England and the searchers had not even found a piece of wreckage after a long quest. On 6 September an all-metal low-winged Junkers left Old Orchard, Maine, bound for the other side of the treacherous ocean. The patriotic name of *Old Glory* was no help; the wreckage of the aircraft was found at sea with its three crew members dead.

'It was like this,' Schiller rumbled, 'I got away from London on 1 September after the usual screw-ups. Then I had a couple of forced landings, so the other guys in the "Carling" beat me to the punch and had left Harbour Grace when I got there on 7 September.' He paused and looked at the dark dregs of his drink as he swilled them around in his glass. 'And then the "Carling" went missing too. Christ, I didn't care! I figured I'd be the lucky one, but . . .'

I leaned forward. 'But what?'

'Hell, the damned sponsors told me my flight was just an invitation to suicide and they didn't want to be responsible. So they told me to come back.' He paused, obviously still angry, then gave me a rare smile, and said, 'But I'm getting a bellyful of the North Atlantic with the Command.'

'Yeah,' I replied slowly, 'but on the other hand you're still alive.'

'Shit,' he replied, to show what he thought of my opinion.

Yet in the long run the Atlantic killed him too when he was making a single-engined landing at night in a Cat after returning to Bermuda.

I twisted the sheets as I tossed uncomfortably, trying to think about happier times. I punched the lumpy pillow under my throbbing head as I recalled that the hotel was only a few miles from Father Point, where the big ocean liners took on a river to guide them upstream to Quebec City or Montreal. So it was logical that that was the place for the pioneer airmail flights to start. In September of 1927, that vintage year, a Curtiss HS2L flying boat piloted by H. S. Quigly and Stuart Graham had made the first of ten experimental flights to Montreal. The flights saved three whole days on the transatlantic mail, and so the south shore community had a long history in Canadian aviation.

Canadian Transcontinental Airways then began the first winter mail service of any kind from Quebec City along the rugged North Shore of the St. Lawrence all the way to Blanc Sablon, which was only a few miles from the wilderness of Labrador. After a tough winter, in the spring of 1928 they inaugurated an air service from Quebec to Magdalen Island then south to the Maritime provinces. Schiller was part of the operation.

Then on 15 April the attention of the world was focussed on remote Greenely Island, just off the north-west tip of Newfoundland and not very far from Blanc Sablon. A Junkers W33 after being in the air an incredible 37 hours from take-off from Ireland, had crashed there. The forced landing had been witnessed by the local lighthouse keeper who used his dog-team to send the news to the nearest Marconi wireless office. The Junkers buckled its wheeled landing gear, but the three men aboard were uninjured. They were two Germans, Baron von Guenfield and Captain Koehl, and an Irishman, Captain Fitzmaurice.

The world wanted to know more, much more.

So the newspapers began a game to see which would get the authentic news in print first. It turned out that Schiller, who had many contacts with reporters, was hired by a friend of his,

Charles Sloan, who wrote for the *New York World News*. The Duke took over the tale.

'Sloan got hold of me at Quebec City and told me to get my ass down to Greenely Island, wherever in hell that was, get the story and get it back to him. Don't spare the horses and the hell with the expenses.'

I looked at him as he recounted this bit of authentic Canadian history. 'What about Romeo Vachon?' He was also a well-known bush pilot.

'Romeo got going just after I did,' the Duke drawled, 'but the weather was real crappy, so I was the first one to get to the accident. Gotta say that Dr. Cuisinier had a lotta guts too . . . He came with me and helped me gas up from his caches along the way. That Fairchild FC2WA of his never missed a beat either.' He tugged on his ear, which I figured was his usual gesture when describing a dangerous flight.

Now I was almost breathless with anticipation. 'Then what happened? I heard Arctic explorer Bernt Balchen was involved too.'

'That's right. There were a lot of famous names involved in the whole operation before it was finished. Anyhow, I got down on the little frozen lake they'd landed on and found they were all OK. I made sure that the crew was OK. Then I flew Fitzmaurice back upriver to Murray Bay where he could use a phone to order parts to repair the Junkers. When I got there both Balchen and another explorer, Floyd Bennett, were waiting with a Ford Trimotor to see what they could do to help. It was the same Ford that Admiral Byrd had used on some of his exploratory flights in Antarctica, and he'd loaned it for the rescue mission.'

'What a story!' I exclaimed. 'Did you get it out all right?'

'Yep, Sloan got his scoop from me and the whole thing was plastered over all the newspapers of the world, so he was happy.' He paused, then, his voice slowing, said: 'The only really bad thing was that Floyd Bennett had pneumonia, and knew damn well he shouldn't have been flying. When he finally got into a hospital at Quebec City he was in real bad shape. Even the special serum that Charles Lindbergh flew in for him did no good.'

'Lindbergh!' I said in an awed voice. 'What happened to Bennett?'

Schiller threw me a scornful glance. 'He died, you dummy.

But at least the Americans named an airport after him.'

The insult didn't stop me. 'What happened to the Junkers . . . they called it the "Bremen", didn't they?'

Schiller had a wry grin. 'They couldn't fly it out, so they finally got a barge and took it out to the Ford Museum at Dearborne, where they make all those tin lizzies. There it sits, stuffed and mounted, if you want to go and feel it.'

'Maybe I will,' I said slowly. Then by a coincidence, which some people might call strange, the Duke's fund of flying stories ran dry just as my bottle of liquor did the same. We both hit the hay. I never saw him again.

At Rimouski the hotel phone rang with such startling loudness that maybe George himself jumped. I know I did. It was Captain Ray Roy bubbling away on the other end of the line. How about having lunch with him at the Hotel du Havre? They served great food, and he'd pick me up in his car and tell me about some really great ideas he'd come up with. Mutually beneficial, of course. I said I'd do it because I really did admire him and his agile brain. He'd been dubbed 'the Eagle of the North' by some newsman, or maybe it was a newswoman with a taste of old-time romanticism. Although many in the aviation fraternity scoffed at the description, as is their wont with anything unusual, I thought he deserved the high-flying sobriquet. He only grinned when I called him 'De Heagle of de Nort.'

Like me, he had come up the hard way after learning to fly in Montreal and then serving his time as a ground helper in the bush with old-timer Arthur Fecteau who was an excellent teacher. Then, stage by stage, he'd progressed after getting that elusive Commercial Flying Licence, finally with Canadian

Pacific Air Lines both in the bush and with their Air Observer
School in Quebec City. Then he'd helped businessman Roland
Sanson set up Northern Wings, who were my competition in
the fur business out of Seven Islands with their nice shiny new
Noorduyn Norseman. Sanson could, and did, put away a 40 of
scotch a day. But he had powerful political connections. I had
no political connections of any kind, but I did have a valid
licence to fly 'for hire and reward' with my Stinson Reliant.
Northern Wings started their operation without the formality
of an Air Transport Board licence, which I had, and I filed a
complaint.

Guess who won? It sure as hell wasn't me. But the tangle got
sorted out when my pilot Jim Lewington hit an extra-hard
ridge of snow called 'sastrugi' on take-off and wrote off my
aircraft. Ray Roy showed up at remote Sandgirt Lake in
Labrador and flew my men out to civilization and never even
sent me a bill. It was the type of thing that people in the bush
automatically did for one another, even if they were stiffly
competitive for every paying mile of charter.

As you go through life you find people whom you just
cannot stand, even if they could be of value in the world of
business. So you cut them off, due to personal animosity.
Probably a mistake. On the other hand there are some people
who have what might be called the 'Indian Sign' on you. Even
if their ideas are wrong or half-baked you try to give them a
break. Ray Roy had this effect on me. Besides, he was a natural
pilot. In return for his Norseman rescue I'd checked him out on
my DC3 free of charge. He'd proven to be a quick learner, a
pilot whom I could turn solo without worrying. In the air he
was not only skilful but lucky, which is even better. On the
ground he was just as hard a driver as he was in the air, and was
anxious to get into business for himself, which made him act as
a bit of a con man. All would-be entrepreneurs must have this
trait.

Certainly all these facts were racing through my mind as I
climbed into his car. He had brought along his wife Stella, a
stunning natural blonde, either to take my mind off business or
to add a touch of normality to his proposition. Roy was of
average height, and rather muscular, which he needed to
survive as a bush pilot far from any assistance. He had jet-
black hair and deep hypnotic eyes and was as handsome as any
actor playing the part of a French Foreign Legion officer in a
Sahara desert thriller.

When we got to the restaurant the owner, who also occasionally acted as maitre d', swept us to a damask-covered table adjacent to a large plate glass window which gave us a sweeping view of the harbour for which the place was named. Roy thanked his friend the owner, who left us while Roy skilfully switched our conversation from old flying stories to a rather theatrical production he obviously had planned well in advance. He used the waiter as his straight man as he turned to me and pronounced: 'Don, for us this is a great occasion. We must have a suitable drink.'

The garcon standing at attention nodded his agreement.

'Sounds like a good idea to me,' I replied. 'Watcha got in mind?' I was ready. Any thought that drinking before noon and before a business discussion being not too smart had fled my mind. Also that famous cure for a hangover of 'a hair of the dog that had bit me' was becoming more and more necessary. My hangover was still throbbing away at a high rate of revolutions per minute.

'Bon,' he said with a wide smile, rubbing his hands, then turned to the attentive waiter. 'Did you put that magnum of Mums champagne on ice for me, as I asked?'

'Oui, monsieur Roy,' the waiter replied as he returned his smile, and bobbed a little as he did so. It was becoming very impressive.

'And the stout?' Roy continued.

'Certainment, mon capitaine.'

'Parfait! Now chill three large wine glasses, bring them to the table, then bring the champagne and stout.'

The waiter scurried away and quickly returned with the glasses and dark brown ale. Then he served the large bottle of Mums properly in a silver ice bucket, nested in clear, white ice. While he drew the cork with proper reverence Roy looked at me with a question in his eyes. I nodded my head as if the operation was unstoppable, then raised my right thumb in the universal sign of approval. The waiter was silent as he poured the rich, dark brew into our glasses, then carefully added the clear champagne. The two liquors were the most unlikely blend I had ever dreamed of. While the champagne continued to fizz in the brownish liquid Roy raised his glass. It was obvious he was about to make a toast so Stella and I raised our glasses as well. 'With this "French 75" I wish our venture every success,' he said, now very serious. We all clinked our glasses and drank to the venture, although I hadn't the least idea what it might be. The mixture went down with absolutely no trouble, very smoothly, with just a tickle to our palates. It would prove to be just as lethal as the famous French Army artillery gun for which it was named.

I drained my glass. 'Ray, this stuff's not bad,' I said, which for me was a great compliment.

He replied with that old aviator's saying. 'Don, a bird can't fly on one wing,' as he signalled the waiter to refill all our glasses. That old bromide might have a touch of truth in it but somehow nobody ever mentioned the fact that a bird can't fly—with four or five or more wings either.

Finally he sprang his idea. I should rent him one of my Norseman aircraft on skis, with no money in advance. He would take the plane to Thessalon, Ontario, on the north shore of Lake Superior, and use it to fly woodcutters and their supplies into the bush. He knew his friend Gerry Joncas would give him the business because Roy had hauled him out of some tight squeezes up north in the past. This part was quite believable as bush pilots performed many mercy missions each year as part of their more or less normal routine.

I noticed that his wife wasn't as enthusiastic as Roy was, but discounted her reaction because no doubt she'd heard many other of his schemes which she considered hair-brained. Wasn't that what wives were for? Besides, she didn't know that I had no business lined up for those two bush aircraft. Then Roy took his plan a step further, and suddenly I heard myself agreeing to let him lease my DC3 CF-FKZ to fly the bushwhackers from Matane to a large cow-pasture he'd found near Thessalon. There was a great lack of land airports all the way from North Bay to the Lakehead. I felt that Ray could fit the big aircraft into just about any field safely and he proved me right later. It was a good idea to keep the woodsmen in one bunch under surveillance because if they'd taken the train a lot of them would have gone missing in the fleshpots of Montreal, from which they would have to be rescued at great cost. Besides, it would take a week or so in the bush when they finally arrived before they could produce their quota of cords.

Roy thought his present employer wouldn't mind because they couldn't take CF-FKY, the DC3 I'd sold them, off the trans-river run if they wanted to give reliable service. I believed him, but it turned out later they weren't too happy with his side deals.

Now that business was out of the way I decided to investigate a subject which had always interested me. I put down my drink and leaned forward. 'What did you think of Ernest Gann's book *Island in the Sky*. You were part of that rescue operation, weren't you?'

For a moment he hesitated, then answered: 'I thought he got the feelings of the pilots well, and he sure knows his weather.'

This wasn't enough for me. I pressed on: 'But don't you think he short-changed the efforts of Canadians like yourself and Norm Forester?'

'Maybe you're right.'

'Damn right I'm right. Norm was the very first to find that downed Consolidated bomber, the C87, remember? The Yanks finally had to admit they never knew where the hell they were on their search patterns, never mind where the four-engined plane was.'

He scratched his head, obviously not at ease, then added, 'Well, you know it was only a novel. That's fiction isn't it?'

I was becoming angry with his modesty, so I blared right back, 'Sure it was only a novel, right enough, but Gann's own foreword says the story is based on a true incident, because, as he said, "he knew it best".'

'That's right, he *was* involved.

'Besides, the places and characters he writes about are pretty thinly disguised. The real idiot pilot who got lost was named O'Connor, and Gann's man was called Dooley. Pretty obviously Irish, right? And if the plane was coming from Greenland obviously "Sparkle 20" just has to be Bluie West Eight.' I laughed grimly and added, 'God knows I've been there enough, but anyone with an ounce of brains could figure it all out.'

Roy grinned crookedly. 'Well, the Americans gave all of us Canadians one of the Air Medals, anyway.'

'Not much of a deal, I'd say. They gave away millions of those medals during the war, but better than nothing, I suppose. The Montreal newspapers gave you some coverage, and the Canadian Pacific Air Lines house paper *The Honker* gave a nice write-up. I saw that Forester and his crewman Norman Crewe were in Barkley-Grow CF-BMG. At least it had two engines. But you flew an old Fairchild 82, CF-AXE, one engine and Pete Midlidge as your crewman.'

'I was glad to see the engineers get mentioned for once.'

'I agree,' I answered, because without the help of my crews during my Ferry Command days I could have been in serious trouble. Then I went back to the burr which was under my saddle. 'But according to Gann the Americans spent several days milling around before they wised up and called in you bush pilots who knew the country. Even Ferry Command was in on the search but they were useless too. I guess a lot of people don't realize that you can't really do a good search over featureless lake-filled country, without even a good map, while you're drifting along a couple of miles in the air and doing three miles a minute.'

'You're right. You gotta get down to spot even a big aircraft like a C87. Especially when the snow's been drifting in the wind during a big storm, which happens a lot up there.'

I nodded, then blurted what I really felt. 'But a lot of people will never know the true story because Gann's books sell in the thousands. So, as usual, Canadians get short-changed while the Americans take all the credit.' I was getting well warmed-up. 'It's just not fair.'

Roy's voice was low as he tried to cool me off. 'Who said that life was supposed to be fair, Don?'

'Well, if we don't try . . .' I decided to drop this contentious subject and get some more detail from a man who'd been there. 'What happened to you and Midlidge? You were missing for a long time, weren't you?'

He flushed a little as he replied. 'Well, we got away from Seven Islands a day ahead of Forester, and we had three steel 45-gallon drums of gas in the fuselage, just in case. We landed at Nitchequon, a trading post just about 200 miles north-north-west of Seven Islands. It was the closest settlement to the radio fix they had on the C87.'

'How far were you away then?'

'We figured the bomber was about 100 miles further west. When we got to Nitchequon we refuelled as fast as we could, then took off again. But then the weather went sour and finally darkness set in. I turned back.'

I leaned forward. This I'd never heard about. 'Then what happened?'

'Well, Nitchequon had no radio, so I asked them to light as large a bonfire as they could, figuring I could see it after dark. But we never did spot the blaze, so, like we usually did if we were stuck, we just sat down and made camp.'

'Seems reasonable. What did you do the next day?'

'We got off and did another search. But we pretty well got lost ourselves. Our compass was screwed up.'

'You must have been used to that, after flying in an area where there are lots of iron ore mountains.'

He glared at me. 'Of course, of course. But this was different. The damned thing never would settle down. Midlidge and I figured it out later that those steel drums must have thrown it off. Anyway, we were twelve days in the bush before I saw the St. Lawrence again. We sort of wandered southwards in the bad weather another storm brought, and finally we came out at Havre St. Pierre.'

'Jesus! That's almost 75 miles east of Seven Islands!'

'Right. Even I don't know how many miles we flew.'

I was shocked, because Roy was one of the best bush pilots. 'So you never did even see the lost aircraft?'

Roy rubbed his chin hard, a sure sign he was upset. 'No we didn't. But we sure gave it our best shot.'

I paused before answering, wanting to put my true feelings in just the right words, then said slowly, 'So for you there really was no Island in the Sky.'

By now he had recovered his customary aplomb, and grimaced as he looked me squarely in the eye. 'Don,' he said with conviction, 'for pilots like us there never was an Island in the Sky.'

I had no answer, except to drain my glass once again, as did Roy and Stella, all in a dead silence.

Chapter 5
Cornell Carnival

Charter business for big aircraft like a DC3 was mighty scarce in late 1948, so I was glad when CF-FKZ climbed strongly out of Toronto's Malton airport. The gear had come up with no trouble and now we were established on Green One Airway, Canada's only east-west instrument route. As we reached cruising altitude I reset the power and did a quick scan of the engine and flight instruments. All was in order, so I turned to my copilot, little Alphonse Elie. He might have been small in stature but on a delivery flight he never wasted a minute and always got to his destination, even if it was in a Beech 18 to far-away Turkey or Eqypt, or in a little single-engined Bonanza to some South American Country.

'I guess the Babb Company knows what they're doing,' I shouted over the roar of the Pratt & Whitney 1830s. 'They've bought a lot of aircraft and this batch of Cornells will no doubt make them a few bucks.' I shook my head and added, 'But while I know we can find our way to Mossbank on the bald prairie of Saskatchewan, can those 26 heroes back there find *their* way back to Montreal again?' I flicked my right thumb over my shoulder to emphasize my doubtful feelings.

Elie squinched up his dark-brown eyes. 'Why do you say that?' What he actually said was, 'What for you say dat, you?' The meaning was clear.

'Well they are a real mixed bunch. Some of them have done a tour of ops, some have flown fighters and some have other good experience, but there are quite a few who never have done a long cross-country flight of any kind. They'll miss mother Royal Canadian Air Force holding their hands.'

Elie wasn't worried. He said, 'Maybe, but for sure that Fairchild Cornell is an easy one to fly, just like a de Havilland

Tiger Moth or a Fleet Finch. Now if they were getting Harvards . . .' I agreed. Bad news.

'I don't think some of them have even got road maps. What they *do* have going for them out of Mossbank are the section lines that divide the land into square mile areas. The lines are true north and south and east and west. Winnipeg should be a breeze for starters.'

Elie nodded. 'That's right. But from Winnipeg east it's some different. Nothing but bush and rocks and lakes. The airports are pretty far apart too. No section lines or roads to follow there.'

I reached forward and gave the Sperry automatic pilot a tweak. 'So for them it's gonna be the iron compass. CPR VFR or CNR VFR, and hope that no station agent throws the switch the wrong way.' This was a slightly exaggerated way of saying that the railways weren't always infallible guides. I continued my wasted briefing, as none of the 'heroes' could hear me. 'And they better watch the weather. Reminds me of a chickadee mother sending her chicks out solo for the very first time.'

Elie just shrugged, as it obviously wasn't our problem. I reached up and cranked in the frequency of the four-legged low-frequency range at Muskoka. We heard the steady whine which meant we were on course. Then I leaned out the engines just a shade more past auto-lean. Although we had a six-hour flight plan and a theoretical nine hours of fuel; old habits die hard, and as a long-range ferry pilot I'd always hoarded my gas.

It was getting late in the fall and the local time was just on midnight. A perfect time to be flying a good old Dakota. Ahead of us there were a string of radio ranges which the Government had built before the war from coast to coast. Trans-Canada Air Lines had used them extensively when they'd started their transcontinental service with Lockheed 14s. Without the ranges the scheduled service would have been impossible. Now all types of aircraft were using them and their associated airports. The radio range operators broadcast the weather of their adjacent stations as well as their own twice an hour at +15 and +45. It was for many aircraft an invaluable service. For people with two-way radio the range operator listened on 3105 or 6210 kilocycles and answered on the low frequency of his individual range. Some stations were getting VHF, a great improvement.

I was giving Elie air time so he could get the DC3 endorsed on his licence so I disconnected the autopilot and shouted the time-honoured instructor's command. 'You got it.'

Elie didn't reply. He was suddenly too busy. Naturally, being a hard-shell instructor type I couldn't just turn over the controls to a student without some words of wisdom, so I leaned over and shouted, 'Don't try and fly her like a light plane. Let her do the work. Otherwise we'll have a bunch of sick kids in the back. Smooth, that's the way. And hang onto that on-course like you're aiming for Ascension Island.' I paused to let this sink in, than added: 'Furthermore, I don't want to see that altimeter more than plus or minus 20 feet from 10,000.' I looked at my watch and gave him the remaining piece of our flight plan puzzle. 'We should be over Muskoka in 24 minutes.'

Elie nodded without replying, just hunching forward a little. He was going to do all right, so I unlatched my seat belt, raised the hinged arm of my seat and wriggled around the pedestal, then walked back to see how our pilots were doing. The door was a bit tough to open, as usual, then I stood in the front of the noisy cabin and shouted just as loudly as I could: 'How's it goin'? Everybody happy?' Standard Air Force jargon.

It appeared that no one was 'happy'. Some told me about the hard metal seats with the famous bucket shape, which fitted parachutes but not the human posterior. Others moaned about the lack of heat and the noise. One fellow even complained there was no stewardess to serve him coffee. Another scruffy-looking type then insinuated that I'd better get back in the cockpit because he was sure we were already lost. Finally, as I began to back away from this barrage a pilot said they were obviously getting paid for the ride out, and the ferrying would be pleasure and for free. This made me grin. It reminded me so vividly of my similar remarks when I'd been returning in the bomb bay of a cold and noisy Liberator bomber during the late unpleasantness. I certainly did not trust the British Overseas Airways Return Ferry flights crews, and more than once they proved to me the hard way that my distrust was well founded.

There was no point in arguing with my vociferous passengers, so I waved at them and returned to my 'office.' When I belted up I reflected there was nothing to worry about. Just as in a naval ship at sea, everying is copacetic — normal — when the crew is bitching. It is when the men become silent and surly that the Captain had better watch out.

Besides, my passengers — being typical pilots — felt they had to conceal the pleasure they were feeling at being 'ungrounded'. For them it was just great, really marvellous to be back in the air, even if it was just to drive a humble Cornell.

The Dakota we were driving through the night had been chartered at the Air Transport Board rate of £1.10 per statute mile by the Babb Company, an American-controlled company headed up by old timer Charlie Babb. He was well known and well liked in the aviation trade and had helped the Canadian Government locate twin-engined aircraft for training schools in 1939 and 1940 when none were available domestically. I had flown in both a Lockheed 10 and a Boeing 247D he had located for No. 2 AOS (Air Observer School) at Edmonton when even the Avro Ansons shipped from England were in short supply. The Canadian-built Ansons were still in the future at that time.

Post-war, Babb and acquired numerous aircraft, now surplus. There were many Catalina Cansos, Fleet Finches and many other purchases, but his big investment was in North American Harvards, which had been built by Canadian Car and Foundry at Cartierville, near Montreal. There were over 500 of the single-engined advanced trainers in his lot. Most of them had been ferried from remote airports back to the factory for refurbishing to the standards of various foreign governments around the world.

There were 101 Cornells in this particular batch and winter was coming. They were parked outside. By spring they probably would need major repairs. So the Canadian part of the Babb Company, headed up by Chester Newhall, a small man with the tragedy of a misshapen back, decided that a mass move was necessary. Ches, as he was known in Canada, had flashing intelligent dark eyes and a devastating sense of humour. He never let the fact he was a hunchback affect his speech or his conduct. He was assisted by a dark, handsome man named Jack Beacham who had done a great job as Lockheed's representative with Ferry Command.

The paperwork for what became to be known as 'the Cornell Carnival' was considerable, so they had contracted with Gilbert 'Peanuts' Tobin, a fellow Ferry Command pilot, to handle the job. He had located the ferry pilots, made sure their licences were valid and their medicals up to date and told them they'd get the princely sum of fifty bucks and their expenses once they got their aircraft safely to St John's, just south of Montreal. We were flying at night because that saved 26 hotel rooms, and the pilots had been told to pack their own lunch. Normally they would have been sent by airline or train, but the journey to the remote airport could have been a lengthy one as it was far off the beaten path, south of Moose Jaw, which was south of Regina for those who didn't have an atlas handy. So this chartered aircraft was not such a luxury as might first appear. Some of the pilots were happy to cut their journey time as they were doing the flying away from their normal job, commonly referred to as moonlighting.

North Bay had passed below and now we were heading into the real bush; trackless, timeless and remote. The only signs of civilization would be the small towns scattered along the Canadian National Railroad, and a lot of those were 'company towns', owned by large American companies engaged in harvesting the woods for newsprint. The company controlled every facet of the community, maybe a lot like a Russian Gulag. If you lost your job you were on your way outside on the first train. At Earlton the airway began to curve towards the true west, following the outline of Lake Superior to the south. Porquis Junction was just a pinprick of light in the darkness, and then it was Kapuskasing, a TCA gas stop with paved runways. Pagwa and Nakina were reminders of the native Indian the white man had exploited. Then Armstrong's weather report told me that the forecast warm front was really there. It was time to tighten up seat belts as the grey cloud began to bounce us around. The cockpit began to leak and the Douglas product began to groan, proving we were in a Dak. She carried herself with a sort of ponderous grace, ironing out the heavy turbulence, and we were glad we couldn't see the wingtips flexing out there in the darkness. An application of alcohol to the props and windshield and the light rime ice was taken care of. The rubber boots on the wing and empennage inflated and deflated, breaking off small hunks of flaky white crystal. I always figured that if you ever really had to rely on rubber boots in heavy ice you were just deluding yourself, and they would let you down when you needed them most. The best thing to do when heavy ice made its frightening appearance was to change altitude in a hell of a hurry. There were, fortunately, only rare meteorological conditions which produced heavy ice, and a change of altitude soon got the aircraft into a layer of safer air. Finally, as we passed Sioux Lookout, the cloud began to thin out and soon we were over Kenora. I wondered if it had ever been possible on any given day or night to fly from the east to Winnipeg, 'the Gateway to the West' without plugging through at least one zone of frontal weather.

Behind us the sky was turning pink, and, just as the sun peeped over the horizon, we circled and landed at Stevenson Field, west of Winnipeg. It had been named after a World War I fighter ace. A voice from the control tower on its unique spindly steel legs welcomed me back with a cheery greeting. That pleasant welcome came because I had been the officer in charge of the tower when it was first built, and controllers remembered one of their own who had escaped from the tension-filled glass cage to a pilot's life.

With full wing tanks, and bellies rejuvenated by hot coffee courtesy of the Winnipeg Flying Club, we got airborne on the final leg. I had decided to go direct in the daylight, and give the boys in the back room a chance to inspect the countryside they'd soon be flying over on their own. It was an elementary navigational exercise because all I had to do was follow the section line which marked the 50th parallel of latitude. As we passed Portage la Prairie, a sure reminder of early colonization, the blue waters of Lake Winnipeg spread to the north. It was there that what I considered the most delicious of fish, the Winnipeg Goldeye, were caught. After we passed Brandon the country became flatter and flatter with only an occasional range of low hills or patches of woods to relieve the monotony of the prairie. The border between Manitoba and Saskatchewan couldn't have been detected from the air — and for sure my birthplace, fifty miles or so to the south in the town of Oxbow, would have been hard to distinguish from any other raw prairie town. Unless you could see the name on the side of the massive grain elevators, of course.

It took us only two hours to complete the flight, but the monotony of the earth below made it seem longer. Perhaps night flight is the best. Below, you expect nothing of note but, above, the stars are always steady in their places in the firmament, giving a sense of confidence to a wandering aviator. A large dried-up patch of whitish earth with small puddles of brackish-looking, alkali-laden water was the best guide to Mossbank, which was perched near its southern flank.

The lake was named 'Old Wives Lake'. I wondered if some puckish explorer had so named it because they were both sort of dried up.

Mossbank airport had a standard three runway layout. It was just like the dozens of others from which a multitude of aircraft had flown many hundreds of thousands of hours in the British Commonwealth Air Training Scheme, which had graduated the amazing total of 131,553 airmen. A high percentage of the graduates had given their lives in the battle to preserve freedom and democracy. There had been many types of training schools, from the Instructors' School through the Elementary Flying Training Schools, the Service Flying Training Schools and finally, for pilots, the Operational Training Units. Then it was overseas postings. For navigators there were ten Air Observers' Schools and six advanced Air Navigation Schools. One Flight Engineers' School and four Wireless Schools took care of those trades. Mossbank had been one of eleven bombing and Gunnery Schools, located, as were so many of the other schools, on the prairie where there was enough space so that the aircraft had little danger of running into one another. For each small town the infusion of the money and the people of an adjacent school had given a big boost to their local economy. That excitement was all over. So now the weather, the wheat crop prospects and cattle health would once again become the main topics of conversation.

When we landed there was no delay after I shut down the engines and shouted, 'Everybody off for the City of Mossbank', a rather feeble joke. The big cargo door was thrown open and then the metal ladder attached to the door sill. Soon our passengers were spilling out of their magic chariot (although that's not what they would have called it).

Their reactions varied considerably when they met W. P. Dunphy, the 'B' engineer in charge who had signed out the aircraft, and learned which number was theirs. Some seemed a bit unsure. So it was for real? They began a careful inspection while other eager beavers had their props turning even as I taxied the Dak out for take-off. We would be back home in less than ten hours, but for the Cornells, even aided by the usual tail-wind it could be two full days, provided they didn't get lost too often.

Now eastbound at last, we landed at Winnipeg for gas. Elie and I had both been on the move for more than 24 hours.

Probably we should have checked into a hotel. But we didn't. The weather and winds were good, and we were both eager to get home to a hot shower, a hot meal and something else hot, but not necessarily in that order. It took us just six hours and fifteen minutes to get back to Dorval, and the Dak loved every minute of it, which, of course made me love her.

While we were waiting for the ferry pilots to make it back east and then go to Mossbank for another batch of Cornells, the Government finally, after three years of screwing around after the war, got around to offering us a hangar at St. John's, which the French insisted on calling St. Jean. It was just a short hop south of Dorval, where we had fought the elements for so long outside in rain, snow or wind. Our aircraft weren't much of a problem to ferry down and the big double hangar took them with space to spare. It had a leaky roof and no heat. The rent, which for us was non-negotiable — although people like American Can got a break — was a high $400 per month. It doesn't sound like much, but somehow it adds up to $4,800 bucks a year, and that amount of money doesn't come easily in our line of business. The airport was managed by Tommy Wrathall, a World War I fighter pilot, and his son Derek was his assistant. They both seemed like nice guys, and might have turned out to be good neighbours in other circumstances.

St. John's had been the home base for No. 8 Air Observers' School, where day and night dozens of Avro Ansons set off with the idea of getting the sprog navigators lost so they could find themselves over Germany. Crown Assets had disposed of most of the Ansons and now the Babb company had a hangar near ours, while Aircraft Industries had another. Babb were strictly in the surplus aircraft business, but Aircraft Industries, who retained a lot of No. 8 personnel, were in the overhaul, repair and conversion business.

The Canadian Government had been left with billions of dollars worth of war fighting equipment such as naval ships, tanks and aircraft. Their method of disposal was to send out descriptive listings to various interested people who had to respond with a 'sealed bid' which would be opened in front of several people in Ottawa on the appointed day. The lucky (?) winner would be given a short period of time to remove his new property, or else. I never found out how much naval or army surplus stuff was disposed of, but I did know of the aircraft the RCAF sold. They were of various vintages and some were of no commercial use whatsoever, but a surprising number of entrepreneurs bought a surprising number of aircraft from the total listing which comprised the following: Airspeed Oxford, Avron Anson, Avro Lancaster, Boeing Flying Fortress, Bristol Beaufort, Bristol Bolingbroke, Cessna Crane, Consolidated Catalina, Consolidated Liberator, Curtiss P-40, de Havilland Mosquito, de Havilland Tiger Moth, Douglas 8A, Douglas Digby, Fairchild Cornell, Fairchild PT-19, Fairey Battle, Fairey Swordfish, Fleet Finch, Fleet II, Handley-Page Halifax, Handley-Page Hampden, Lockheed Hudson, Lockheed Ventura, North American Harvard, North American Yale, Short Stirling, Stearman PT-27, Supermarine Spitfire, Vickers Wellington, and Westland Lysander. To that impressive list other aircraft would be added at a later date, such as the Douglas C47 and the North American B25, etc. Only the C47, the Catalina and the Mosquitoes interested me.

On 5 October we got away for the remainder of the Carnival. Now each pilot seemed like an old friend, and insults were exchanged in the old style, such as 'Never thought I'd see you again,' and more of the same. Once more we flew through the night and when we got to Mossbank we found the operation had already spawned a good collection of stories. The best one was that of one of the dumber pilots, who was briefed to use section lines for navigation. He took off on a section line, all right, only it was the straight north one. One of his buddies saw him disappearing towards the North Pole and took off after him. A long stern chase ensued before the would-be rescuer got formated with the hapless northbound driver. Hand signals and an effort to stick his right wing in the dummy's left ear to rotate him 90 degrees had no effect. Finally, they both landed about 60 miles north of Mossbank and had a little chat and the disorganized pilot fell in behind the man with the map. Then there was the Cornell with the busted prop at Sioux Lookout, and the one abandoned by the DOT inspector at Kapuskasing because he had to report back to work. As a matter of fact each flight could have had some adventure story if the pilot had chosen to loosen up.

After the long flight Edmonton seemed just a hop, skip and a jump, so two and a half hours later I was phoning my father, surprising him once more. As usual, he was pleased to see me. Then it was time to party with old friends such as Don McLaughlin, who was trying to sell my Western Bonanza demonstrator with a notable lack of success. He introduced me to one of his prospects, an amiable man named Herb Peets who was in love with aviation. His greatest hope was to fly in and land a DC3. Elie found a little two-seater Swift to ferry, so Peets and I made the long flight home together. He was good company, although I discovered his navigational ability was about nil.

In Montreal the moving was going well, so Loretta, Peets and I concentrated on moving my ham radio equipment of VE2WW from the chicken coop on Noel Brossard's farm to the lean-to of our new hangar. It took more than a few trips, but I still managed to get on the air before much else had been installed. Loretta seemed a little mystified by this attitude, but I told her 'First things first.' She was still finding out that ham radio was a powerful rival.

Ten days later a long-awaited phone call came through for me to report to San Diego for Convair 240 familiarization. Old friend Captain Ron George of KLM would help me become qualified on the new aircraft, which WWA had contracted to fly from the factory to Zurich for Swissair. I rubbed my hands in anticipation at the thought of flying a brand-new post-war design. So it was down to La Guardia in a Bonanza, because Colonial Airlines had no seats available. This time my chauffeur was Steve Brody, who'd survived the war and a tour with Bomber Command. His nickname was 'Guv', which suited his reserved manner and sense of humour. The only problem was he couldn't fly very well. I wondered how in hell he'd completed a tour, but didn't say anything at the time. This politeness cost me a bent Bonanza some time later when Brody ran off the runway at St. John's. Which proved that friendship should never intrude when a pilot's ability is being questioned.

Chapter 6
The brightest stars in the sky

The stewardess's welcoming smile changed to a frown as she advised the passengers aboard the Lockheed Constellation at La Guardia airport to fasten their seat belts. As I obeyed I felt a vibration in my bottom and glanced out of the window where No. 1 propeller had disappeared as the Wright engine belched a characteristic cloud of blue smoke. Just like the Bostons, the Mitchells and the Forts and Hudsons of Ferry Command. Why Wrights smoked on starting and Pratt & Whitney engines didn't was a question engineers seemed to be unable to explain. Soon all four were turning and we began to taxi past the Marine Terminal which catered for the fast-disappearing flying boats using the harbour. There was a rather long pause as the Captain and Flight Engineer ran through their pre-take-off checks. Then we swung out on the runway and powerful acceleration pushed me back in my seat. The gear came up with a thump and we turned west over the canyons and towers of Manhattan. Los Angeles here we come! It was time to relax. The pilot in command of a flight with other pilots on board probably never realizes just how much assistance he gets from the boys in the rear.

The Constellation, well named as a collection of many stars, was the most modern aircraft in the air, well ahead of the Douglas DC6 and the Boeing Stratocruiser. The Loughead brothers had begun to design aircraft before World War I, then late in the 1920s had gone their separate ways. Allen, the aviation-minded brother, had legally changed his surname to Lockheed because he was tired of being called Loghead. Very few people realized that the proper pronunciation was 'Loch' as in Loch Lomond. When I learned of this I felt some sympathy because a lot of people tried to call me McIvor, or to stick a 'k' into McVicar. I rather sarcastically told them that the ones with the 'k' were the *rich* members of the clan. So some of them wandered away, sort of bemused, and obviously wondering what sort of a nut they'd encountered.

Lockheed had decided to name his newly designed aircraft after first magnitude stars rather than unromantic numbers. The first was called 'Vega', a high-wing, beautifully streamlined wooden plane of outstanding aeronautical design by Jack Northrop. It first flew on 4 July 1927, an appropriate date for an aircraft made in America. Although the first Vega, 'Golden Eagle', was lost in the Pacific during the Dole race to Hawaii, the second soon redeemed the name. Hubert Wilkins and his pilot Ben Eielson had just returned from a frustrating attempt to fly from Alaska to Spitzbergen across the North Pole, having cracked up three aircraft in the process. While Wilkins was recovering from his ordeal in San Francisco he chanced to glance out of his hotel window one day and saw what he called a bird of paradise. It was a Vega. He traced the plane immediately and bought it on the spot. In the process he sold his three-engined Fokker to Australians Charles Kingsford-Smith and Charles Ulm. These two adventurers went on to complete safely the first flight from Oakland to Sydney, Australia, across the wide and dangerous Pacific. The Fokker was registered VH-USU and named 'Southern Cross'. It left North America on 31 May 1928, and landed in Hawaii after 271/2 hours, aided by ground directional bearings. The next leg was the toughest, 3,200 miles to Suva in the Fiji Islands. But American navigator Harry Lyon did not let the flight down. Just as they were sure they were about to run out of gas they sighted the island and came in to a risky landing on a 1,300 foot long strip cut through a race track. Although the weather threw them off course on the next leg, Australia was a target impossible to miss and they were back home by 9 June, welcomed like the heroes they were. Two pilots, a radio man and a navigator had combined their efforts to make the long flight successful.

In the meantime Wilkins and Eielson had flown the bright orange Vega, equipped with extra gas tanks to extend its range to more than 2,000 miles, to Point Barrow. Eielson was the pilot and Wilkins the navigator, a strong team. On 15 April 1928, a clear day, they set out to find if there was any land in the high Arctic. Beset by storms near Ellesmere Island they pressed on over the top of Greenland before finally being forced down by yet another storm. Through the turbulent clouds they spotted a flat stretch of snow and Eielson set the Vega's skis on it safely. They had been in the air 20 hours and 20 minutes, the longest flight yet carried out in the Arctic. They waited out the storm and Wilkins got a fix. They were only five miles from their destination. Veteran Arctic explorer Amundsen, who had publicly said the flight could not be accomplished, now said that no flight had been made anywhere, any time to compare with it. Admiral Byrd called the flight the greatest ever in the Far North. A few weeks later Wilkins was knighted by King George V.

The Vega was now shipped to the South Pole where the same team succeeded in photographing 100,000 square miles of unknown territory. So before they were a year old the swift Vegas had been at the top and bottom of the world. Domestically, they astonished everyone with their performance. There were only 144 built but they went on to set no less than 34 world records. Various pilots on different occasions held the transcontinental record using Vegas. In

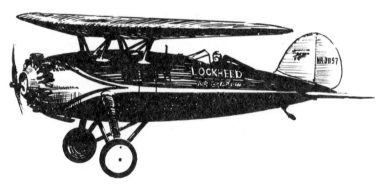

1929 the first non-stop race from Los Angeles to Cleveland (which became the Bendix I once competed in) was won by a Lockheed Air Express, which was a Vega with a parasol wing, in 13 hours and 15 minutes. Another Air Express came in second. That was the meet where Jimmy Doolittle took his P-1 Curtiss Hawk up and had it shed its wings. He baled out and got another aircraft to continue his usual dazzling aerobatic exhibition.

Aided by a new engine cowling Robert Caldwell won the Civilian Cabin Ship Race with a Wasp-engined Vega, bettering by ten miles per hour the previous record of 142.9 miles per hour set by a US Marine Curtiss Sea Hawk fighter. Then in the 'free for all' in which military and civilian planes competed against each other there were some big surprises. Douglas Davis flying a Walter Beech-designed Travel Air Model-R 'Mystery' craft came first, with a speed of 194.4 mph on the closed course. Lt. R. G. Breene, flying the Air Corps' best, a P-3A Hawk came second at 186.8. Then Roscoe Turner, flying his Vega, was third at 163.8. In fourth place was Commander J. J. Clark, USN, at 153.4 in a Curtiss Hawk F6C-6. It was a stunning victory for the civilian aircraft, the first time they had defeated the Armed Services' best. Beech and Lockheed! Leaders in the field! It was time for the military to do some serious thinking if their designs were slower than civilians.

In 1930 Wiley Post flew his Vega *Winnie-May* to first place in the Los Angeles-Chicago cross-country race in 9 hours and 9 minutes. As a matter of fact, the first four finishers flew Vegas, and Roscoe Turner was fifth in a Lockheed Air Express. There were no Vegas in the closed course race that year. After all, they had been ahead of the field long enough, some said. However, a Lockheed Altair flown by Ira Eaker, who went on to fame in the USAAC, did finish a not too poor fifth in the closed course Thompson in 1931 at 196.832 mph.

At Detroit in 1931 Amelia Earhart blazed a record closed-course speed of 174.897 mph, while fellow aviatrix Ruth Nichols set a new altitude record for women of 28,743 feet. Both in Vegas, of course.

A year later Earhart would take her Vega from Harbor Grace, Newfoundland, to Londonderry, Ireland, in the fast time of 15 hours 48 minutes to become the first of her sex to fly the Atlantic solo. Bernt Balchen, a pioneer pilot and explorer who had been one of the early Catalina delivery pilots with Clyde Pangborn for the Ferrying Service in 1941, had gone to Newfoundland with Earhart to give her confidence. He also had constructed her flight plan and told her what courses to fly. Like Charles Lindbergh's record-setting flight from New York to Paris in 1927 she would fly dead-reckoning courses with no radio or navigational aids. Lottsa guts, those two!

Chapter 7
Wiley Post – America's
one-eyed ace

My first sight of a Lockheed aircraft would remain engraved in my mind for the rest of my life. It was love at first sight. The occasion was on 1 July 1931, just nine days after my sixteenth birthday, and perhaps it was excusable for an impressionable teenager to fall in love with an inanimate thing like an aircraft. One good reason was that girls, the normal object of a boy's affection, seemed far out of reach. The 'big guys' of 18 and 19 had all the luck. I was at my usual hangout at Edmonton's airfield when suddenly a white, beautifully streamlined high-wing monoplane swooped out of some wispy grey clouds. It circled, a bit like a lonely seagull looking for a safe haven from the storm. Then the pilot lined it up into the wind and set it down with a mighty splash on the grass field. For a moment it seemed to hesitate as the mud sucked at its wheels, then we heard the roar of a powerful engine as the pilot opened the throttle wide to keep moving. Using bursts of power sufficient to progress, yet not strong enough to put the bird on her nose, he skilfully half-flew, half-taxied towards the safety of the hangar's concrete ramp.

The crowd was deathly quiet after the propeller shuddered to a stop. What superman had brought this Lockheed Vega from Alaska to our small town? The name *Winnie May* was painted on the side, and everyone knew it was on an attempt to break the round-the-world speed record held by the dirigible Graf Zeppelin of 21 days, 7 hours and 21 minutes. Then the cockpit hatch opened and Wiley Post appeared, stretching his cramped limbs. As he waved at us, in my youthful eyes his confident manner and the patch over his blind eye made him seem like the incarnation of an Elizabethan explorer from the days when men were indeed men.

Post smiled briefly at our cheers, then seemed to become very serious as he looked back at the swamp that had almost trapped him. Finally he climbed down, and at the same time his navigator, Australian Harold Gatty, emerged from his cubby-hole behind the huge gas tank that filled the fuselage. It looked as if half the population of Edmonton had turned out on this rainy day to greet the famous airmen. We had all read about other record-setting flights, but this was *the real thing*. Heroes in the flesh, like seeing the parade with the Prince of Wales chugging down Jasper Avenue on his royal tour back in 1927.

There was a surge to get close to the famous men and the crowd easily burst through the cordon of police. Naturally I was in the van, paying no attention to the threats of the law because this was one aircraft I just *had* to see close up. To feel, even. Maybe somehow its closeness would help me on my aviation career.

Meanwhile the ever-present photographers, radio announcers and newspaper reporters were elbowing their way to the plane to get the obviously exhausted crew's attention. I began to believe what many pilots had said, that the ground interviews were more tiring than the actual long-distance flying. In response to the many questions Post had little to say, still quite concerned with the condition of the landing surface. Once before on this flight they had almost lost their attempt on the record because of gumbo mud at Blagoveshchensk in the wilds of Siberia. They had been delayed for 12 hours and 21 minutes while waiting for a tractor that never appeared. Finally some horses borrowed from a droshky had hauled them out of the mud to firmer ground. They had staggered off once more, but this time there were no droshkies, and no firm ground either. No wonder Post looked downhearted, because, ironically, by far the most dangerous parts of his flight were now behind him.

Canadian immigration and customs formalities were rushed through by friendly officials and then the two airmen were conducted to the office of Jimmy Bell, the airport manager. The news people were quiet while Edmonton's mayor, James Douglas, and the acting premier of Alberta had a lot of nice things to say, most of which probably sailed right by the airmen's slightly deafened ears. Mud. Mud. Mud. That was the problem.

Many opinions were expressed by the aviation people crowded into the small office, and finally it was a Canadian Airways airmail pilot who made the suggestion which was to save the day. The prairie airmail service had just been started, and I still remember how impressed I was when one of the airmail planes, a Boeing 40H-4, had landed at night aided by just a bunch of oil flares. The pilot sat in the slipstream, while the mail was inside, and the big engine shot out streams of purple flame. The name of the man who made the suggestion is not recorded, unfortunately. Maybe it was Ted Stull, who had just made the first flight using the experimental radio beam from Winnipeg to Moose Jaw. Or maybe it was 'Punch' Dickins, famous World War I fighter pilot and record-setter in Canada's bush. Or it could have been 'Tommy' Thompson, another fighter pilot, and the man who had hired me in 1941 when I went to fly for No. 2 AOS, then run by Canadian Airways (Training) Limited. Or maybe it was Herbert Hollick-Kenyon, destined to go on to fame for both his Antarctic and Arctic flights. Or it could even have been Norm Forrester, one of the nicest men I'd ever met, both while he was Operations Manager with the AOS and later in civil life. Whoever had the idea, they certainly had lots of experience landing in semi-improved grass fields on wheels instead of on their more normal and more popular lakes and rivers using float planes. Why not use Portage Avenue?

This wide boulevard, all that remained of an overly-optimistic real estate developer's dream, ran straight as an arrow from the airport's boundary towards the city. There were no dream houses or other obstacles to obstruct an aircraft or to set up air currents which would be dangerous to the heavily over-loaded plane. When he heard this Post brightened up and said it sure sounded like a hell of a good idea to him. He was game to try anything to get going. When they saw his reaction the mayor and the airport manager quickly got crews busy taking down the electric light wires that crossed the boulevard. The relieved aviators, now just about out on their feet, were whisked to a suite in the MacDonald Hotel, Edmonton's finest, built by the Canadian National Railways on a sheer cliff overlooking the North Saskatchewan River. Post and Gatty later reported that they had never been treated better any place in the world.

As the cavalcade escorted by the Royal Canadian Mounted Police disappeared down the runway-to-be, I hung around the aircraft trying to be useful. Like a 'gofer', in other words. One who gets no pay, just the satisfaction of being a small part of an operation with the opportunity to go for whatever the big shots might need. I managed to climb up and inspect the cockpit where Post had removed the usual tin bucket type of pilot's seat and replaced it with a comfortable soft chair that had arm rests, and which reclined. Even with the upholstered chair he had to do isometric exercises in an effort to keep his muscles from tightening up. And, more interesting, in his instrument panel he had instruments I'd only read about. The leading edge of technology. There were the blind flying instruments from Sperry which Jimmy Doolittle had helped develop. In addition to the normal airspeed indicator, engine instruments and so on, he had an artificial horizon and a directional gyro, both powered by an externally mounted propeller driving a vacuum pump. He also had one of the first models of Kollsman's sensitive altimeter. Even with these aids he had always to be on the alert to make it through the worst of stormy weather, of which he'd had plenty. The big gas tank just aft of his seat plus his wing tanks gave him more than 20 hours of flight endurance while burning about 22 gallons per hour. His true airspeed of 150 mph was a good 50 miles per hour faster than other planes I had seen, such as the Junkers, Fairchilds and Fokkers. Lockheed had jumped far ahead of its rivals.

I climbed down and went aft to inspect the navigator's compartment. In my opinion, if Post's cockpit was the heart of the effort then Gatty's station would be the brains. Through a small window I could see a clutter of maps and navigational tables — and then I saw my very first sextant. It was a real thrill because I had learned the stars with my local Boy Scout troop, and some of the theory marine navigators had used. This sextant had a glass bubble, which meant that it didn't need a fixed horizon such as seamen used. There weren't many in the world at that time. Gatty also had a duplicate set of basic flight instruments, although I couldn't see another magnetic compass. The crew had to communicate with a long speaking tube between the two positions, just like the Gosport tube used in open-cockpit trainers. Gatty would shout up his courses and trust that Post would steer them. From a navigator's point of view this left a lot to be desired, as some pilots were quite sloppy about steering a given course. As a matter of fact, Post had complained that Gatty had given him too many course changes during the early part of their flight over Europe and so they were zigzagging across the terrain. I wished I could have been there to hear the navigator's reply! There was a small clear opening in the roof for star shots and two small clear openings in the sides of the fuselage for map-reading and pin-pointing. Compared to sitting in the cockpit the view of the ground was dismal, lacking distance and continuity. Gatty had also fitted the wind-drift meter so essential to dead-reckoning navigation with a very ingenious clockwork device which gave him his ground speed as well as his drift angle. There also was a low-powered transmitter and companion receiver fitted. He admitted he rarely used them. As an avid radio experimenter on my way to my amateur radio operator's licence I found this attitude very odd. Even without a direction-finding loop he could have used Morse code with the ground to get valuable bearings. Every little bit of information helps the safe completion of any flight.

Very early the following morning Post and Gatty were driven back to the airport, appearing much refreshed, even if their sleep had been interrupted many times by unthinking reporters anxious for a 'scoop'. This time *all* of the population of the city seemed to be awake to see them off. Naturally I was among the throng, and was pleased to see that all the mud, mire and grass had been washed off the *Winnie May*. Gatty was heard to remark that she reminded him of a little flower girl dressed all in white, at a wedding. They climbed in and settled down. As the electric starter, among other things, had been removed to save weight, a local mechanic had to swing the prop. The engine started with a roar that made some of the crowd wince, and as Post ran up the engine, checking the magnetos, oil pressure, head temperatures and all the other details so necessary for a safe take-off, the rain finally stopped. It seemed like a good omen. In an automobile rather than on their usual horses, a couple of Mounties were dashing up and down the boulevard clearing away sightseers. When all was ready, Post was towed out on the gravel road from the hangar apron to the broad street where the *Winnie May* sat parallel to the unused street-car tracks. He made one final engine check and let the white aircraft have her head with full power. After a long run,

because Edmonton is over half a mile above sea-level, Post
lifted off, having successfully avoided the telephone poles and
sidewalk kerbs. Everyone in the huge crowd gave an
involuntary sigh of relief. Post turned south down 101st Street,
then flew over the MacDonald where he rocked his wings, the
universal signal to ground people that all is well. Edmonton's
motto was 'The Gateway to the North'. Normally we thought
of that as meaning northbound, but in this case a gate could
swing both ways.

They flew back into the rain, but that didn't bother them
now, Post reported they even had a tail wind, which he thought
was highly unusual. Most pilots feel that there are more head
winds than tail winds in the world and maybe, in spite of
scientific proof to the contrary, they could be right. I'm sure
my experience has been that if I wanted to steer a course to
some destination all I had to do was point the aircraft into the
wind. Well, maybe not *every* time. Now the navigation was
simple, with flat prairie crossed by section lines a mile apart.
Gatty decided to joke with his pilot. 'Steer 83 1/2 degrees,' he
instructed.

He got a rise. 'What do you mean, one half?,' Post replied,
thinking that just to steer within a degree was hard enough.

They flew over Saskatoon right on time, then as the weather
began to clear, flew across Manitoba, and finally into 'the good
old USA', as Post described it, near Bessemer Junction,
Wisconsin. He opened up and ripped the air apart before

landing at Cleveland. They were trying to make New York before dark. With a fresh load of gas they were off in just half an hour, in spite of the usual reporters and radio announcers. It was now dusk and the revolving airmail route beacons guided them on. When they sighted New York it was for them the biggest thrill of their lives, just seeing the big city from the west. They managed to avoid the squadrons of welcoming aircraft and set down at Roosevelt Field for a record, which smashed the Hindenburg's all to hell, of 8 days, 15 hours, 51 minutes. On the ground once again, the police were helpless to protect them and Post shut off his whirling propeller while still on the runway before some fool walked into it. The usual ticker-tape parade was a fitting end to their marvellous feat.

In 1933 Post decided to fly the *Winnie May* around the world in a new record time, *Solo!* He was going to show the world how flights could be scheduled through bad weather by day and by night. In order to do this he had his usual advanced blind-flying instruments and the prototype of Sperry's newly developed automatic pilot. Now he could nap in flight safely. He decided he didn't need astro and relied on dead-reckoning aided by an experimental radio direction-finding receiver loaned to him by the US Army Air Corps. It would enable him to home on any commercial broadcast station.

Now he had a rival, Jimmy Mattern, in another Vega. However, Mattern did not have the advanced equipment Post did, and eventually he crashed his aircraft in bleak Siberia. But he did have the right aircraft.

On 15 July 1933 Post took up a renovated *Winnie May* with more fuel from Floyd Bennett, Long Island. Less than 26 hours later he landed at Berlin, the first to fly the long trip non-stop. From Tempelhof airport onwards his troubles were many. First 'Mechanical Mike', as he named his automatic pilot, malfunctioned, delaying him in Moscow. Over Alaska's cloud blanket he became hopelessly lost when his radio malfunctioned. Totally fatigued, he circled until, purely by chance, he spotted a short strip through a break in the clouds. Then he ran off the end into a ditch, damaging his right landing gear and bending his prop. This time it looked like it was all over for sure. But enthusiastic local men hoisted the *Winnie May* out of the ditch while pioneer Alaska pilot Joe Crosson and mechanic 'Hutch' Hutchinson flew in a new prop from

Fairbanks, 300 miles away. Overnight the two saviours made the aircraft airworthy, and Post took off for Fairbanks and another load of fuel and oil. There bad weather delayed him another eight hours, after which he made Edmonton with no trouble. The grass was now firm, as I well knew, as 'Moss' Burbidge, chief instructor of the local aero club had soloed me in an ancient Cirrus Moth a month or so previously. Post was gone in 90 minutes, and when he landed at New York at midnight he had a new round-the-world record of 7 days 18 hours and 491/2 minutes.

With his speed records behind him Post searched for new skies to conquer. Very little was known of the effects on men and aircraft of the rarefied atmosphere where oxygen must be used, so he decided to experiment with the dangerous flight regime. He wanted to stick with the *Winnie May*, but her wooden fuselage couldn't be pressurized, so Post had a special suit built for his flights. If the engineers were right, it would keep his body at an altitude of 5,500 feet even when he was flying eight miles high. It was his intention to prove that high-altitude flight would be the key to high-speed public air transportation high above the storms and turbulence of frontal weather.

It was a daunting task.

No less than four times he set out to break the existing transcontinental speed record, and four times, for various reasons, he failed. But he did prove his point on one memorable occasion when he recorded a ground speed of 340 miles per hour, a record at the time. Many people of judgement consider that Post's high-altitude research constitutes his most valuable contribution to the progress of aviation.

After its outstanding career the *Winnie May* was honourably retired. She is now in an uncharacteristically static position in the Smithsonian Museum in Washington. Her registration NR-105-W is prominently featured, and her silver Hamilton-Standard propeller and reliable Pratt & Whitney Wasp engine seem ready to respond to the next challenge, whatever it might be.

Chapter 8
Charles Lindbergh's Favourite Crew

I glanced out of the window as the sun burst through the ragged clouds we had been flying through. At our 20,000-odd feet altitude we had avoided the terrors of the early airmail route through Pennsylvania and the treacherous Appalachian Mountains. Many a pilot had paid the final price after trying to stay in contact through the difficult passes in foggy weather. As we passed over Cleveland, site of the National Air Races, I could see Canada across the grey waters of Lake Erie. This made me remember other events in which Lockheed aircraft had played a very important part.

Their engineers were well satisfied with the record-breaking performances of the Vega. But they could see that the future lay with low-wing aircraft. So they took the thick, strong wing from the top of the Vega fuselage and installed it on the bottom of no less than three newly designed fuselages. Thus three new stars in the sky, Sirius, Altair and Orion, were born.

Charles Lindbergh had captured the imagination of the world when he flew his high-wing Ryan-built *Spirit of St. Louis* non-stop and solo from New York to Paris in 33 1/2 hours on 22 May 1927. His flying gas tank with its limited visibility from the cockpit had ignited a fierce fire of enthusiasm for aviation that would burn forever. When he saw his first Sirius he was impressed and immediately proceeded to set a new transcontinental speed record, in spite of the fact that his landing gear was not retractable. Highly streamlined wheel pants had helped, and at the same time he must have appreciated the superior visibility from his cockpit high on the fuselage.

Lindbergh had been contacted by energetic Juan Trippe of Pan American Airways and had agreed to act as technical adviser on new routes and new flying equipment. While on a survey flight to South America through Mexico he had met, courted and married Anne Morrow, a petite woman who had been brought up in reserved diplomatic circles. It seemed she should have been more at home on the ground, entertaining her husband's business acquaintances. But her delicate appearance was deceptive. She learned to fly and volunteered to accompany her famous husband whenever he set out on his next pioneering flight.

Lindbergh took her at her word. He put his Sirius on floats in preparation for a flight across the Great Circle route to the Orient, partly sponsored by Pan Am, who were looking at the Pacific as their next target in a world-wide expansion. He installed a more powerful Wright Cyclone engine and carried extra fuel in the float compartments so that he now had a range of 2,100 miles. He also put dual controls in the rear cockpit so his wife could fly while he used his sextant or took photographs. He also installed a two-way radio for her to operate. She had mastered the Morse code up to 15 words per minute and passed a third-class radio operator's test. This was a feat to be admired, although I wondered how Lindbergh had convinced her, because with my copilot, Loretta, I had had no success. Indeed she had put up a fierce fight when I tried to make her memorize what the dots and dashes stood for. To me, knowing the Morse code was as natural as learning to ride a bicycle, being able to drive a car, or being capable of touch typing.

Pan Am installed their standard high and low frequency receiver and their CW telegraph transmitter with coils to operate on 333, 500, 3130, 5,615, 8,450 and 13,240 kcs. The low frequencies were mainly for direction finding from ground stations. Generally speaking, the higher the communication frequency the longer the distance covered. They also fitted a fixed-loop direction finder, which required the aircraft to turn to get a null in the signal. They began their trip from College Point, Long Island. Lindbergh lifted off with a minimum of effort, but the tyro radio op in the rear cockpit had trouble. Each frequency required a separate set of coils to be fitted into their proper sockets. The master oscillator controlled the frequency and the power amplifier beefed up the output. There were so many of them that she came to remember them as Tweedledum and Tweedledee. For a time she was thoroughly confused. Then she discovered the plugs were different so that it was impossible to plug Tweedledum into Tweedledee's sockets. Step One accomplished. Now she had to reel out the trailing antenna to the proper length so the final amplifier was in proper resonance, otherwise the radio frequency power would be wasted. She counted out 48 turns very carefully, which was correct for 3,130 kc. Then she called the ground station WOA to give them a position report. No luck. Lindbergh passed her a note from the front cockpit telling her not to worry, they'd find the trouble when they landed at Washington on the Potomac River. There they picked up all their visas and permits, then set off for her home at North Haven in Maine. This time she had better success with the radio, actually getting out some position reports and copying several garbled lines from New York and Bangor, Maine, through the static. She was learning that operation in flight was a lot different from on solid ground, but she was a good learner.

The next day, on the flight from North Haven to Ottawa, Ontario, she paid no attention to the scenery because she was beginning to master her radio. She was in contact with one or other of two ground stations every fifteen minutes of the flight and was able to send 'psn' (position) reports her husband gave her. It gave her great comfort to receive 'dit-dah-dit' (R) from the ground, which meant that her message was received OK. She was slowly beginning to recognize whole words instead of single letters, although she soon discovered that the radio layout in her cockpit was so arranged that she had to cross her hands while tuning and sending, like a pianist playing bass with his right hand and treble with his left. Doggedly, she decided that she would become a radio operator, even if she looked more like a pianist.

That night they were invited to a reception in their honour. A group of assorted Canadian experts, men who knew the north, were arguing with Lindbergh. They wanted to know why he had chosen *that* route. He replied that it was the shortest. They told him of some of the disadvantages: desolate country with poor maps, heavy tides in Hudson's Bay, quicksand and bad fogs, unreliable magnetic compass readings, and finally the vicious mosquitoes. Lindbergh was unimpressed and told them they'd all got back safely, hadn't they? Finally they used their last argument: They wouldn't

take *their* wife over that route, no sir! Mrs. Lindbergh felt
strangely flattered, as she once had at the age of fifteen when
she had walked into an elevator and a man had taken off his
hat for her. Her husband had parried with the remark that *she*
was *crew,* which made her feel even more flattered because now
she was considered to be on an equal footing with men. Finally
Lindbergh lost his patience and snapped that if they wouldn't
let him take the Canadian Arctic route he'd go over
Greenland. That did it. Better to let this madman go his way
and try to help him after all.

The next day they got away to Moose Factory on James Bay,
and that night they reached Churchill where the 'terrible' tides
were for real. A good tie-down enabled them to sleep fairly
comfortably that night, but the water was rough in the mouth
of the Churchill River the next morning, making their take-off
more dangerous than any before. All that day they flew over
miles and miles of flat, treeless land, mottled with lakes and
muskeg. That evening they came upon a grey lake bounded by
harsh rocky shores little higher than the muskeg. They had had
their first taste of the remote, friendless land called the
Barrens. On shore there were a few scattered white buildings
with a Union Jack flying from a flagstaff. They had reached
Baker Lake, where Revillon Frères had one of the few fur
trading posts in the Arctic not controlled by the Hudson Bay
Company. Although it was in the middle of summer they were
told that the yearly re-supply vessel was still expected. That
night, at an impromptu dinner, they tried to bring the Padre,
the Mounty, the Parson and the fur traders up to date with
what was happening 'outside'. They were astonished to learn
that the accepted method of reading the daily newspapers was
on its published date, but one year late. What did 'outside'
news really mean to people in isolation anyway?

Lindbergh used the gas drums he'd had sent north to fill the
Sirius' tanks to the top. This next leg to Aklavik was a long
one. There the mighty Mackenzie river finally found the Arctic
Ocean. His flight plan would be just over 12 hours and he
began to realize why the bureaucrats in Ottawa were worried
about him. If he went down, there really would be a shortage of
suitable aircraft and aircrew to go looking for his, even if he did
get down safely on one of the millions of unmapped lakes. He
had painted his aircraft with bright orange wings and

empennage, but even that bright colour would be as hard to spot as the proverbial needle in a haystack.

It had been only three years earlier, in August 1928, that C. H. 'Punch' Dickins had made the first flight from Baker Lake westward across the Barrens to the Mackenzie river, on a survey flight for Lt. Col. C. D. H. McAlpine, a courageous mining promoter. The flight which Dickins made without accident was considered so hazardous that he was awarded the Trans-Canada (McKee) Trophy that year. Then in 1930 the same intrepid McAlpine had chartered two float-equipped aircraft to survey the Coppermine and Coronation Gulf areas, near to the north-west of Baker Lake, for mineral deposits. Both aircraft force-landed, lost and out of gas, and the rescue expedition had many difficulties before the people in the first two aircraft were finally flown out.

It was generally agreed that the late start of the McAlpine expedition in September was a major cause of their troubles. So Lindbergh had not made that mistake, realizing the float season in the Arctic was of very short duration. And Aklavik itself had only been reached by air by the same pioneer, 'Punch' Dickins, in Fokker Super-Universal G-CASM on Dominion Day, 1 July 1929.

Aklavik had no weather station so Lindbergh had to take off with a very minimum of Met information. It things got too bad he could always land, just as Canadian bush pilots did quite frequently. Then they would live on emergency rations until the clearing weather beckoned them on again. There was no real night at that latitude so he would have to depend on his sun compass for lines of position. His magnetic compass would be difficult to read so close to the magnetic pole. It had been only a year earlier when W. E. Gilbert, a well-known bush pilot, had flown over the mysterious pole on King William's Island, which was just a few hundred miles to the north of Baker Lake.

When I had made the first flights in 1943 from Europe to Canada's west coast in an obsolete Handley-Page Hampden bomber, my track from Coral Harbour on Southampton Island in Hudson Bay to Edmonton and Fort Smith N.W.T. had taken me just south of Baker Lake. I had used exactly the same navigational technique as Lindbergh had: dead-reckoning, drift sights and sun lines. The maps I'd used weren't much more detailed than those he'd used, so dead-reckoning wasn't very accurate. And, of course, if clouds hid the sun that meant no lines of position. It was a great relief to fly onto a chart which gave accurate ground features, but the main body of the Barrens would remain unmapped for many years.

So Lindbergh planned his flight to lessen chances of becoming lost. It was almost certain he would not know exactly where he was for long periods. He got off the grey water in front of the trading post at Baker Lake and flew slightly north of a direct course to Aklavik. That would cut down his time over the featureless Barrens and he would be able to locate himself when he found the open water and well-mapped shore of the Coronation Gulf. With bleak Victoria Island to starboard he followed the shoreline of Amundsen Gulf, named for the Norwegian explorer who had first sailed into the area. Then he cut across the tundra to the delta at the mouth of the Mackenzie, where he had to find the one proper channel in hundreds as the big river slowly wound its way to the Beaufort Sea, much like the Mississippi finding its way leisurely into the Gulf of Mexico.

His loyal crew was becoming more adept with her radio, and the call KHCAL, which spelled out his initials, was heard widely. She also relieved him on the flight controls while he had his charts on his knees or when he slept for a few moments. Then he would fly again while she slept,and so, by a real team effort, they continued to function at maximum efficiency. It was three o'clock in the morning when they finally found the settlement, which was big for the north, with about 20 or 30 houses, two churches, radio masts, and even another plane pulled up on the sloping river bank. It was still so light that people ran out with their cameras to take pictures.

Then the last river boat of the season arrived, to great excitement, but that night even the usual howling of the husky dogs was not enough to keep them awake. But now they faced another problem. They would need full tanks to make Point Barrow, America's farthest north settlement, where many other Arctic voyages had started or ended. The weather was cloudless, but windless too. So the water was flat, glassy. They were there for three days before Walter Gilbert and his crewman Lew Parmenter offered a solution. (Parmenter was very experienced in the bush and was to go on to become one of Ferry Command's senior flight engineers). The two aircraft taxied out together and Gilbert's Fokker G-CASK, already famous in the north, added to her laurels. Gilbert taxied rapidly in circles creating some waves, then led Lindbergh so that his propeller slipstream enabled Lindbergh to get on the step of his floats. Then the expert pilot carefully nursed the overloaded aircraft into the air. Gilbert turned south and flew up the MacKenzie, eventually reaching Edmonton in record time. There *Edmonton Journal* reporter Gordon McCallum filed his story, which told the world how the famous couple were doing on their epic flight.

Actually, just then they weren't doing too well. There were long patches of dense sea fog which Lindbergh attempted to fly under, as he had no intention of being caught on top with no sure way of knowing where he was. Descending blind under those conditions had terminated many a pilot's flying career. He had had plenty of experience in this dangerous type of flying when he was flying the US Airmail by night and day from St. Louis to Chicago and return in 1926, using rickety de Havilland biplanes with no radio and only elementary flight instruments. In fact he had even baled out when the weather closed down at his destination and his fuel had become exhausted. Now, in the rear cockpit his wife, his crew, and his radio operator, all rolled into one fragile woman, was justifiably nervous. She glimpsed the metallic scales of the sea, which she knew were as hard as steel. But she did not lose her nerve as she tried to hear the Barrow weather, without which they would have to turn back. They were flying so low that

Lindbergh told her to reel in her antenna. That meant she could not send, but she let out just a few feet so she could receive, and finally she copied the Morse which told them that the fog was lifting and the visibility had increased to two miles. She'd done it!

She poked her husband excitedly with her message pad and when he read it he nodded. They'd press right on. They landed in a lagoon where the radio man in his khaki mackinaw stood out against the Eskimos in their parkas and sealskin mukluks. They were received as the heroes they were into the Doctor's house, where they sat down to a real Thanksgiving dinner with all the inhabitants pooling their supplies. But there was one sad note. The *Northland,* the yearly supply boat, was stuck 100 miles down the coast waiting for a wind change to blow the pack ice off-shore. It also carried their gasoline supply, the lack of which made the next leg to Nome very trickly. They got away finally, but had misjudged the time of sunset as they were now flying south. So, with their fuel running low, they had to land on Shishmaref inlet on the coast of the Seward Peninsula, more than a hundred miles short of Nome. Lindbergh had made up his mind to force-land so quickly that his wife barely had time to reel in the trailing antenna after she had told WXN in Nome they were on their way down. Whether the people anxiously waiting their arrival got their message she could not tell. Anyway, she soon had other troubles as the floats spanked the water when Lindbergh landed down-wind in the gloom of the mountain-surrounded inlet. After he shut off the engine the silence was dramatic. He threw out the anchor, and they were safe, temporarily at least. At Nome the welcoming bonfire lit an empty shore as the welcoming crowd straggled home. In their aircraft they made a sleeping place in the baggage compartment out of their parachutes, flying suits and sleeping bag, and so they slept. But not for long. Some Eskimo duck-hunters dropped by to say hello and a guttural voice woke them. Finally the hunters left and sleep came, doubly welcome. The most dangerous part of their flight was behind them. Or so they believed.

They would keep going to find out. That was what pioneers were for, wasn't it?

The next morning, after an uneventful flight, they landed on Nome's 'Safety Harbour' and spent three days getting used to the sight of roads and automobiles. Then it was an eleven-hour hop across the Bering Sea to the harbour of Karaginiski in Russian Siberia. When they flew through the 180 degree line of longitude they lost a day, so it wasn't until 16 August that they experienced the true Russian hospitality at Petropavlosk. Then, after six hours in the air with the Sea of Okhotsk to starboard and the blue Pacific to port, they were forced by their old enemy, dense sea fog, to land on the northernmost of Japan's string of Chisima Islands. It was just a volcanic peak called Ketoi sticking out of the ocean. Anne had been able to contact Radio JOC in Tokyo, who dispatched the two-masted ship *Shinshuru Maru* to help them after they had managed to anchor on the lee side of the island. Then they could not start their engine and soon ran their battery down. The *Shinshuru* to the rescue! After a bad storm had passed, cutting their anchor rope in the process, the Japanese ship had secured them with another anchor and then towed them to nearby Buroton Bay, where their next cache of gas was located. There in the protected harbour scooped out of a volcano they refuelled and recharged their battery.

They had hoped to reach Tokyo on the next leg. But it wasn't to be. The weather forced them to land in various strange harbours no less then five times. Once they slept in a fisherman's simple hut, and the rest of the time they toughed it out in the aircraft's fuselage. It was during one of those hairy descents alongside a mountain, in and out of fog, that Anne decided that she would never fly again. However, when they finally reached Tokyo and civilization the incipient mutiny died out. But Lindbergh almost made her change her mind when he was interviewed by reporters. He said it was just a 'pleasure trip'. Maybe her knuckles were white, but she kept her mouth shut. Maybe they were even as white as they had been when they were tobogganing down the side of a volcano.

After more than two weeks of meetings and parties in Tokyo, where Lindbergh sounded out the Japanese on direct flights to America, they set out for China. But not before a would-be stowaway was found and ejected from the baggage compartment of the Sirius. It was ironic that he thought he was going to America. And so they flew due west until they saw the brown waters of the Yangtze river darkening the blue waters of the wrongly named Yellow Sea. Then they flew up the majestic river until they were able to land at Lotus Lake, near Nanking.

The great river was in flood and the Lindberghs offered to help in flying medical supplies and doctors to remote spots. After one landing the aircraft was almost swamped by hungry peasants in their sampans. Lindbergh had to fire warning shots from his .38 revolver to frighten them away. Fortunately, this time the engine started on the first try and so they made their escape. They moved up-river to Hankow and made many more mercy flights; and it was at Hankow that fate finally finished their flight. The British aircraft carrier HMS *Hermes* had lifted their aircraft aboard for safety overnight, away from the endless sampans in the river who had little regard for the fragility of aircraft. While they were slinging the Sirius over the side next morning, with Lindbergh and his wife aboard, a hoisting ring jammed. Lindbergh got the engine started but he was too late to offset the swift current. A wing went down and they had to jump. Anne remembered no fear, only thinking as she gulped down mouthfuls of dirty polluted Yangtze water that she'd been religiously brushing her teeth with boiled water for weeks.

The Lindberghs took a ship from Japan back to American while the *Hermes* delivered the wreckage of the Sirius to Shanghai, from where it was shipped back to the Lockheed Aircraft factory in Burbank for a complete rebuild. (The *Hermes* was sunk near Trincomalee, Ceylon, on 9 April 1942 by bombers from carriers of the Japanese Imperial Navy commanded by Admiral Nagumo. He was the man who commanded the sneak attack at Pearl Harbour on 7 December 1941. But the United States Navy got revenge for both Pearl Harbour and the *Hermes* at the Battle of Midway in June 1942, when they sank all four of Nagumo's carriers and killed the majority of his airmen).

Lindbergh had proved the Great Circle route to the Orient could be flown. But, being the realist he was, he reported that until aircraft were developed which could overfly the ice-packed harbours and pervasive fog the route was impractical. There were also political difficulties. The Russians refused to discuss landing rights in Siberia because the United States still refused to recognise Lenin's successors and the government they had established by revolution fourteen years before. The Japanese, polite and mysterious as ever, declined to talk about routes or bases in their country. In fact they were fortifying their mandated islands, contrary to League of Nations directives, in preparation for the war which they had already decided was inevitable.

Pan Am turned their attention to the Atlantic, where more than a quarter of a million passengers were being carried each year by ships between the United States and Europe.

And again they turned to Lindbergh to make a survey flight in 1933 along the Great Circle route to the east instead of the west. Lindbergh had funded most of his flight to the Orient from personal resources, but this time Pan Am was firmly behind him. They chartered a Danish steamer *Jelling* to act as 'mother ship'. It would carry the fuel needed, thus getting away from the long and tedious business of shipping drums to remote locations. It would also carry mechanics, a radio station and an operator, as well as a physician. It even carried a spare plane, which fortunately was not needed.

Lindbergh stayed with his two best assets — Anne, his favourite crew, and the rebuilt Sirius, which was still on floats. He felt that his flight would make an even greater contribution to the advance of aviation than his solo flight of 1927.

Complete with the same radio and emergency equipment but without parachutes, which Lindbergh felt were useless in the cold Arctic seas, they got away from New York on 9 July 1933. They visited Halifax, then St. John's in Newfoundland, then made their way up the rugged Labrador coast, landing at Cartwright, Hopedale and Hebron. Anne kept the *Jelling* and Pan Am abreast of their progress. If she had been classified as a tyro on her first flight she could now be called an expert. They had the usual difficulties with fog, too much wind and no wind at all. Finally they made it across the Davis Strait to Godthaab in Greenland. Finding no good anchorage or area suitable for an airport there he flew north to Godhaven, where he decided it was too dangerous to land. So he turned south and put down at Holsteinsborg, a small coastal settlement.

He was only a few miles from the Sondestrom fjord, where Bernt Balchen would establish a secret landing base on the USAAC's 'Crimson Route' during World War II. Its code name was Bluie West Eight and it would be from there that I would make the first flight from Greenland's west coast to Iceland in a lumbering Catalina amphibian early in 1942. Lindbergh did the initial survey flying, but it wasn't until the urgency of delivering aircraft to the war fronts that the authorities would spend the huge amounts of money necessary to establish land airports.

Lindbergh was aided by the reports of Arctic explorer Vilhjalmur Steffanson, who had made two ground expeditions sponsored by Pan Am in 1932. And he needed all the information he could get, because he proposed to fly across the forbidding, unmapped Greenland ice-cap to survey the east coast. It took him over seven hours to reach Ella Island and then he went on to Eskimonaes, which at 74° North latitude was his farthest north penetration. It was also the site of a secret weather station established by the Germans in 1941. It would take Bernt Balchen and a squadron of Liberators to eradicate them.

Now Lindbergh started south. He landed at Angmassalik, which I would know by its code name Bluie East Two, then slipped across the ice-cap once again to Godthaab to make sure all his observations were correct. Then it was south to Julianthaab, which was inland on the Nararssuak fjord. Close by would be built the staging post of Bluie West One, familiar to thousands of airmen who used it in World War II as a stepping stone from Goose Bay, Labrador, to Iceland, on their way to Prestwick and the war.

The *Jelling* was faithfully tracking the Lindberghs and their versatile aircraft as he turned north again. It was at Angmassalik that an Eskimo boy gave a perfectly suitable name to the black and orange plane. He called it 'Tingmissartoq' which meant 'the one who flies like a big bird'. When the lad painted the name on the fuselage it was a little crooked, because he had lined up the letters with the water instead of the flight line and the floats always sat lower in the water to the rear. The Lindberghs loved the rustic touch.

Then they turned their backs on Greenland's deep fjords and featureless ice-cap as they flew across the Denmark Strait to the remote island of Iceland. There were meetings with the officials at Reykjavik and then Lindbergh decided to check out an alternate anchorage at Eskifjordur on the east coast. But the harbour was exposed to the Arctic storms sweeping down the Norwegian sea, so he turned south and checked out both the Faroe and Shetland islands, where he found the prevailing weather just as atrocious.

Finally they landed at Copenhagen and began the really important talks with the Danes who controlled Iceland and

Greenland. Anne now changed from her flight suit, helmet and goggles into a formal gown and became the gracious, diplomatic helpmate her forthright husband needed. It was a role for which she was well suited. They met the King and Queen of Denmark, then the prime minister, and finally the mayor of Copenhagen. Everywhere they were hailed and in some cases plagued by enthusiastic crowds numbering in the thousands. It was a pattern which would be followed all through their landings in Europe. Being famous wasn't all fun. After a week in a luxury hotel they set off again, this time to Helsingfors in Finland. After receiving hard-to-get flight permits they dropped in to Russia's Leningrad, and finally Moscow. When they landed on the Moscow river with the cold, stern walls of the Kremlin in the distance their welcome was still warm. After the usual round of vodka-soaked receptions which the Lindberghs found slightly boring they flew to Tallin in Estonia and then across the Baltic to Oslo and Stavanger. Southward across the North Sea they found a snug harbour at Southampton where transatlantic flying boats not yet built would land in time to come.

All Britain was air-minded and they were received by royalty and Prime Minister Ramsay MacDonald and thousands of common citizens. More to the point for Pan Am, the 'Lone Eagle' had meetings with George Woods-Humphries, the managing director of flag carrier Imperial Airways. When they compared flying boats on the drawing board the Englishman wasn't exactly ecstatic with joy when he realised how far ahead the Americans were, and that they were likely to beat his airline in the Atlantic race.

Lindbergh was always proud of the Irish side of his ancestry so he flew to Galway to give the Emerald Islanders a glimpse of his plane as well as Anne and himself. Then, after having checked out the landing facilities in Ireland, he flew up to Inverness in Scotland, which could be an alternate landing spot. He found the Firth of Inverness well protected and listed it for future use, although it was never used until the start of World War II, and then only for military aircraft.

Now he turned south again, right across the English Channel, until he could see the Eiffel Tower and land on the River Seine. Paris was *en fête* for the pair of globe-trotters and they spent several days there mixing pleasure with business.

Then it was over to Amsterdam where the mechanics of

KLM gave the Tingmissartoq a thorough check. Pioneer Dutch Aircraft designer Tony Fokker understood the advantages of the new American aircraft designs and soon would sell a fleet of Douglas DC2s and then DC3s to various European flying companies. The Dutch had had their own aviation heroes but were unstinting in their praise for Lindbergh's achievements.

The next stop on their itinerary was Geneva, Switzerland, but it proved difficult to reach. On their first try the weather was so bad that they were forced back after some hours of instrument flight in turbulent clouds. Anne had another attack of white knuckles but gamely decided not to desert the ship.

Finally they made it through the passes of the Alps onto Lake Geneva. The Swiss were most pleased to meet them, although they had no aspirations at that time for a transatlantic route. Swissair, the national flag carrier, was already operating sister ships to Lindbergh's Sirius on their domestic flights. The Sirius had been built primarily as an airmail carrier and so the pilot's cockpit was far to the rear of the wing, which meant visibility was poor.

So when Lockheed enlarged the fuselage to accommodate passengers they placed the pilot up in the nose just behind the engine, where he belonged. They called the sister ships the Orion and folded the landing gear neatly into the wing.

This arrangement was popular with the pilots who always got the blame if their aircraft ground-looped or slipped off the common grass fields. The graceful lines of the aircraft also pleased the Swiss, who were growing increasingly tired of their clumsy Fokker F.7Bs. Passengers liked the fact that the Lockheed Orion was a good 60 mph faster than *any* aircraft flown by competing European airlines. So, with the compliments of the Swiss still ringing in their ears, the Lindberghs turned their faces to the west, homeward bound.

On the way they stopped at Santana on the coast of Spain, then hopped over to Portugal's Rio Minhot and Lisbon, still showing the American flag. Everywhere the unique husband-wife team was received with rapture. They had been the greatest ambassadors of goodwill the United States would ever have, or hope to have.

But the flight back would not be an easy one. The prevailing wind across the North Atlantic was westerly. It had helped Lindbergh greatly when he flew the *Spirit of St. Louis,* but now it was dead against him. So he flew to Horta in the Azores, which would shorten his long Atlantic flight leg by a significant amount. But, as would happen often in the future, with even much larger flying boats, other problems prevented his take-off. The local sheltered harbour was too small for the heavily laden Sirius. Out in the open sea there was plenty of room, but the heavy swells rolling in all the way from North America made a take-off so hazardous as to be unthinkable. The Sirius could have returned as deck cargo, but the Lindberghs didn't want to end their odyssey that way. They decided to fly via the South Atlantic, where the winds and seas were not so terrible. They knew it would add 7,500 miles to their journey and take an extra month. But they felt the extra effort was worth it, as they would arrive back in the aircraft they had started out with, and also that the information gained on their southerly flight would be valuable to Pan American.

So they pointed the nose of the Tingmissartoq south and landed at Las Palmas in the Canary Islands, then dropped in at remote Villa Cisneros in Rio de Oro on the edge of the Sahara desert. Then they flight-planned for Santiago in the Cape Verde Islands, where they believed the French had a base for their transatlantic flying boat operations. But when they got to the remote rocks they found that the harbour at Porto Praia was not as attractive as it appeared on their navigation chart. It was too exposed and confined, and it appeared the flying boats had landed and taken off in the lee of the islands. Once again the ocean swells were a dangerous hazard, and when they finally decided to land Anne thought their pontoons must surely collapse under the pounding of the seas. A small rowboat towed them into the harbour where they managed to set up a secure anchor.

But the small Portuguese outpost had few amenities. It appeared the transatlantic flying boat operation had ceased operations some time previously. On shore the Lindberghs found their quarters extremely distasteful and elected to sleep on board their aircraft instead of fighting the hordes of black bedbugs. The *Jelling* was now just a fond memory. How they could have used her! But the island was a good 200 miles closer to Natal in Brazil than any other African harbour, so Lindbergh was determined to try a take-off. Two hundred miles meant about two hours in the air, a significant margin for a safe westerly flight. But in the end he had to give up the idea of a heavy take-off, because the winds never stopped, and the rollers never became less. Maybe that was the main reason the French had abandoned the base.

However, there was a powerful radio station, so permission was sought to make a light take-off to Dakar. After an agonizing wait the permission to land was denied because there was an epidemic of Yellow Fever there. They could be quarantined for an indefinite period. So that was out of the question. Back to the radio station, who contacted Bathurst in Gambia, a British possession. Yes, the Governor would be pleased to grant authorization for the flight . . . Kindly advise time of arrival . . . Good news. Great news. But the danger of the take-off still loomed in their minds.

They were towed out of the choppy entrance to the harbour into the open seas with the aircraft wallowing in the heavy swell. When they started their take-off run the water rushed over their wings as they got up on the step. Then the pontoons once again had to withstand the heavy whacks of the waves, but Lindbergh skilfully stalled the aircraft off and finally they were in the air. The endless wind was now behind them. Anne contacted CRRK at Porto Priaia with their estimate at Bathurst, where they were received in Government House by his Excellency the Governor and his wife. A delicious fish lunch was followed by a wallow in a hot bath. Maybe these English were all right, after all!

But if there had been too much wind in the Cape Verde Islands, now the problem was just the opposite. No wind. Not even a breeze to ruffle the flat surface of the big harbour. They tried several times to get off, both by night and by day, but with no success. And this time they had no friendly Canadian bush pilot to produce an artificial wind. Lindbergh had cut back his gas to the limit of safety, and now decided that a really intense lightening of his load would enable him to get away. Every day wasted made his flight that much more difficult because the moon would soon be setting as it waned. His flight plan would be 16 hours, so he needed the moon either for take-off or landing in the black waters of the harbours he had to use. He was ruthless: he left behind most of his tools, nearly all of his emergency rations and a host of smaller items such as their cameras and personal clothing.

What he did not leave behind was their rubber boat and their emergency radio equipment. This equipment had been designed by Mr. Hugo Leuteritz, Chief Communication Engineer of Pan American Airways. It weighed 44 pounds and comprised a transmitter set on 5,515 kc and 8,340 kc with a companion receiver tunable from 320 to 555 kc and from 4,614 to 11,110 kc. The sets were in a watertight and padded aluminium box. During their tests they were dropped 18 feet onto a concrete floor and continued to function when they were set up again. The box was also submerged for 24 hours in water and worked perfectly when brought to the surface.

When they taxied out on the night of 6 December they were using up the last of the moon to illuminate the surface of the harbour. The long take-off run was a full two minutes, but finally they broke clear. The 200 pounds left behind had made the critical difference. But, as is usual in these cases, there was a last minute fright. Just as they broke water the engine began to splutter. Lindbergh pressed on, sure it was just a bit of water or air in the gas line. He was right, but Anne wasn't so sure. She put the thought of a balky engine out of her mind as she began to operate her radio. Schedules had been set up for position reports on the hour and half hour with Pan American stations, using Morse, of course.

Through the usual tropical static crashes called 'QRN' she listened for PVC in Natal as she used her ship's callsign of KHCAL. For a long time she could hear nothing but static; then, dim and faint, she began to hear some 'faint squeaks, no

more than a twig tapping on a window-pane during a storm.'
The air was rough, but she concentrated on the weak signals
and eventually was able to get her position reports through.
Then suddenly she heard WCC calling her. She found it hard
to believe, because that station was at Chatham,
Massachusetts, nearly 4,000 miles away. They wanted to
conduct an in-the-air interview, but Anne told them she was
too busy. But the reporters got their story anyway, because it
was a long-distance record for an aircraft in flight contact with
a ground station. But as the sun came up the propagation
changed. Even when she changed her frequency and coils and
reeled her antenna in and out she was out of contact. So she
tapped out her position 'blind', hoping that some Pan
American station would copy them, even if she couldn't hear
their acknowledgement, that dit-dah-dit (R), she so prized. It
turned out she was right, and that most of her positions *had*
been copied on the ground.

Then Lindbergh started a series of sun shots while Anne flew
the aircraft. Even as she concentrated on holding her course
she left her earphones on and the trailing antenna out. After a
long time she worked her old friend CRKK, which was now
further from the aircraft than Natal. But the contact faded out
with no useful information exchanged.

There is a general call for *any* station, using the letters CQ.
She tried that — with no luck. So then she dropped KHCAL
and signed 'the Lindbergh plane', which she had found in the
past had given good results. And once again the ploy worked.
Soon she was talking to DDEA, the SS *Caparcona.* Eleven
hours into the flight she sent her position report to be relayed
to Natal. Only five hours to go. Then they passed over another
ship, the *Aldebaran,* which reminded her of the star. Then she
worked DDWE, the *Westphalan,* which was the German ship
stationed in the South Atlantic to catapult a float aircraft to
shorten the time for mail delivery. DDWE gave them a
directional course to steer for the ship. Radio was now backing
up astro and dead-reckoning navigation. Then the ship gave
them a bearing for the island of Fernando de Noronha, off the
coast of Brazil, and then to Natal.

So, just 16 hours after leaving Africa they landed alongside
the PAA barge in the river at Natal. The navigation during the
flight and the teamwork between the two Lindberghs was so
exemplary that Lieutenant Commander P. V. H. Weems used

it as the frontispiece for his comprehensive book, *Air Navigation,* published by McGraw-Hill in 1937.

They continued their survey flight by landing at Belem, then flying up the Amazon to Manaus, a rubber plantation town. Then it was across the jungle to Trinidad's Port of Spain, up the Caribbean to Puerto Rico, and finally back to North America's mainland at Dinner Key near Miami. They visited Charleston and finally landed on Flushing Bay near New York on 19 December, the very place from which they had started five months before.

They had flown more than 30,000 miles without an accident over some of the most dangerous terrain in the world, varying from Greenland's ice-cap to the long, lonely Atlantic and the deadly jungles of South America. Their pontoons had tasted the waters of 21 countries in four continents. New York gave them one of the most boisterous, enthusiastic welcomes on record.

When Lindbergh submitted his report to Pan Am's president Juan Trippe he stressed that the most advantageous route would always be via the Great Circle. He also stated that wheeled aircraft would be the most practical. This was almost heresy in the age of flying boats. But until large land airports were developed he was sure that the big flying boats which the American designers were developing were far superior to those of the British. So the diplomats fought it out during a lengthy stalemate until 1937 when Imperial Airways and Pan American finally started summer-time experimental flights across the North Atlantic.

Winter-time flights would have to wait until the war emergency made the first Lockheed Hudson flights necessary in November 1940. From then on, aided by anti-icing devices and ground navigational aids, there would be a heavy stream of bombers making the long crossing direct from Newfoundland. It wasn't until the spring of 1942 that the Greenland-Iceland route was proven practical, and I was proud to have been part of those pioneering flights.

Chapter 9
The lure of the Great Circle

The air had become a little choppy and the Captain's announcement that we were now letting down and that we'd be on the ground at Chicago in fifteen minutes shattered my thoughts of the genuine heroes of the pre-war days. But not for long. Wiley Post had been right. The combination of pressurization and high-altitude flight had made my trip of 800 miles almost pleasurable. And Lindbergh had been right too. Wheel-equipped aircraft had replaced flying boats on the shortest distance between North America and Europe, with the result that large numbers of passengers had overcome their fear of flying and were deserting the luxury liners. I had always avoided ships because of their slow progress, and I hated to be laid out for days by seasickness. No doubt now a lot of other people were beginning to think the same way.

Through my association with Ferry Command I had been fortunate enough to meet many famous pioneer aviators and when I heard 'Chicago' it reminded me of Bert 'Fish' Hassell, who came from Rockford, just 50 miles to the north-west of the Windy City. In 1928 he and Parker 'Shorty' Cramer had left Rockford bound for Stockholm, Sweden, in a Stinson Detroiter single-engined aircraft on *wheels*, of all things. They intended to be the first to traverse the dreaded Greenland ice-

cap. They had spotted fuel along their route, and also had had their mechanic set out a snow runway near Sondrestrom fjord, that very familiar name. It was there that the University of Michigan had set up a geological and meteorological research station, so there was a small body of men to help.

They crashed on their first take-off attempt on 26 June, because they were heavily overloaded with 400 gallons of fuel. But, nothing daunted, they repaired their aircraft and took off again on 16 August. This time they skimmed over the fence at the end of the runway, which the citizens of Rockford had lengthened, with just 250 gallons on board. This was enough to take them to Cochrane, Ontario, where a longer runway had been prepared. For two days they waited for a good weather forecast which was bound to be not very accurate because of the lack of reporting stations. When they got away they flew in cloud with no navigation aids except a drift meter they couldn't use. After 20 hours they found themselves over Greenland, a flight of 2,100 miles, but lost. They searched for the 120 mile long fjord, much as I had done on more than one occasion. I was luckier than they, because I always made it, but after looking for four hours Hassell decided to set the landplane on the ice-cap. After two weeks of jumping bottomless ice crevasses and detouring for endless miles around icy, water-filled fjords, the smoke of the airmen's campfire was spotted by a band of Eskimo hunters who reported it to the university camp. Soon they were on their way back to civilization, but not without a further adventure when the boat taking them out sank on a reef. However, their welcome in Denmark must have made up for a lot, as the Scandinavians had a deep interest in one of their descendants trying to reach Sweden rather than France, Germany or Great Britain.

I met Hassell during the war at Goose Bay and Frobisher, when he was a Colonel in the USAAF putting his Arctic knowledge to work. He was a really rugged man with what seemed like an infinite capacity for booze and a vocabulary which could be described as 'colourful', an understatement if ever there was one. I thought he would have been right at home in the free and easy environment of Ferry Command, although the thought of Clarence 'Duke' Schiller and him together in the Piccadilly Club at Montreal was more than a little frightening.

Cramer was still obsessed with his Great Circle flight. He

made a second attempt in a twin-engined Sikorsky flying boat in 1929, but it sank at anchor during a storm off the coast of Labrador. Then in 1931 he and Canadian radio operator Oliver Pacquette set off in a Bellanca 'Pacemaker' with a 225 hp Packard diesel engine. On 5 August they made it across the ice-cap, the first to do so. But they had little time to enjoy their triumph because they were lost on the last leg of their flight from the Shetland Islands to Copenhagen when they flew into a violent North Sea gale and were never heard of again. Bits of their aircraft were discovered a month later off the Shetlands.

In the meantime there were efforts to fly the Great Circle track from east to west, led by German Wolfgang von Gronau in 1930. He used the same flying boat, a twin-engined Dornier 'Wal', that had taken Amundsen almost to the North Pole in 1926, but the methodical pilot had added an experimental model of an artificial horizon, a precision altimeter and a gyrocompass. He would need all of these blind flying instruments as he flew through the treacherous weather that always lurked on his route. His three crewmen, a copilot, a radio operator and a mechanic, had been briefed to keep their mouths shut about their itinerary because neither von Gronau nor the German Government wanted the blame if the flight failed. Certainly a very Germanic attitude! And just the opposite to that of Canadians or Americans. They staged through Reykjavik harbour, then flew across the Denmark Strait, sometimes almost on the surface in fierce and turbulent clouds. However, they managed to land at Ivigtut on Greenland's south-west coast after a nine-hour flight. Another fog-filled flight and they were able to reach North America at Labrador's well-protected harbour at Cartwright. Then they landed at Halifax, and finally circled the Statue of Liberty at New York, eight days and 47 flying hours after leaving the Fatherland.

Von Gronau knew that the old Wal with its 500 hp BMW engines could not top the ice-cap, so in 1931 he set out in a new Dornier flying boat with 700 hp BMW engines. He passed Cramer in the Faroe islands, determined to be the first to cross the ice-cap from east to west. He flew from Iceland to Angmassalik, then north to Scoresby Sound. His instructions from the German Government were to investigate the climatic conditions for an air route to America, and he had the same crew as on his previous flight to assist him. But it wasn't going to be easy. The Dornier took off on 15 August after a long run, full to the limit with gas. Then it took an interminable time to get to an altitude which would clear the 10,000 foot peaks of the ice-cap. I knew exactly how he felt, and I always considered that a minimum altitude of 14,000 feet was safe, and never mind what the charts said. Von Gronau was right to demand more powerful engines, because from time to time he had only 600 feet clearance and had to change course frequently to avoid uncharted mountains of ice. He flew on instruments for over an hour in a snowstorm. Without his modern instruments he surely would have crashed. It took him ten hours to make it to the west coast; then he flew across the Davis Strait to Ungava Bay and then to Hudson Bay and finally south to Chicago.

As the Connie landed with a small bump I reflected that Ferry Command's first east and west flights across the icecap in 1942 had been damn near as dangerous as that of von Gronau. Ours' were only the third eastbound and the fourth westbound flights over the route. I always thought that the third westbound flight was probably the most interesting. John Grierson had flown solo in a de Havilland Fox Moth in 1934 'over the top' from England to North America. For some reason his flight did not receive the publicity it deserved. As far as I was concerned, survey flights in multi-engined aircraft aided by trained crewmen are one thing. Solo flights in single-engined aircraft are certainly birds of another colour.

Because I had cleverly obtained a window seat, even the hustle and bustle of departing passengers being replaced with new ones failed to divert my mind from another famous Ferry Command pilot. He was Senior Captain Clyde Pangborn who had contributed so many acts to the Gates Flying Circus in the 1920s he'd become known as 'Upside-Down Pangborn'. In 1931, with another Ferry Command Captain, Hugh Herndon Jr., Pangborn had set out to beat Wiley Post's round-the-world record. They had flown in a red Bellanca on wheels named *Miss Veedol*, and 30 hours after leaving New York they circled down through a hole in the clouds, wondering where they were (like most aviators of the day). They discovered they'd made it to a farmer's field near Moylegrove in Wales. They got to Croydon the next day, and then it was Berlin. A rough flight to Moscow was followed by a rougher flight through a pass in the Ural mountains to Novosibirsk. Then, while Pangborn napped, Herndon lost the way and they landed somewhere in Mongolia. They made it to Chita and then to Khabarovsk which was to be their last stop in Siberia. As seemed normal for remote Russian airfields, this one was covered with several inches of mud. When they touched down they hydroplaned and slid off the end of the so-called runway. They were now firmly stuck and it wasn't until the next day that several hundred volunteers dragged them back to the airfield and into a small hangar. The field was too much of a swamp to take off even then, and, as they were now 27 hours behind Post and Gatty, they decided to give up the speed attempt.

They decided instead to proceed to Japan and try for the $25,000 prize offered by the Japanese newspaper *Asahi Shimbun* for the first non-stop flight from Japan to the USA. Without proper clearance, which they thought the American Embassy had obtained for them, they were detained by the police for a month as suspected spies when they landed at Tokyo's Tachikawa airport. They readily admitted they had used their cameras, just like any tourist. When they appealed to the Embassy they were told they were out of luck because they'd violated Japanese laws. It was a typical embassy-type reaction in my estimation. Finally, Pangborn's Washington friends got through and on 2 September 1931 they were given permission to leave. But they must be successful on their first, and as far as the Japs were concerned, only, attempt. Oriental thinking, no doubt.

They flew to Sabishiro which had a long stretch of sandy beach. They would need it because the Bellanca would have to carry 915 gallons of gas and 45 gallons of oil, enough (barely) for 4,500 miles to Boise, Idaho, the home state of their friend Senator Borah. It was on the morning of 1 October that Pangborn began the hazardous one-time take-off. Acceleration was painfully slow. But a mile and a half down the beach he began to rock the plane from wheel to wheel, which is a trick water flyers use to unstick first one float and then the other. Finally, with less than 200 yards of beach remaining, the plane staggered into the air. Pangborn was in no mood to abort the take-off. He said he'd had more than enough of the Japanese. With the engine roaring at full throttle and the plane wallowing it was several long minutes before he could turn on a Great Circle course of 72 degrees True, which would take them by the shortest route to far-away North America.

Pangborn had another trick up his sleeve to lessen the wind resistance. He would drop the landing gear. But when he pulled the release pin two of the struts failed to release. This could be a serious problem, not only for drag but as a sort of spear into the fuselage in the event of a belly landing. They started to pick up ice as night fell, and finally topped the cloud in intense cold at 14,000 feet. Then Pangborn performed a fantastic feat. He let Herndon fly and climbed out into the bitter slipstream and freed the two struts, which dropped into the cloud below. Perhaps his many years of wing-walking (which Lindbergh had also done) while barnstorming had helped him keep his balance.

Over the storm-lashed waters of the Gulf of Alaska the engine quit twice. Pangborn had to dive steeply to get the prop windmilling again. On one occasion the black, deadly waters were only 1,500 feet below. They continued towards Boise, but it was socked in with fog. There had been a news flash when they left Japan and an amateur radio operator's report that he'd heard an aircraft overhead at False Pass in the Aleutians, and that was all. Now, 40 hours later, it was time to get down. Pangborn chose Wenatchee, Washington, where he knew the airfield, and incidentally where his mother and brother lived. He got down with some damage. They had been in the air over 41 hours and had won the $25,000. The Bellanca was repaired and sold to Dr. Leon Pisculi and Edna Newcomer, a practising nurse. They renamed it *The American Nurse* and set out to fly the Atlantic to Italy. But the plane and its passengers were lost at sea with no trace ever found.

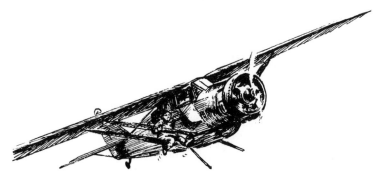

Now Pangborn was at a loose end. His barnstorming days were over and he'd made his imprint in the history books. At 35, and in the middle of the Depression, he had to search for ferrying jobs with some airmail flying in between. Then early in 1934 he heard of the World's Greatest Air Race, which was the MacRobertson Trophy from England to Australia. There was a $75,000 prize for open speed and handicap entrants. He wanted to fly that trickiest of aircraft, a Gee Bee Super Sportster, but his backer quit. So Pangborn decided to throw in with flamboyant Roscoe Turner, who had leased a brand new Boeing 247D airliner from United Airlines. He would be copilot-navigator while Reeder Nicholls would operate their radio. It looked like a well-balanced crew. They flew the aircraft to New York where it was loaded on the tennis deck of the SS *Washington* rather than being flown over. Perhaps Turner thought the North Atlantic flight was too risky, and besides there was no prize to be gained there. When they got to Southampton there was no suitable crane to unload the awkward cargo, so they continued on to Le Havre. But there they encountered the first of many difficulties because the French authorities wanted a $20,000 bond while the aircraft was on French soil, even if it was just in transit. Naturally Turner didn't have that kind of cash. Finally the huge harbour crane at Le Havre safely placed the aircraft on a floating lighter for just a few hundred francs. Then they were towed across the English Channel without ever touching French soil, and so to England.

At a military airfield called Mildenhall, which was still under construction about 75 miles north of London, all entries were assembled for inspection. The Royal Aero Club was in charge and in late July announced there were 63 entries from 13 countries. The competition consisted of a speed section, for which only five intermediate stops were allowed on the 12,314 statute mile course, and a handicap section that allowed for 23 stops. Naturally, any landings tended to slow down the speed of the contestants.

Finally, on the departure date of 20 October only 20 entries were flagged away. Many of the drop-outs had legitimate reasons but, as is usual in such a much-heralded event, others had entered just for the publicity. The Boeing, registration NR275Y, racing number 5, got away second. There was a bit of confusion with numbers because Turner wanted to display '57' prominently on the nose of his aircraft as he had some sort of a deal with the Heinz company who had made that particular number famous.

Turner and Pangborn figured their toughest competition would be three specially built de Havilland Comet racers, which had been built from design to flight in the remarkably short time of nine months to carry the Union Jack. These all-wood aircraft were the first built in the British Empire to feature variable pitch propellers, wing flaps and retractable undercarriage. They were the precursors to the de Havilland Mosquito, the most versatile and useful aircraft of World War II, and with which I had a long and intimate relationship.

Another tough competitor would be the KLM entry of a Douglas DC2 airliner PH-AJU, racing number 44, named the 'Uiver', which meant Stork. The aircraft would be flown by experienced Dutch pilots K. D. Parmentier and J. J. Moll, both navigators of note. The Philips 80 watt radio would be handled by Van Bruge, while mechanic Prins would keep the engines turning. The Uiver would have a significant advantage because KLM had since 1928 been operating the longest scheduled air route in the world, from Holland to Batavia, Netherlands East Indies, which was about three-quarters of the way along the chosen route.

All the survivors suffered from tired engines, muddy fields, equipment breakdown, enervating fatigue, and, most of all, from being lost a good deal of the time. With no radio aids and not very reliable maps it was a wonder they finished at all. In the event a Comet, 'Grosvenor House', registration G-ACSS and racing number 34, was first across the finishing line. The tired crew, C. W. A. Scott and T. C. Black, who had no radio to aid them, had taken only 70 hours, 54 minutes and 18 seconds from England to Melbourne.

The DC2 came in second and took first in the handicap, while the 247D came in third and so took second in the speed section. Comet G-ACSR, racing number 19, flown by O. Carthcart-Jones and K. F. H. Waller was next in, followed by another de Havilland product, a Dragon flown by New Zealanders J. D. Hewett and C. E. Kay. Entrants drifted into Melbourne at intervals for almost a week.

The third Comet, 'Black Magic', G-ACSP, racing number 63, was forced out of the race at Allahabad by burnt-out engines. The flight crew were the husband and wife team of J.

A. Mollison and Amy, the former Amy Johnson. They both held a cluster of long-distance records gained before and after their marriage. American racer Jacqueline Cochran tried in a Gee Bee racer with Wesley Smith, but gave up in the insufficiently tested tricky low-wing when they landed at Bucharest, slightly off course. Several others suffered similar misfortunes but, remarkably, there were only two fatalities — H. D. Gilman and J. Y. C. Baines, who crashed their open cockpit biplane, Fairey Fox G-ACXX, racing number 62, on take-off from Rome.

Turner and Pangborn split the £7,500 they had won and went their separate ways. The faithful 247D flew the line for United for many years. Pangborn came with Ferry Command in the early days, acting as a publicity agent to secure experienced American pilots before he made the pioneer Catalina deliveries across the Pacific to Singapore. I often wondered why Turner didn't join us. He would have fitted right in, just like his perennial racing rival Earl Ortman who gave five years of his life to delivering the bombers so desperately needed during the war.

Another famous pilot/navigator, who led the first seven Lockheed Hudsons across the North Atlantic on 10-11 November 1940 for the first winter crossing, was D. C. T. Bennett. He was an Australian who had set several long-distance records, including one from England to South Africa in a float plane. In addition he had been the pilot of the Mercury, the upper component flown on take-off and climb in conjunction with a powerful flying boat. When he got to his chosen height he uncoupled from 'Mother' and went on his lonely way across the North Atlantic to Canada and the USA with his load of airmail. It must have been a testing experience, but he was an expert radio man and navigator as well as a skilled pilot. When I was a radio operator at Cranbrook in 1938 I had bought his comprehensive book *The Complete Navigator* to go with my book by another famous navigator, Weems, who had written *Air Navigation, British Empire Edition*. The stars had always held a strange fascination for me.

There were other members of Ferry Command who had some claim to fame, as well as the outstanding ones. Why, even our boss, Air Commodore 'Taffy' Powell, had been an Imperial Airways flying boat captain pre-war and held an east-west speed record from Ireland to North America.

'Punch' Dickins was every Canadian boy's hero after his exploits as a fighter pilot in World War I and in the Arctic.

And there was Captain/Navigator P. G. Taylor, who would go on to fame for his flying and be knighted after the war for his efforts. I remembered he'd called his Catalina 'The Frigate Bird', when . . . oops, the Wrights fired up and we began to taxi out on Chicago's busy airport, ready for take-off. So I had to stop dreaming of the past for a short period while I assisted the Captain on his take-off, as always.

With my assistance he made a nice departure and soon we were back at about three miles high with nothing to worry about except the bum-numbing nine hours plus flight ahead.

It was reminiscing time again . . .

Chapter 10
'The Frigate Bird'

Ferry Command had pioneered many long-distance routes from the Arctic to the tropics, so it was only natural that they should be called upon to make the first flight by an alternative route from North America to New Zealand and Australia. This 'all-red' route, so-called for the British Empire countries coloured scarlet on all maps of the world, would use British Honduras and then drive westward to pick up the well-established route at Fiji. The French-claimed island of Clipperton, about 700 nautical miles south-west of Acapulco, Mexico, would have to serve as a refuelling point for the Catalina flying boat to be used. Our boss, Air Commodore 'Taffy' Powell took the Liberator 'Commando' and led a small armada to Mexico City to iron out the diplomatic difficulties of using neutral soil at Acapulco as a supply base. Sqn. Ldr. L. L. 'Slim' Jones, a fellow Saskatchewan native, would be captain-navigator for the long flight, and he used an amphibious Canso FP532 to set up a fuel cache on the tiny island. At the same time Captain Al Torrey had a Dakota to use for liaison. Torrey had checked me out as an instructor in Ferry Command and was a handsome, Spanish-speaking pilot who knew the ropes at Mexico City and Acapulco.

But suddenly the plan was cancelled because the Americans decided that Clipperton was in *their* area of operations, in accord with the Roosevelt/Churchill agreement that the whole Pacific, except only for areas adjacent to Australia and New Zealand, was an American operational zone.

Finally, after some diplomatic manoeuvring, the Americans gave permission for the survey flight to take place over 'their' ocean. But then the Australians got in the act and one of their civilian Ferry Command captain/navigators got the job. It was tough on Slim Jones, who had already made one Cat delivery to Australia and was a trained astro-navigator, as every RAF Coastal Command flying boat captain had to be. However, the Australian, Captain P. G. Taylor was eminently qualified to carry out the flight. He had been a fighter pilot in World War I, flying a Sopwith Scout and shooting down a German Rumpler in flames. He had been a flight crew member on many historic flights, and as navigator on the Fokker tri-motor 'Southern Cross' on a flight across the Tasman Sea in 1933 he had checked out his self-designed drift sight and

improvised bubble sextant. On another flight in the venerable Southern Cross he had been copilot/navigator to Sir Charles Kingsford-Smith, the famous Australian aviation pioneer. This time the starboard wooden propeller had broken, so they had to shut the engine down. Then the port engine had started to smoke heavily as it ran out of oil. The centre engine would not keep them aloft alone, so Taylor had gone out into the slipstream with a small container to carry oil from the useless starboard engine to the port engine. It had been a courageous act, and it enabled them to make a safe landfall.

Then he had teamed up with Kingsford-Smith in 1934 to attempt the first Australia to North America flight. This time they used a new Lockheed Altair, whose modern retractable landing gear gave it a speed edge over most other aircraft. They fitted extra gas tanks to VH-USB for the long legs, as there were no airports between Australia and Honolulu. Taylor was to be relief pilot and navigator. In mid-October they flew all day from Brisbane to Fiji, where Smith put down in only 300 yards on a clearing which included a cricket pitch. Then with the remaining fuel they flew light over to the beach at Naseli where the hard grey sand gave them a long run, sufficient even for their heavily overloaded aircraft. Cross-winds delayed them for a week, but finally they staggered off on the long haul to Honolulu.

The aircraft had two cockpits in tandem, and Smith did most of the flying while Taylor navigated, occasionally relieving Smith on the long flight. During the night they flew into a violent tropical storm and somehow Smith let the aircraft get into a spin. Usually a spin under those conditions was fatal, but luckily this time, at a dangerously low height above the hungry sea, Smith recovered. He told Taylor he had inadvertently selected his flaps down while groping for the landing light switch so that he could inspect the storm clouds to try to seek a way out. It was a simple error which could have had fatal results, but simple errors are not allowed in the air.

Soon after the spin they broke into clear air with all the stars in the heavens welcoming them. Polaris, the North Star, was low on their port bow, while on their starboard beam Sirius, the brightest star in the sky, was in a perfect position for an astro fix. When Taylor, working with his sextant and a board across his knees, crossed his two lines of position he knew exactly where they were, and how they were doing. At the moment they were right on their flight plan. He used the heavenly bodies as they flew along, until finally, just as the eastern sky started to show pink, he got his final fix. The procedure was the same as I had used many times during my flights from Goose or Gander to Prestwick. A reliable star fix just before dawn a hundred or so miles from the destination, close to landfall, and then the searching, searching, waiting and wondering until finally the purple line of land appeared just where it was supposed to be. After landing, there was always cause for celebration.

When the Altair landed safely on Wheeler Field on 29 October after their 2,795 nautical mile flight they believed they still had their planned two-hour gas reserve in their tanks. After they disembarked they were greeted with the traditional garlands of leis by the cheering spectators. They were the first international aircraft to pass through immigration and customs in Hawaii. So then Smith, in spite of the fact he'd had no sleep for almost two days, volunteered to take the mayor of Honolulu on a local sightseeing flight. He was airborne for less than three minutes when suddenly all was quiet as his engine stopped stone-cold dead. With his prop windmilling he turned back, wound his landing gear down and settled gently on the grass. They dipped the gas tanks. Shock and horror! Nothing left but fumes. So they had flown over the shark-filled ocean for more than 25 hours and landed with just five minutes of petrol remaining. What the mayor thought is not recorded, but Taylor and Smith were badly shaken.

The United States Army Air Corps engineers checked the tanks and found that a too-prominent rivet head had rubbed through one of the tanks, allowing the precious fuel to leak away. In the cockpit the loss went unnoticed as they had no fuel gauges for their long-range tanks. While the cooperative military made the necessary repairs, Smith and Taylor must have offered thanks to God, or perhaps to some personal joss.

Even with only one engine the 15 hour flight from Honolulu to Oakland was a piece of cake, with a succession of star fixes. Welcoming throngs of Americans gave them the Royal welcome they deserved.

In the long run, the law of averages caught up with Kingsford-Smith. While he was attempting to set a new England-Australia speed record in 1935 he went missing on his Allahabad to Singapore leg. All that was found was the main landing wheel of his favourite Lockheed Altair.

Taylor went on to other rewards, flying many aircraft, including his Percival Gull to a solo record from Java to Sydney in May 1937. He also made the first survey flight and crossing of the Indian Ocean from Australia to Mombasa, Africa, in 1939. The aircraft he used was the Catalina 'Guba', which eventually Ian Ross ferried from Newfoundland to Scotland for the very first Canadian Pacific Air Services delivery in October 1940. Later, RAF Ferry Command took over, in June, 1941.

Taylor made some further survey flights in the Pacific during the early years of the war, and then, late in 1942, he joined my outfit as a captain-navigator, of which there were very few in the Command. He delivered some Liberators and Catalinas and also flew some RY3 flights for Command Squadron, but his most memorable flight was the Bermuda-Clipperton-South Pacific-Australia survey flight.

It was early in October 1944 that Air Chief Marshal Sir Frederick Bowhill, the Commander-in-Chief of RAF Transport Command (formerly Ferry Command), told his subordinate, Air Vice-Marshal Reggie Marix, that it was time to issue Captain Taylor with a Catalina and a crew to carry out the exploratory flight. Taylor set out from Bermuda in JX275, which he had named *Frigate Bird* because he admired the bird's effortless flight. The 2,330 mile flight across the Gulf of Mexico proved to be simple, giving him time to shake his crew and his aircraft into shape for the longer flights to come. He landed at Acapulco, refuelled and then made a shuttle to the tiny island of Clipperton, which was really just the top of a defunct volcano sticking up from the Pacific a scant 20 feet or so. The enclosed water of the lagoon gave a run of only a quarter of a mile on a southerly heading which could be increased only by making a step turn, a tricky manoeuvre. In addition there were coral heads to be avoided. Any one of them could tear the belly out of the flying boat.

But then Taylor's troubles started. He was delayed for almost a week because when his engineer was changing two spark plugs they broke in the cylinders. Replacements had to be brought by a reserve Cat standing by in Mexico for just such an emergency.

Then there was a hurricane and they almost lost both Cats. Only some heroic work by the flight crews saved the aircraft. Taylor had not paid much attention to the words of the old *Sailing Directions* for the island which said the 'mountainous seas sometimes sweep right over the island'. Now he found that the warning was true. The ancient mariners knew what they were talking about.

When the hundred-knot gale died down they checked their engines, which had been semi-submerged for days. They seemed undamaged by their salt-water bath. Finally, on the morning of the 14th conditions seemed perfect for take-off for their 2,940 mile flight to Bora Bora. At noon Taylor taxied away from the anchorage where his own heavily weighted buoy had kept him safe. This flight would bring him to the Marquesas by the following dawn and to Bora Bora in the French-owned Society Islands. It was known that Bora Bora had fuel and a seaplane anchorage, and possibly a radio beacon.

But the island was reluctant to let him go. The auxiliary power unit would not start but they got the starboard engine going on the ship's batteries. Then the port engine starter would not engage, so copilot Birks stood on the wing and engaged it manually, avoiding falling off the wing with a display of agility. Navigator Henderson quickly cast off the mooring and they were free. Or were they? On run-up, engineer

Jock Hogg saw the starboard engine almost vibrate out of its mounting as Taylor checked the left magneto. It was back to the mooring, where the fault was thought to be fouled spark plugs. Hogg located three cold plugs and quickly replaced them. Surely this was the answer. But it wasn't. On run-up there was still a heavy misfiring on the left mag. The right one was perfect. Taylor was determined to press on so he did not check the left mag again, thus confusing his crew into thinking all was well. It reminded me of the old adage in cases such as this, which went: 'If you can't change the left mag, check the right one twice.'

Besides, in flight the fault might clear itself. Maybe it was sea-water soaked ignition leads? Taylor looked at his copilot who was in on the scene and told him they'd check the mag again at Bora Bora. Birks nodded. If his Captain made a tough decision like this, the least he could do was agree. It was time to go.

I put myself in Taylor's place. The Cat would be well overloaded and riding low in the water. Each little wave would wash over the cockpit. When the throttles were opened she would plough heavily through the water with a deluge of spray, so that I would have to rely on the directional gyro to keep a straight course. To the thunder of the engines the bow wave would commence as she got on her step and I'd be able to see forward again. It would be time to signal for floats up, which would be dangerous but which would cut the resistance and give more lift. Now with aileron control, it was time to ease her into a gentle turn and take four more inches than Pratt & Whitney recommended for full power. Otherwise, without the necessary airspeed the wing couldn't lift her. A light pull back on the control column and there would be a feeling of sudden release as the hull left the sucking sea. It was always the most marvellous feeling finally to get into the air after the ground-induced delays.

Taylor was now faced with the same problem that faced all Catalina captains on Ferry Command's long-distance North Atlantic delivery flights. He had standard fuselage overload tanks which gave him 2,130 US gallons of fuel. Even with the most careful use of his engines he needed a tail wind to reach his destination. On the North Atlantic we had the best forecasts available, although at times they were pretty inaccurate. But for the remote South-East Pacific Taylor might as well have read the old *Sailing Instructions*. His experience as a crack navigator now stood him in good stead. Although the wind near the surface was southerly he'd checked the cloud formations — fair-weather cumulus whose tops sloped away from the north, which indicated a reversal of wind. He decided to go for this so-necessary wind and climbed straight up to 4,500 feet before levelling off. He knew, as I did, this was usually exactly the wrong thing to do. It was always better to stay low while the engines ran themselves in at the power necessary to maintain the desired 105 knots indicated at the heavy take-off weight. But that tail wind was more important. Below, the sea showed white-caps from the south, so, at 4,500 ft, the *Frigate Bird* was in a favourable air flow.

Now Taylor began to keep an accurate record of the engine power settings and fuel consumption. He found he was using less than 600 hp per engine at 2,000 rpm and 29 inches of manifold pressure. His consumption was 85 gallons per hour. It was all so familiar. At that power setting and airspeed he could not reach Bora Bora, just as I could not have reached Prestwick on my flights. But the consumption would become less as the fuel burned off and the weight decreased, and, by God, there had to be a tail wind out there somewhere. It was just a matter of finding the right height. Sun observations confirmed the wind was generally behind the Cat, but it would take a good three-star fix to derive a really accurate position. So they flew on, with radio op Bligh contacting the stand-by aircraft who relayed the flight's progress to main base at Dorval. Maybe if they went down there might be some lone ship that could be diverted to search for their dinghy. That was about all the help that Dorval could offer.

Finally the sun set and their first three-star fix showed they were now in a head wind and only averaging 98 knots since their last sun-line. That was bad news. So they had to find a better level. The method of finding the wind was to use the

double-drift method. The course would be altered 60 degrees to starboard and a flame float dropped, and then the drift sight would pick it up and give the drift. Then the course would be altered 120 degrees to port and the process repeated. It was tricky work, and required accurate piloting and skilful use of the drift sight, which was in the rear of the aircraft. When all the information was placed on the Dalton computer the wind speed and direction could be established. Taylor felt his way down to 3,000 feet where he found the wind he was looking for, north-east and right up his tail. He stayed there in intermittent cloud and continued turbulence while his ground speed regained the margin he needed. It was navigation of the highest order.

Then Hogg reported that the oil pressure on the starboard engine was running low. I'd been in that pickle more than once myself. Taylor told his engineer to disregard it, which was exactly my reaction. What could be done anyway? The oil temperature was staying in the green. So maybe it was the gauge? Pilots are great optimists. Henderson got two more excellent three-star fixes that showed their ground speed was away down again. This time Taylor was down to only 600 feet above the dark sea before their double-drifts showed an easterly wind again.

Each member of the crew had done his share. The navigator with his sextant and charts had found their position. The engineer in his tower was monitoring his dials, alert for any strange vibration. The radio operator with his earphones was remote from life in the cockpit, living for the sounds of stations he hoped to hear and which should help the progress of the flight. Only the two pilots, high on the flight deck which reminded me of the bridge of a small ship, were in contact with the surrounding air as they tried to fly their courses and hold their altitude.

They made their landfall at Fatu Huka in the Marquesas right on flight plan, shortly after dawn, just as planned. They had been flying for 20 hours, and still had almost a thousand miles to go. Hogg, doing double duty as cook — as Bill Baker had done for me — served hot coffee and bacon and eggs. With the autopilot doing all the work it seemed like a good time to relax. But there is never a time to relax on a long flight. It looked as if high cloud cover would mean loss of the sun, which was serious because they needed it to hit Bora Bora. Maybe the radio could come to the rescue.

But when Bligh finally raised Bora Bora the news was not reassuring. The ground station had no HF/DF and their radio beacon was on 1,668 kc. The Cat's upper limit for that frequency band was 1,500 kc. So Bora Bora was useless for radio navigation. But good dead-reckoning and plenty of drift sights enabled Taylor to spot Mount Temanu, which caps Bora Bora, in clearing weather. Birks and Taylor looked at each other, then Taylor reached up and checked the left mag on the starboard engine. There was just a barely perceptible drop in revs. The pilots smiled at one another, and Taylor began his descent onto the blue waters of the lagoon. When they landed they had been in the air just over 27 hours and they had enough fuel for three or four more hours.

The *Frigate Bird* visited other islands in the Marquesas, then Tahiti, Tonga, the Kermanecs and other remote reefs, which could be valuable if a service was established along the route. Then the crew received a hero's welcome in Auckland, New Zealand, and an even bigger welcome in Taylor's home town, Sydney, Australia.

Quantas engineers did a complete inspection of *Frigate Bird* and found everything in good shape. Then Taylor was off again, this time along the route he and Kingsford-Smith had pioneered in the Altair. They rested at Pearl Harbour, then checked into the Ferry Command base in San Diego after a flight aided by numerous radio fixes to back up their astro shots. Then it was across the Rocky Mountains to the lake at Fort Worth, a quick refuelling and on to Elizabeth City, and, finally, the full circle to Bermuda, where the ramp rats hauled *Frigate Bird* up on the ramp of Darrell's Island.

Meanwhile the Americans had reacted. Clipperton was placed out of bounds. The Daks that were to fly in materials to build a landing strip were recalled to Dorval.

Maybe Admiral King of the US Navy didn't want British influence in 'his' ocean, or maybe it was General Douglas MacArthur, not the greatest lover of the Union Jack the world had ever seen, who closed the door. But I always thought it was Juan Trippe of Pan Am, whose dreams of a 'chosen instrument' forbade all foreign competition, who used his connection with the White House to shut us out of the Pacific.

Chapter 11
Lockheed never named one of their aircraft 'The Phoenix'

As we floated along in Lockheed's latest airliner design I reflected that to name an aircraft for the ancient mythical bird, which had risen and flown from its own ashes, might not have been such an impossible idea. The depression which had started in 1928 had just about wiped out Lockheed. Even with their 'star' aircraft, which were the fastest in the sky, the company went bankrupt in 1931. It was Robert E. Gross who winged to their rescue, symbolically in an Orion flown by Varney Speed Lanes. In July 1932 he heard the judge in a Los Angeles courtroom confirm he now owned the crippled company — for the magnificent sum of just $40,000. For partners he had designer Lloyd Stearman and airline operator Walter Varney.

Bob Gross, Chairman of the Board, set the sales policy. Single-engined passenger aircraft were now obsolete. Look for a niche where Lockheed could fit. Let Douglas court the big airlines with their new DC series. Hope that Boeing doesn't

come up with anything better than their 247D. Go after the little guys with a speedy airliner, not too big, and at a low price. Stearman and Hall Hibbard had the answer. It was a metal, twin-engined aircraft with Wasp Junior engines and they called it the Electra Model 10. But the newest star had birth pains. With a single rudder and one engine out it wouldn't maintain straight flight. That was when a new engineer named Clarence 'Kelly' Johnson joined the company and put twin tails on the Electra, which solved the directional control problem. Kelly Johnson's brilliant designs would keep Lockheed in the forefront of aviation for many years, in both the civil and military fields and against some really tough competition from America and the rest of the world.

The Electra was flown for the first time on 23 February 1934, and its performance could only be called superior. It cruised at an honest 190 mph with a top speed of 200 and was the first multi-engined aircraft to do it. Within a year 40 of the Electras were flying with Pan Am, Northwest, Braniff, Mid-Continent and Delta. Canadian Airways Ltd., was the first Canadian customer, and in 1936 they bought CF-AZY and CF-BAF for their Vancouver-Seattle run. They had their sights set on a transcontinental route, but in 1937 politician C. D. Howe decided that a government-owned airline was the way to go. He set up Trans-Canada Air Lines, who took over the two Electras and the routes. TCA bought three more Electras, CF-TCA, CF-TCB and CF-TCC. When the Model 14 Super-Electra was produced in 1938 TCA equipped their whole fleet with them, and when the slightly larger Model 18 Lodestar came out they bought those too. So, until 1943 when they got the Avro Lancastrian for transatlantic flying, TCA was an all-Lockheed airline.

Meanwhile, in 1936 Lockheed had produced the Electra Junior, Model 12, which carried six passengers at a top speed of a current fighter, or 219 mph. It was meant to tap the executive market, catering to those people who were sure they were so important they couldn't waste time with normal scheduled airlines. The Canadian Department of Transport bought one, CF-CCT, which completed in one day the first survey flight across what was to be the Trans-Canada Airway, astonishing the public. J. H. Tudhope was the captain and John Hunter the copilot, with Arctic veteran engineer Lou Parmenter along to keep the aircraft airworthy. The passengers were C. D. Howe, C. P. Edwards, head of the Department of Transport, and H. J. Symington, who came from government-owned Canadian National Railways to be president—of TCA.

They were impressed with the little airliner, as was I, even after flying VP-TAI for several hundred hours with British West Indian Airways. There we often had to land in strips cut out of the jungle at various small islands. The little aircraft was very manoeuvrable and when I let out the full Fowler flap it came down like an elevator, which was necessary when we approached over some high cliff or other obstacle.

In Europe many airlines followed the lead of Swissair and their Orions. North American designers like Douglas and the Lockheed men were far ahead of their European counterparts.

As a matter of record, it was Lockheed 14 Super Electra G-AFGN that carried British Prime Minister Neville Chamberlain to see Adolf Hitler in Germany, in September 1938. When the gullible Englishman returned home he proclaimed: 'Peace in our time'. Eleven months later Hitler attacked Poland and World War II began. But surely Lockheed couldn't be blamed for that piece of monumental misjudgement? And besides, when the war started it would be Lockheed Hudsons, a derivative of the Model 14, that would be the first American-built aircraft to carry the war to the Third Reich.

The feeling of security as the four powerful engines hummed through smooth-as-glass air made this part of the flight almost enjoyable. Far below I could see the cup-cake shapes of white, fair-weather cumulus. I was reminded of Amelia Earhart's description of them when she was on her round-the-world flight using a Lockheed Electra in 1937.

She had called them 'little lamb clouds'.

Chapter 12
Amelia Earhart - a comet burned out?

Independent, striving, courageous, modest, bright, articulate, truthful, dedicated, unobtrusive. All these adjectives had described Amelia Earhart at one time or another during her career as the female equivalent of Lindbergh. She was born in Atchison, Kansas, in 1897 and brought up by an alcoholic father and a doting mother. A pacifist, she felt compassionate enough to serve as a nurse's aide for the Red Cross in Toronto's Spadina Military Hospital from 1917 until the end of the war. AE, as she preferred to be called, visited a local airport one bleak November day when the snow on the ground was thrown into her face by the ski-planes. The cold shower somehow ignited a burning fire within her to fly one of the rickety machines.

   She worked for her flying time and finally got her licence in 1922 and appeared in a few local air meets, setting a new women's altitude record of 14,000 feet. But there seemed to be no need for her flying skills so she drifted between college courses. Then in 1928 she took the opportunity to fly as passenger for Mrs. Frederick Guest, a wealthy socialite who had bought Byrd's tri-motor Fokker Friendship with the idea of becoming the first woman to fly the Atlantic. Mrs Guest's relatives and friends had convinced her that the flight was too dangerous. But that didn't stop AE. As the flight was delayed she wrote what she called 'popping-off letters', which reflected her philosophy and were to be delivered in the event of a fatal crash. Pilots Wilmer Stultz and Louis Gordon, with radios dead, finally set down at Burry Port, Wales, after a flight from Newfoundland of 20 hours, 40 minutes. AE became an instant celebrity, which she hated, saying it was only an accident of sex that made her the chief performer in what she called 'our particular sideshow'.

But she had done more than be a performer in a sideshow. She had galvanized women's interest in aviation. Obviously, if a woman had flown the Atlantic as a mere passenger, next time one must do it alone. The next year AE entered the first Women's Air Derby along with 19 others from Santa Monica, California, bound for the National Air Races at Cleveland. Will Rogers had wryly dubbed the event the 'Powder Puff Derby'. It was really an endurance marathon, because each day the contestants had to rise at 4 a.m. and fly more than 300 miles a day for nine days. It called for dead-reckoning navigation with sectional aviation charts and Rand McNally road maps. During such a tough flight there were bound to be accidents. Bobbi White crashed during a forced landing, Florence 'Pancho' Barnes crashed into a parked car, and Ruth Nichols clipped a tractor beside the runway at Columbus, Ohio, almost within sight of the finish line. Margaret Perry flew on for two days with a high fever until finally she was hospitalized at Fort Worth, Texas, with typhoid. There was only one fatality, which was amazing considering that the qualifications for entering the race only stipulated a pilot's licence and 100 hours' solo. Marvel Crossen baled out of her crippled plane at too low an altitude and was killed when she hit the ground, wrapped in her partially opened parachute.

So 15 flyers flew across the finish line at Cleveland. Louise Thaden was the winner, Gladys O'Donnell was second and AE finished third. There was another spin-off when four Derby participants and 22 other women met at Curtiss Field in Valley Stream, Long Island, to form an association of women flyers called the Ninety-Nines. The name derived from the number of charter members, and the new association was largely responsible for changing the attitude of the press towards women flyers and making them an accepted part of aviation, including competition flying. For a time Ruth Nichols led the field, but a crash of her Lockheed Vega 'Akita' and its eventual loss through an in-flight fire extinguished her dreams of flying to Paris.

AE plugged doggedly on. She set several speed records in her Lockheed Vega, which was the leading aircraft of the day, and became a sort of roving ambassador from the sky. She became aviation editor for *Cosmopolitan* magazine and wrote of her experiences in the 'Friendship' in a book aptly titled *20 Hrs 40 Min*. Then, to the astonishment of her friends who knew how much she valued her freedom, in 1931 she married promoter and publisher George Palmer Putnam. He had asked her to marry him in 1929, when, perhaps coincidentally, he had separated from his first wife. AE wasn't having any. But Putnam proposed six more times before she finally accepted him. But she had her conditions and wrote them out for the prospective bridegroom. They were tough, unique; but they were AE to the core. 'Dear G. P.,' the declaration began, 'you must know again my reluctance to marry, my feeling that I shatter thereby chances in work which means so much to me. I feel the move just now as foolish as anything I could do. In our life together, I shall not hold you to any medieval code of faithfulness to me, nor shall I consider myself bound to you similarly. I may have to keep some place where I can go to be myself now and then, for I cannot guarantee to endure at all times the confinements of even an attractive cage. I must exact a cruel promise, and that is you will let me go in a year if we find no happiness together. I will try to do my best in every way.'

AE thought she needed Putnam's help in her flying and he was more than happy to shine in the reflection of her glory. She accepted the commercialization of her career in order to raise money for flights she considered serious, but she grew weary of what she called 'the zoo part' of her work. The thought of love was missing in their relationship; in fact, Putnam had lined up so many engagements for her that there was no time left for a honeymoon.

Then, one morning in 1932, she asked Putnam if he would mind if she flew the Atlantic solo. He agreed, even showing enthusiasm, probably realizing that had he objected AE would have made the flight anyway.

She knew she needed expert help, so she enlisted the aid of Arctic and Antarctic flyer Bernt Balchen who was one of the most experienced pilots and navigators in the world. He fitted blind flying instruments, a new engine, and enough gas to make a flight of over 3,000 miles in her tricky-to-fly Vega. They left Teterboro Airport near New York City on 19 May and had an uneventful flight to Harbour Grace, Newfoundland, where so many other flights, both tragic and successful, had started. The next day Balchen checked over the aircraft and prepared her flight plan, which would give her proper magnetic headings according to the forecast winds and changes in variation. With no radio it would be dead-reckoning all the way. But then again, Europe is a hard target to miss, she thought as she took off.

AE had her troubles. First her altimeter ceased functioning, then she got a dose of heavy ice and spun down to just 3,000 feet above the hungry waves. Then blue exhaust flames from a broken weld on her engine exhaust manifold gained her rapt attention. If they had continued to burn through the heavy metal manifold she would have been finished. Her comments were very much those of an intrepid pilot: 'I didn't want to look at the flames at all,' she said dryly, 'because at night they looked so much worse than they did in the daytime.' Then her cockpit was saturated with gas from a leaking fuel line. She was now certain she would never make her planned destination of Paris, France, so she turned due east and finally landed safely on a long, smooth, sloping pasture near Londonderry, Ireland. The flight was the fastest on record, just 15 hours and 18 minutes. She was awarded the Gold Medal of the National Geographic Society by President Herbert Hoover. Typically, she made light of her achievement. 'Some features of the flight I fear have been exaggerated,' she said with a smile. 'It made a much better story to say I landed with but one gallon of gasoline left. As a matter of fact I had more than a hundred. I did *not* kill a cow in landing — unless one died of fright.'

Meanwhile, on the other side of the Atlantic more women were proving they were just as skilful and daring as men aviators. Amy Johnson made it safely in a single-engine Gipsy Moth to far-distant Australia in 1930. She took 19½ days, failing to beat the record of her male rival, Bert Hinkler, by four days. Now she proceeded to set records to Poland, and then to Tokyo, taking only 10 days for the 10,000 mile flight to Japan's capital. Then she married James Mollison, holder of many long-distance records. The 'flying sweethearts', as the press dubbed them, flew together and solo as they both continued to smash long-distance flight records. Mollison became one of the early pilots in what was to become RAF Ferry Command. Certainly he had the qualifications, having flown the Atlantic *three times* solo while many other aviators were being swallowed up by the hungry Atlantic waves. Jean Batten, New Zealand's gift to the flying world, took her place with solo flights to Australia, then New Zealand, and threw in a hop from England to Brazil and on to Argentina to prove it was no fluke. Her book *Alone in the Sky* was a sensitive account of a brave woman's effort to pioneer. There were other English women who were joined by their compatriots from Germany and France in pioneer flights.

Meanwhile AE was busy setting new transcontinental records with her trusty Vega. But somehow they lacked the punch, the excitement, of over-water flying. So in December 1934 she loaded a brand-new Vega on Matson Line's SS *Lurline* bound from Los Angeles to Honolulu to attempt the first woman's transpacific flight, which carried a $10,000 prize. She was accompanied by ever-present husband Putnam and, more importantly, another experienced pilot to replace Balchen, who was unavailable. He was Paul Mantz, who numbered in addition to his skills as a dare-devil pilot the ability as a technical man to advise on navigation and long-range flying procedures. Then the sponsors got cold feet and suggested to AE that she cancel the flight. Resolute AE would have nothing to do with the suggestion and even accused her backers of cowardice: she told them she was going to make the flight with or without their support. The backers, perhaps shamed by her example, decided that after all they would continue their participation.

Mantz made out her flight plan. Now she had two-way radio, yet the flight once again would be just by dead-reckoning navigation. But then again, North America is a hard target to miss. After a difficult take-off from a rain-soaked muddy field she made a safe landing at Oakland of 18 hours and 15 minutes. Another record in her bag. Then she made a flight from Burbank to Mexico City and then direct to New York City. Even Wiley Post's warning of the hazards involved did not deter her. Her last fling was with her Vega, which was now obsolescent, in the 1935 Bendix race. Paul Mantz and a friend occupied her cabin where they poured drinks and played gin rummy. AE landed just two minutes before the deadline at Cleveland and finished in fifth place. What her two passengers thought is not recorded. But what *is* known is that AE met for the first time a potentially dangerous rival in the person of Jacqueline Cochrane who had force-landed her Northrop Gamma at Kingman, Arizona, during that year's Bendix.

Now AE, realizing her Vega was fast becoming a relic, persuaded Purdue University to provide her with a brand-new twin-engined Lockheed Electra, the Model 10. It had a cruising speed of 200 mph and the cabin, which normally accommodated ten passengers, could be fitted with instruments, or, more interestingly, extra gas tanks. She and her copilot entered the aircraft in the '36 Bendix, but again finished a disappointing fifth. It was reported that there was trouble with the fuel system and that the pilot's overhead hatch blew open.

But now AE finally had the aircraft which would allow her to make a round-the-world flight of a different nature — the long way, around the Equator. With the necessary zigzags between landing places the distance would be 29,000 miles. While Putnam made arrangements for fuel dumps, landing permits and all the other paper-work, AE studied her maps and charts. With some reluctance she decided she needed a navigator, especially for the long stretches across the Pacific Ocean. Putnam brought a suitable candidate to assist her with her planning. He was Bradford Washburn Jr, the 26-year-old head of Harvard University's Institute of Geographical Exploration. He was teaching field astronomy, which entailed the use of heavenly bodies for precise ground navigation.

AE was cautious about selecting her new crew member. At the Putnam home in Rye, New York, she traced her itinerary on charts spread out on the living-room floor. Such planning is often the most pleasurable part of any flight. AE's planned route was from Oakland to Hawaii, thence to a tiny island named Howland in the central Pacific, where the US Government had laid out three runways on the coral of the low-lying island. It would be a critical refuelling stop. Then it was across the South Pacific to Lae, New Guinea; then a quick stop at Australia's northern city of Darwin. From there the flight would proceed northwestwards through romantic Bali to Singapore, then across India and Africa, where the South Atlantic to Natal, Brazil, wouldn't present much of a challenge; and then it would be all downhill back to Uncle Sam's land.

Washburn said he stared at the pinpoint of Howland Island, less than two miles long and half-mile wide, then asked AE how she was going to find this needle in the enormous haystack of the Pacific. She seemed confident that she could find it by dead-reckoning alone. He insisted that a radio beacon on the island, which would provide a signal for the aircraft to home on, was a necessity. AE did not think that such a precaution was needed. Washburn, stubbornly insisting it was, went upstairs to bed. In the morning he packed his bag and left, explaining that even with the experience of ten years of navigation he could not find the tiny island without a homing signal.

When AE met with Paul Mantz, who once again was her technical adviser, it was decided that the US Government would station a Coast Guard cutter near Howland with both an on-board transmitting low frequency beacon and a low and high frequency direction finding set-up. The Lockheed was equipped with a specially modified Western Electric three-channel transmitter and receiver of the type being used by some American airlines. Two fixed channels on HF were allocated: 3,105 kc, the channel used by non-scheduled flight for communication with control towers and radio ranges, would be used at night; while 6,210 kc would be used during the day. Each frequency had propagation characteristics making possible reception of AE's transmissions according to the time of day and the distance from the aircraft.

The high frequency channels were crystal-controlled and all the dials were preset for most efficient output into the aircraft's fixed antennas, which ran from the vertical fin then through insulators into the fuselage. But the high frequency receivers were tunable and required a certain amount of skill to set on the desired frequency. AE was capable of setting them up properly. Voice was used exclusively.

The third channel on the set was to be used on the low frequency bands. Pan Am and ocean-going vessels were the big users of this band from 200 to 600 kc and each vessel or aircraft carried a radio operator to tune the sets and translate the Morse code and 'Q' signals used. A long trailing antenna was necessary for efficient propagation on the low band. Generally speaking, the longer the better, up to about 250 feet. This length of flexible copper wire was kept in a straight line during flight by a series of small lead weights, which ensured that the wire did not kink up. AE hated the effort necessary to rotate the small reel in the cockpit that released the heavy antenna in flight. Even more laborious was reeling in for landing. But without the long wire the low band transmitter was almost useless.

In addition, the low band receiver had a rotatable loop, on which AE could get bearings from ground stations. She would tune for the weakest audio response, called a null, and thus could get a bearing, or her course to fly towards the station. The only problem was that the loop was bidirectional and so gave ambiguous bearings. The correct bearing was 180 degrees different from the false one. There seems to be some doubt as to whether AE understood the operation of the loop properly, and as the controls were in the cockpit *she* would normally be taking the bearings.

She had decided that she wanted her navigator to ride in the rear of the aircraft, behind the long-range gas tank where he could spread out his charts. But she had not insisted on an astrodome, where he could use his sextant to take sights on various heavenly bodies. To do that he would have to crawl over the long-range tanks and take his shots through the pilot's escape hatch, right over her head, asking her to crouch down while he did so. It was a very awkward arrangement.

When a flight crew must work in concert, as on a long-distance flight, they should be able to communicate with one another with no trouble. But the sense of isolation was intensified for the navigator because there was no proper intercom fitted. Messages were to be passed by means of the line of a bamboo fishing rod fastened to the roof of the fuselage. It reminded me of the 'clothes-line' we had to use in the old Hampden bomber when the wet-cell battery froze up. It really wasn't very satisfactory. The navigator had a chronometer and airspeed, altimeter and outside air temperature gauges. He also had a pelorus, a sort of telescope with a graduated base which he could use for bearings of objects not directly overhead. He also had the essential drift meter to check on what the wind was doing to him. That was good, but what was not good was that he had no magnetic compass to tell him what course AE was steering.

At Oakland the problem of navigation was supposedly solved by hiring *two* navigators. They seemed to be under the impression that two navigators are twice as good as one. I believe such an assumption is false. Maybe they would flip a coin to see whose course would be flown . . . The chief navigator of this small vessel would be Harry Manning, a sea captain on leave from American President Lines whom AE had met on her ferry trip to Hawaii. He had extensive sea experience, but very little in the air. The additional navigator was Fred Noonan, who had had lots of experience in the air. In fact he had been in charge of navigation while Pan Am were laying out their routes in the Pacific for their long-range flying boats.

On 17 March 1937 the Electra roared off Oakland's runway with Mantz in the captain's seat and AE acting as copilot. The two navigators were huddled in the restricted space in the rear. Mantz wanted to get her away to a good start and had done the take-off because AE had been slow to master the transition from single-engined aircraft to the two throttles of her Electra. She kept trying to correct any swing on take-off by juggling the throttles. The engines are always slow to respond, and very soon anyone trying this would find the aircraft swapping ends in a ground loop. A lot of military trainees found that out the hard way.

Once in the air, AE took the captain's position so she could legally claim to be in charge, and the flight proceeded smoothly. The silver Electra's registration, NR-16020, would soon be a familiar sight on airports around the world, just as its radio call sign KHAQQ would soon be heard in many pairs of earphones. The flight to Honolulu was uneventful, taking less than 16 hours, although Mantz was distressed to see how the strain of preparation and the long flight had worn AE down. He was pleased that the new Sperry automatic pilot worked so well. She would certainly need all the help she could get on the longer legs to come. He made the landing, but this would be the last time he would be able to assist her in the cockpit. The next day he flew the Electra from Wheeler to Luke Field where there was a longer runway.

On 20 March AE ran up the engines, which checked out perfectly after Pratt & Whitney's men had inspected them. Manning was in the copilot's seat and Noonan was in the rear. She had 900 gallons of fuel for the 1,800 mile leg to Howland. Mantz and a collection of military personnel watched as she taxied out on the wet runway into a slight cross-wind. AE opened the throttles and almost immediately the aircraft pulled to the right. The spectators could hear her engine power changing as she started to jockey the throttles. Mantz cried out a warning, but of course AE couldn't hear him. Now the Electra, with its centre of gravity far aft, began swinging to the left; and this time there was no stopping it. As the ground loop inevitably progressed, the right landing gear was wrenched off and both props hit the ground. The right wing and vertical fin were bent, but though the gas spilled out there was no fire. The three crew members scrambled out unhurt. They were lucky, just as my two crew members and myself were at Churchill, Manitoba, when my Hudson's belly tank had ruptured on take-off and spewed gas ankle deep in the cabin. Let's change that from 'lucky' to 'very damned lucky'.

Mantz surveyed the wreck and decided it could be rebuilt, so he had it dismantled for shipment back to the Lockheed factory. AE, Manning and Noonan were aboard the cruise ship *Malolo* by noon that day, bound for California, but determined to try again.

Except for Captain Harry Manning.

He'd had enough. In addition to almost killing him, AE had refused to fly one of his courses on a previous test flight off the coast of California. From an unknown position far out in the Pacific she'd consistently drifted to port. She said he'd miscalculated by almost 200 miles. He said she couldn't fly a consistent heading and in the process added a few adjectives to those previously mentioned. He called her 'bullheaded' as well as having a very big ego and being a prima donna. Perhaps there's nothing like almost being burned up in an aircraft to bring out the honest opinions in a navigator about his captain.

That left AE with Noonan and his drinking problem. He promised to quit boozing during the upcoming flight and she believed him. Maybe memories of how her father had needed help with the very same difficulty swayed her judgement. But still, she knew very well Noonan's drinking was the reason Pan Am had fired him.

On 21 May she took off from Oakland after $25,000 worth of repairs to her Electra. She was lucky it was a 10E, which meant it had the more powerful 550 hp S301 engines. With those engines she not only had a faster cruising speed if she wanted to pull the power, but also a respectable single-engined ceiling of 9,500 feet at maximum all-up civil weight of 10,500 lb. The 10A with the smaller 450 hp Wasp Junior SB engines had a single-engine performance at full weight right down there on the surface of the seas with the sharks frolicking just below.

She had decided to fly around the world the other way, ostensibly because the Atlantic weather would be more favourable. That decision was wrong for two reasons. The first was that now she'd be flying south in Asia right through the monsoon season. The other was that now her longest and most dangerous leg to pinpoint Howland was lengthened from 1,900 miles from Hawaii to 2,556 miles from Lae, New Guinea. That additional mileage meant four more long hours in the air. And possibly there was a third reason that Putnam, her husband and mentor, had overlooked. From Hawaii through the south Pacific the prevailing winds are easterly.

When she arrived at Miami Pan Am checked the Electra over. Mantz was astonished because he had not been consulted. He and Putnam had frequently butted heads over AE's plans. But possibly Putnam had another reason for getting rid of Mantz, because when the expert aviation adviser's wife Myrtle had filed for divorce early in 1936 she had named AE as 'the other woman' responsible for the break-up of the marriage. At least that action firmly put to rest rumours that AE was some sort of a lesbian because of her short hair and mannish dress.

At Miami, ostensibly to save weight, the trailing antenna was removed and the Morse key was left behind. This strange decision, which enraged Mantz and mystified many knowledgeable people, meant that for all practical purposes her low frequency transmitter was useless, which also meant that the Coast Guard cutter *Itasca* at Howland could not help the navigation with bearings from its reliable direction finding set-up. Her reasoning was only to emerge later.

While at Miami AE talked with Carl Allen of the *New York Times*. Putnam had given that newspaper the exclusive rights to publish AE's flight reports as she flew around the world. At a price, of course. However, when the reporter talked to AE he found she was very reflective. 'I have a feeling,' she said, 'there is just about one more good flight in my system, and I hope this trip is it. Anyway, when I have finished this job, I mean to give up long-distance "stunt" flying.'

Was this a comet in the last stage of burning out?

In the cool of early morning on 1 June AE lifted the Electra off Miami's long runway with no difficulty, bound for Puerto Rico. Although Noonan missed his ETA by 19 minutes on the seven-hour, 33 minute flight, AE didn't seem concerned. Then it was on to Caripito, Venezuela, where AE curtly refused Pan Am rep's offer of the latest en route weather and airport information. He was astonished as he saw the Electra disappearing in the distance, en route to Paramaribo, Dutch Guiana. Noonan was meeting his old buddies along the route, and probably it was here that he started to drink again. So the crew of the Electra were shaping up as being a stubborn pilot and a drinking navigator. Still they kept going, through Fortaleza, Brazil, and then to the jumping-off spot for Africa of Natal, which would become familiar to thousands of Ferry Command and USAAF aircrew.

At 3.15 a.m. AE pushed the throttles forward and soon they were on their way across the South Atlantic. With little to do for the first hours Noonan just relaxed. AE broadcast her position 'blind' twice an hour, although her voice frequencies were only in general use in the USA and Canada. She reported that she wondered if they were heard at all, or understood if heard. Her inept performance on the radio was in direct contrast to that of the Lindberghs' flight of four years before, across the same lonely stretch of ocean. But the Lindberghs had Pan Am's frequencies, and Anne was a competent Morse code operator. AE had turned down the offer of a crystal for her transmitter in Miami when the Pan Am radio men were checking out her radio installation.

Navigator Noonan was on the ball and gave AE a course towards the end of his ETA for Dakar, which was their target. AE looked at the alteration, mulled it over, and then she decided to trust her own instincts and once again turned to the left; and so disregarded her navigator's course. Just before the sun set she found a small strip at St. Louis, Senegal, and landed. After the 1,900 mile flight she'd landed 163 miles off course, flying that infamous 'left' heading! Although she later apologized to Noonan and admitted she had been wrong, it surely doesn't do much for a navigator's ego to learn his pilot will not steer his course. However, he still stuck with her.

And so it was on across featureless darkest Africa, through Gao, Mali, Fort Lamy, Chad, then El Fasher, Anglo-Egyptian Sudan, and on to Khartoum. She reported 110 degree heat and clouds of dust, which reminded me of my visit there in a Martin B26 Marauder in 1942. Hot, dusty and dirty . . . that defined Khartoum. Then she hopped over to Massawa, Eritrea, and finally left Africa from Assab on 14 June. AE obviously could have skipped over many of those out-of-the way desert stops, by using the Electra's long-range capabilities. But at each dusty airport she filed her flight reports to the USA, and the more she filed the happier Putnam was.

After leaving Assab well before daylight AE staged through her first Asian airfield at Aden, a British outpost in Arabia. Then it was across the Arabian Sea to Karachi, where she learned she had made the first non-stop flight from the Red Sea to India. She took a two-day rest while the mechanics inspected the airplane and installed some much-needed engine parts from a crate Pratt & Whitney had located there just for the Electra. Across India it was a breeze, taking just eight and a half hours for the trip to Calcutta's Dum Dum airport, with rain squalls warning of the monsoon weather she would soon have to brave. Now she had a choice. More rain was coming. Much more rain. And back home Putnam was pressing her to reach the USA before 4 July, as he had great celebrations planned on the nation's birthday. But the rain had soaked the grass field thoroughly. Should she chance a take-off or wait until the field dried out? She decided to press on and remembered that the take-off was precarious. The wheels seemed to stick forever in the sticky mud, before she lifted off with nothing at all to spare over the fringe of trees at the airport's edge.

The Electra made it into Akyab, Burma, where Imperial Airways, Air France and KLM all stopped regularly, and who rushed up to help her. A quick refuelling and she left to try to make Rangoon, in spite of a poor weather forecast. Soon she found that the forecaster hadn't been fooling. The Electra was caught in turbulent air and rain so heavy and relentless it beat patches of paint off the leading edges of the wing. Finally, after a couple of hours of trying to penetrate what she described as 'an unbroken wall of water', she had to turn back. Beneath the cloud, in visibility of just a few hundred yards, Noonan brought her safely into Akyab. This time she appreciated his talents and even praised him as having uncanny powers of navigation. It was quite a change from her usual acerbic relationship with Noonan, but his reaction is, unfortunately, not recorded. On the ground AE was told that the weather she'd just experienced was just the normal monsoon stuff. But, more to the point, she was made to realize it would last for about three months. That delay while the Electra was being repaired was now exacting its inexorable price.

Of course she had to fight on, and she flew through low visibility and turbulent cloud for what seemed endless hours. Rangoon and Bangkok fell behind, until finally the crew of the Electra saw the sun once again at Singapore. Noonan remarked cynically that he really thought there was no more sunny weather left, proving that fatique was starting to affect him too.

It was on 21 June that she set course for Java, landing at Bandung where she decided to spend two days while the KLM mechanics worked on the Electra. And even there she had the questionable pleasure of a phone call from Putnam, who wondered why the flight was going so slowly. On 24 June she tried to fly all the way to Australia, but had to land at Surabaya when one of her flight instruments malfunctioned. No one there could fix it, so, greatly disheartened, she had to return to Bandung. It wasn't until Sunday 27 June that everything on the aircraft was back in order. AE had enjoyed being a tourist, but Noonan had begun to hit the bottle again. Five hours out they landed at Koepang on the island of Timor. The next day they bucked strong headwinds until at long last they landed at Darwin, Australia, where in order to save weight they shipped their two parachutes back to the States. Parachutes wouldn't help them if they came down in the open water that lay ahead of them.

An officious doctor kept them at the airport for 10 terrible hours while he made up his mind that their smallpox certificates were in order. Finally the quarantine was lifted, and after a night's rest they got away, crossing the Timor Sea again, and then the forbidding Owen Stanley mountains of New Guinea. After a flight of 1,200 miles in seven hours and 43

minutes AE slipped the Electra into the short 3,000 foot strip at
Lae. They had conquered the difficulties of 22,000 miles, with
AE handling bumpy or muddy strips with skill and Noonan
doing his share. Only 7,000 miles lay ahead and their epic flight
would be complete.

But the 2,550 miles of open water from Lae to Howland
would be by far the most difficult leg of the flight. Howland
was a tiny target, just two miles long and half a mile wide,
sticking out of the Pacific a bare 20 feet at low tide.

The US Government had done much to help. In addition to
three strips laid out on the tiny island they had stationed the
USS *Ontario*, a sea-going tug, half-way between Lae and
Howland, plus the USS *Swan* half-way between Howland and
Hawaii. But the most important aid to the flight was the
presence of the US Coast Guard cutter *Itasca* just off-shore of
the small island. It had on board not only a low frequency non-
directional radio beacon, but also an excellent low band
direction finding unit. On the island they had set up a high
frequency direction finding unit comprising a radio-
goniometer and four masts supporting wires mounted in the
fashion of the Adcock directional layout. The whole thing was
powered by batteries brought ashore from the cutter and the
sensitive receiver could monitor 3,105 and 6,210 kc. But the
HF/DF was still being developed, with Pan Am's brilliant
engineer Hugo Leuteritz doing much of the pioneer work.
Highly skilled operators were necessary to detect weak voice
signals and come up with usable bearings.

At Lae, which was a frontier outpost serving interior mines,
AE found the Australians very helpful. Guinea Airlines were
operating a sister-ship Electra and their mechanics gave AE's
aircraft a good check-over as they filled the long-range tanks to

1,100 gallons. Harry Balfour, the local radio operator, made arrangements to work AE using his company frequency of 6,540 kc and listening for her on 6,210. Noonan had made a flight plan of 18 hours based on the winds thought to be usual for the time of the year. They called for 18 to 25 knots to the *Ontario* from the south-east, swinging around to 15 to 20 knots from the east-north-east for the remainder of the flight. Just about as adverse as could be imagined. In addition there were heavy rain showers predicted en route, but these were normal for the season. Just as any careful navigator would, Noonan wanted to arrive at Howland after the sun was reasonably well up so he could take a sun shot. Then he would deliberately steer to the right or the left until he crossed his advanced line, so he would know for sure which way to turn. It was the same plan as I'd used when I'd flown my Martin B26 from Natal to Ascension island in 1942, before that tiny dot in the Atlantic had had any radio navigational aids.

Communication between the *Itasca* and AE had been difficult, with several relays involved. Having Putnam, a non-technical person, at Los Angeles in California offering suggestions did not help. Somehow, the fact that the Electra had no means of transmitting on the lower frequencies never got through to the cutter. At this point the real reason for discarding the bothersome trailing antenna was revealed. Neither AE nor her navigator could understand the Morse code! Legally, as a pilot AE was not required to know it, although from a practical point of view she certainly should have mastered it. But she didn't care for code communication techniques, and also had never had bothered to master astro navigation. So she was just a basic pilot. But a person engaged in long-distance flights should surely be *More than a Pilot*. Noonan had passed a slow Morse test in addition to flag and flashing tests when he'd qualified for his marine navigator's licence. But navigators thought they were superior to radio men in the cockpit, so he'd let his Morse slip. What they hadn't realized was that even a long series of dashes on 500 kc could enable marine stations of the *Itasca* type to give them vital bearings. And even on the higher frequency bands a trailing antenna properly tuned is far superior to a short, fixed antenna.

At 10 a.m. Lae time AE climbed into the cockpit while Noonan, reputedly suffering from a hangover, crawled into his flight station. The 3,000 foot runway was almost too short, but she managed to lift off with a scant 50 yards to spare. Then she. let the Electra drop near the sea while she picked up speed, even making spume marks in the blue water. Within the hour AE worked Lae, reporting all was well. Her signals were good on 6,210 which was called the day frequency, while 3,105 was called the night frequency. In reality, the pilots used whichever frequency gave the best results for the time of day or night and the distance to be covered. Trans-Canada Air Lines used 4,330 kc as 'night' and 5,642.5 kc for 'day', as conditions warranted. AE never seemed to understand this simple fact. It was almost as if she considered herself one of the 'old breed', who thought that anything that made a long flight simpler made it sort of 'sissy'.

AE made her half-hourly reports, stating that all was going well. Apparently Noonan was functioning after all. On one of her reports she said she was 'dead on course', an expression I find distasteful, over the Solomon Islands. Actually she was very near the spot where a Lockheed P-38 Lightning of the USAAF would shoot down Admiral Yamamoto in his 'Betty' aircraft in 1943.

Seven hours and 20 minutes into the flight she reported she was now at 7,000 feet and making a respectable 150 knots, and as it was shortly after sunset she was going to change to 'night' frequency. Lae's operator urged her not to switch, because her signals were still very strong, but she ignored his advice and he never heard her again. But she must have continued her 'blind' reports on 3,105 because the radio operator at Nauru island thought he heard her. This tiny island mined phosphate day and night and would have been a valuable check point about half-way through the flight.

Nothing definite was heard for several hours until at 2.45 a.m. Howland time her voice was heard weakly through heavy static: 'KHAQQ. . . cloudy. . . weather cloudy. . .' was all the ship's operators could make out. When they called her there was no response. There was an active front on her track, and if AE had described fair weather cumulus as 'little lamb clouds' she might have called these storm clouds 'hungry tiger clouds'. From time to time the operators aboard the *Itasca* and the direction finding station on the island heard AE making voice transmissions, but they were always too short to enable the operator to get a bearing. She never indicated on what frequency she was listening. The radio men below were becoming frantic, even angry with frustration. They had never been told she did not have 500 kc fitted, nor that she couldn't read Morse.

As the chronometer on the ship's wall ticked away remorselessly the men on the ground were sure that after more than 20 hours she must be down in the ocean. Then, out of the static, her voice came in loud and clear at 8.45 a.m. 'We are on a line 157-337 running north and south.' Noonan had done his duty, but now AE had to follow his instructions. The one thing she should not have done was fly aimlessly north and south. Or did she decide to turn left when she was still to the north-west of Howland?

No one will ever know. After it was realized that her gas must be exhausted a massive sea search was mounted by the US Navy. The aircraft carrier *Lexington* sent her 63 aircraft out, and a battleship, four destroyers and other craft joined the search. They found nothing, not a trace. But such was AE's charisma that many people simply refused to believe their idol had died. Wild rumours were tracked down, but the sea, the remorseless sea, keeps its secrets well.

Some believe that AE got the Electra down on one of the Japanese-mandated Marshall Islands to the north-west of Howland. Fairly substantial evidence was said to have been discovered that a woman pilot and a tall man had come ashore from a wrecked aircraft. The man was beheaded, and the woman died in prison of dysentry. Who were they? The Japanese, the remorseless Japanese, keep their secrets well, too.

Chapter 13
Howard Hughes – Perfectionist

As the Connie droned on, the stewardess now wanted to know if there was anything she could get me. I handed her my business card which said I was President of World-Wide Airways, Inc, and said I'd sure like a chance to inspect the cockpit. She read it and nodded, then went forward after saying she would see if 'his honour' would let me into 'his kingdom'. The gentle sarcasm made me feel I was already part of the flight crew. While I waited I reflected that Howard Hughes, the airline's owner, was an enigma to most people. He was acknowledged to be a secretive genius who had accomplished many things. For instance, the Lockheed Constellation I was riding in had benefited a great deal from his input during planning and construction. Then he'd bought TWA so he could control the main use of his product. It was apparent that he yearned to leave his personal stamp on anything he was associated with. I certainly admired him, even if he had had a hell of a head start over most people because of the money he'd inherited from his father. Howard Hughes Senior had patented a revolutionary oil-drilling bit which could penetrate previously undrillable solid rock. A lot of new oil fields resulted from his invention. He was a very independent man who wanted no partners, and lived his life in high style. He was very clever when he decided to sell the bit, although that would have given him a quick fortune. Instead he leased it out at a very high daily rent and watched the money roll in.

Howard Robard Hughes Junior was born on Christmas Eve of 1905 in Houston, Texas. His birth was so difficult for his mother that the attending physician recommended she have no more children. So he was fated to live his life as an only child, as was I. As he grew up he was bounced around from one school to another, but managed to pick up a hobby which would serve him well in later life. He was just 12 years old when he was granted his amateur radio operator's licence with the callsign 5CY. The fact we were both hams made him seem more human to me. My call was VE4PH, issued in 1933 at Edmonton, Alberta. I had no doubt Hughes had built his own equipment and grown up with the Morse code ringing in his ears. He had used spark transmitters and receivers made with a cat's whisker poked into a galena crystal before vacuum tubes had become available. The closest I had got to 'King Spark' was when I was on board HMCS *Vancouver* which had an arc set for emergency use. But there could be no doubt we both enjoyed talking to the strange signals we pulled in from the ether on our home-built sets. Ham radio attracts many people who otherwise find it almost impossible to communicate with strangers.

He was called 'Sonny', to distinguish him from his father, and had always been a bit of a 'mother's pet'. On 22 March 1922 Sonny received a traumatic shock. His mother had gone to the hospital for what was supposed to have been a simple operation. But she had died under the anaesthetic on the operating table. He was grief stricken, stunned, bereft, alone, after the loss of his best friend. Then on 16 January, just two short years later in 1924, he got another numbing shock when his father died in his office after a sudden heart attack. Now Sonny was really on his own. The premature death of both his parents gave him a phobia of germs. He believed that taking many pills would protect him, and it was the start of a habit which grew to be an obsession.

There were *two* main reasons why I sincerely admired Howard Hughes Jr. The first was that, at the age of 18 when his father died and left him a fortune, instead of taking the money and loafing around he fought to get control of the Hughes Tool Company. To do this he had to get a court of law to make an exception of his age and declare him an adult, normally 21. He accomplished this with difficulty and then proceeded to buy out the other shareholders, remembering his father's advice not to operate with partners. Then he hired a highly competent manager for the tool company and took off for Hollywood. He immediately made a name for himself as a movie producer with pictures such as *Hell's Angels* and *Scarface*. He made the search for 'starlet' talent his personal chore, which probably is the wrong description for his activities. In the process he discovered Jean Harlow. He liked her high, firm breasts which she flaunted without a brassiere. I thought his reaction was completely normal. What growing boy wouldn't?

The second reason I admired Howard Hughes Jr. was . . . Just then my train of thought was interrupted by my now friendly stewardess who conducted me forward to the compartment where three men controlled the destiny of the 40-odd passengers. I introduced myself to the man in the important left-hand seat. When you came right down to it he was the most important cog in any airline operation. He was about my age, with curly blond hair, a pleasant smile and keen blue eyes surrounded by a maze of flight wrinkles. He obviously enjoyed his job, even with the tremendous responsibility it entailed. He swung the third pilot's jump seat into position and as I sat down I felt now I really was part of the crew. Through the windshields the sun was making the snow-capped jagged peaks of the Rocky Mountains sparkle in an awesome vista that stretched to the far-distant horizon. It was rugged country indeed, no place for a forced landing.

The Captain opened the conversation: 'Ever been in one of these before?'

'No,' I answered, then added so he wouldn't think I was a tyro, 'but I've got a lot of time in Lockheeds. This cockpit is almost as cramped as a Hudson's.'

'That's the way Howard wanted it, I guess. By the way, where did *you* get *your* Hudson time? I flew them a little with the USAAF.' He pronounced it 'Yousaf'.

'With RAF Ferry Command on the North Atlantic,' I replied with some pride.

He pursed his lips and nodded approvingly. 'Good for you. Maybe someday TWA will let me go transatlantic in one of these beasts. Got almost enough seniority.' To remove the insult against an aircraft he obviously loved he patted the black pedestal.

'I noticed you called Mr. Hughes, "Howard", just like you know him as a friend.'

He snorted. 'Nobody knows him as a friend, except that the pilots say he's pretty normal when he's not surrounded by a bunch of flunkies. They say when he's talking about aviation, doin' hangar flying', he's a right nice guy.'

This was news to me, so I said, 'I've heard he's hard to meet and harder to figure.'

'True enough, but I've also heard he's shy and sort of embarrassed because he's a bit deaf.' The Captain shrugged his shoulders and philosophized: 'I suppose that genius types by definition have to be different from ordinary mortals.'

I thought that one over for a while, then, still trying to find out what Hughes was really like, added: 'I've heard he surrounds himself with a lot of minions who form a wall around him and keep people who want to talk to him in suspense. They treat them like puppets on the telephone line, dangling them around for days.'

The loyal TWA employee sprang to the defence of his boss. 'Why not? Thousands of crooks are trying to steal his money. Anyway, Howard pays the bills so that makes him entitled to call the shots, don't you think?'

The angle hadn't struck me before. It looked like a diplomatic time to change the subject. I said, 'Is it true he started to fly in 1927?'

'Sure enough. It was at Santa Monica, and he was so intense that he went right on and got his commercial, multi-engine and instrument ratings the next year. He said he intended to become the best pilot in the world.'

'Maybe he made it, at that,' I said, perhaps with a shade of jealously in my voice. 'He sure cracked a lot of records, and finally he got the "Spruce Goose" off the water for a few precious seconds just last year.

'And he's no slouch on the political front either. He got TWA on the Atlantic over all the howling of Juan Trippe and his "Chosen Instrument" of PAA.' I saw a tinge of red creeping up his neck as he mentioned Pan Am, his company's rival.

It was a good time to change the subject again so I told him my favourite story. 'I heard when Howard (he had me doing it) got back in the movie racket just before the war he engineered a brassiere for a super pair, and then went looking for the woman to fill the big cups. Or was it the other way around?'

'It was the other way around, and you know it, you rascal. Jane Russell in *The Outlaw* was the picture. The censors tried to ban it, but . . .' Just then the radio speaker blared his call-sign and he picked up his mike. He motioned me towards the flight engineer who was monitoring his bewildering array of dials and levers. I shook my head in mock dismay and the flight engineer smiled as he caught my meaning.

'They say that Mr. Hughes designed my station and then built the airplane around it. I like this layout better than the Douglas DC6 where the engineer has to reach around the pilots to get anything done.'

'Yeah, sure,' I said a little weakly, because it seemed to me that the Connie engineer had *too* much control. But then of course all pilots thought that.

'Want to hear a Lockheed joke?' His face was split by a happy grin. He saw me nod, because aviation 'in' jokes are pretty scarce, so he continued, 'Weeeel,' stretching the word for maximum effect, 'a lot of people think that when a Lockheed engineer goes to heaven he'll have to go through a hydraulic check valve and an electrical relay.'

'Very good,' I replied sincerely, then, as the flight deck crew were getting busy, I said goodbye to my new friends and wandered back to my seat. I noted that the alert stewardess seemed to think a lot more of me because of my lengthy stay in the cockpit.

I reclined my seat to a comfortable position and began to sum up Hughes's records and achievements to date. He had started out in January 1934 by winning the All-American Air Meet in Miami, flying a Boeing P12 fighter which he'd souped up according to his own ideas. It was the first of many such modifications.

Then, flying an H-1 racer built to his own design, and aided by the engineers of the California Institute of Technology in Pasadena, he had smashed the world's speed record for land planes by scorching across a measured course at 353.39 mph. The H-1 was loaded with advanced aerodynamic features. Some said it was the prototype for the Jap Zero. Then just to prove he wasn't perfect, he ran out of gas and had to make a forced landing.

While the H-1 was being rebuilt he borrowed a Northrop Gamma from Jackie Cochrane and promptly set a new transcontinental record of 9 hours and 27 minutes from Burbank to New Jersey. On his way back to the West Coast he casually broke the New York to Miami record as well as the Chicago to Los Angeles record.

When his own H-1 was rebuilt he took it to high altitudes and, in spite of having trouble with his oxygen mask, broke his own record from L.A. to Newark with a new time of 7 hours and 28 minutes, averaging a hot 332 mph over the 2,500-odd miles.

Courageous to a fault, he insisted on test flying all his own aircraft. So it was perhaps inevitable that he was involved in several accidents, some of which injured him. The worst one was when he made the first flight on his revolutionary XF-11 fighter on 7 July 1946 at Culver City, California. He completed his usual long and meticulous ground taxi check and then told his engineer Glenn Odekirk to climb out. Then he roared away to a perfect take-off. The spectators thought the beautifully streamlined plane could easily exceed 400 mph in level flight, right up there with the de Havilland Mosquito. It featured two propellers on each of its twin engines, and, well into the test flight, that was where the trouble started. Hughes suddenly felt as if there was a large object such as a barn door tied to his starboard wing. In the cockpit all his instruments were normal, except the airspeed which was unwinding almost as fast as his altimeter. Later it was discovered that the rear prop of the right engine had slid into reverse pitch, which meant the engine power was supplying two props that were fighting each other.

A less courageous man would have baled out and let the aircraft go. But not Hughes. He rode it down, aiming for the level ground of a golf course. But it was not to be. His wing caught a house and the plane crashed — hard — very hard. There was a thunderous noise and very quickly the wreck

caught fire. A Marine sergeant named Lloyd Durkin courageously braved the flames and danger of explosion as he pulled Hughes out of the conflagration. At the hospital the doctors thought the pilot would surely die from his many injuries. He was a 'basket case' which meant a lot of loose parts thrown into a container, with not much chance of a rebuild. But he hung on gamely, confounding the experts yet again, and was even able to fly another XF-11 successfully just a year later.

But during his many pain-wracked months in intensive care wards he had been pumped full of powerful drugs. In many cases that is how drug addiction sets in, and it is possible that Hughes was no exception.

It seemed that when he became engrossed in whatever task was in front of him at the time he could work a legendary 40 hours at a stretch. Or maybe he didn't care to be interrupted while using his casting couch to test fly some aspiring starlet? Who could blame him? Anyway, I always believed that superior pilots also came equipped with a superior grade of sex drive.

The flight that caught the attention of the world and catapulted him to the pinnacle of fame was his record round-the-world epic, which started from Floyd Bennett Field on 10 July 1938 at 7.20 p.m. local time.

Hughes had been planning his attempt for a new record for three years. It was not his nature to belt off on a long flight without adequate weather information. But there was a problem. North America and Europe had a network of weather stations, which reported regularly via radio or teletype to forecast centres. At sea, ships were content with slow forecasts which would be useless to a fast aircraft. Hughes was not satisfied with the capabilities of the Government forecasters, so he, typically, recruited the best in Dr. William

C. Rockefeller. As time went on the centre of control became established at the headquarters of the upcoming World's Fair in New York. Grover Whelan and Fiorello La Guardia liked the idea — and the publicity associated with the Hughes name and the adventurous flight.

But Rockefeller needed lots of reporting stations to draw the synoptic map which would enable him to tell Hughes about the winds he could expect aloft, possible dangerous icing conditions, weather to be expected en route and at his destination, and all the other essential information for a safe and successful flight. So he turned to amateur radio. An east coast control station was established at the site of the World's Fair manned by Tommy Thomas W2UK. He and the other operators at the operating position, which was open to the public, controlled transmitters and receivers at W2GOQ, set up in a location favourable for radio propagation and equipped with directional antennas. Four National HRO receivers were manned to receive the coded weather reports from London, Berlin, Paris, Rome, Moscow, Manila, Honolulu, San Francisco and Arlington.

Sample code numbers were 486 for New York, 627 for Montreal, 149 for Paris, 612 for Moscow and 295 for Los Angeles and these reports were decoded and plotted on a weather map, with special attention to the flight in being and the planned next leg. It took a long six hours each day with steady copying of Morse at 30 words per minute to record this essential information for the forecaster.

This is what the code consisted of:

The Weather Code. —The meteorological observations are made simultaneously at a large number of stations at certain hours. The observations are transcribed into coded messages, which are broadcast regionally. The following code is used:

$IIIC_LC_M$ $wwVhN_h$ DDFWN PPPTT UC_Happ RRjjj.

The letters have the following meaning:

III = Index number of station
C_L = Form of low clouds
C_M = Form of medium clouds
ww = Weather at the hour of observation (present weather)
V = Visibility
h = Height of the base of low clouds above the ground

N_h = Amount of low clouds
DD = Wind direction
F = Wind force
W = Past weather (since the last observation)
N = Amount of clouds
PPP = Pressure
TT = Temperature
U = Relative humidity
C_H = Form of high clouds
a = Form of barogram
pp = Barometric tendency
RR = Amount of precipitation.

The meaning of jjj differs with the type of station. For inland stations jjj = MME, where

Minimum temperature in the morning reports
MM = Maximum temperature in the evening reports
E = State of ground.

When I was a radio range operator I used to get the information from the station teletype and plot stations, even making up my own forecasts. The one number that stuck in my mind was 03 for overcast condition, and present weather, which was WW. Once I got the barometric pressures plotted it was interesting to try and figure out when and where the weather fronts would move.

The scheme for universal plotting of information around a station looked like this:

Scheme of Arrangement of Information around the Position of the Station

Station Model. The circle denotes the position of the station. *In the Station Model the letters have the following customary meanings:*

PPP = Pressure. pp = Tendency.
TT = Temperature. T_1T_1 = Sea Temperature.
ww = Present Weather. W = Past Weather.
a = Characteristic. E = State of Ground.
$C_LC_MC_H$ = Form of Low, Medium and High Cloud.
T_sT_s = Dew Point Temperature.

Station Model

N = Total Amount of Cloud. V =
Visibility.

N_h = Amount of Low Cloud. RR =
Rainfall.

h = Height of Low Cloud.

Also (w) = That part of ww which refers to the last hour but not to the time of observation.

U = Humidity is alternative to T_sT_s

Where lack of space necessitates a modification of the Station Model a deformation of it without permutation of the places allotted to the individual elements, is permissible.

If only one colour is used it should be black. If two colours, black and red, are used then red should be used for one or more of the following:-

(1) For C_H (2) For W (Past Weather)

(3) For TT, T_sT_s (4) For V

(5) For pp *when pp is negative.*

Red should *not* be used for PPP, ww, C_M, C_L, T_1T_1, N_h, h.

There were no less than 99 types of present weather to choose from, and this is how the first sixteen went:

Code for ww (Present Weather)

Code Figure	Description
00-19	*Abbreviated description of sky and special phenomena*
00	Cloudless
01	Partly cloudy
02	Cloudy
03	Overcast
04	Low fog
05	Haze (but visibility greater than 2000 m.)
06	Dust devils seen
07	Distant lightning
08	Mist
09	Distant fog
10	Precipitation within sight
11	Thunder, without precipitation at the station
12	Dust storm visible but not at the station
13	Ugly, threatening sky
14	Squally weather
15	Heavy squalls in last three hours
16	Waterspouts seen in last three hours

The range operator reported the weather, of course, and I think I used every 'present weather' number listed above, except 16. Being in a valley between two ranges of mountains, we didn't see too many waterspouts!

The transmitting schedules and frequencies were recorded in various publications such as the Swiss 'Berne' listing, and all countries were bound by international agreement to supply the weather reports. But it soon was apparent that the Russians, in the usual Russian manner, were not cooperating. Rockefeller's map had a huge white spot, which resembled Siberian snow. Representations through diplomatic channels brought no help. In the usual manner of diplomats the matter would be brought up 'at an opportune time'. That wasn't good enough for Hughes. Through his involvement with International Telephone and Telegraph, the communications giant, he got a message through to the Kremlin, or wherever else the Russians controlled their lack of cooperation with other countries. Shortly thereafter no less than 250 reporting Russian stations bloomed like flowers in the previously pristine whiteness of Rockefeller's map.

Communication with the aircraft would be backed up by Charles Perrine's station W6CUH in California manned by crack operator Dave Evans, W4DHZ. This was a powerful station with a water-cooled tube in the final amplifier, and possibly that is where the term 'California Kilowatt' originated. The normal limit of one kilowatt of power was set by the FCC. Both ground control stations would transmit on the bottom edge of the CW band using Morse code, which always was more reliable and punched through better than voice. The frequencies were 7,000 kc and 14,000. When the aircraft was out of range of one frequency the other would normally take over. The ground stations would transmit every fifteen minutes when the aircraft was in the air so the airborne operator could tell which band was favoured by good propagation at the moment. 'Q' code signals would be used because they were international. Thus if the aircraft transmitted QAM, which means 'Can you give me the latest met weather for — (placed desired)?', the ground station in Moscow would look it up in the code book to see the request in Russian and reply with figures for ceiling and visibility. And in Paris the French operator would find the same thing in French.

When he first planned the flight, Hughes had decided to use

a Sikorsky S-43 twin-engined amphibian which would have given him a wide choice of landing places. But while he was waiting for government approval for his flight this slow and bulky aircraft was involved in an accident. Perhaps this was fortuitous because Lockheed had just manufactured the first Super Electra Model 14, the fastest airliner in the sky. Hughes got one of the early models and immediately set about putting his mark on it. More powerful Wright engines were installed and long-range fuel capacity was added. The cabin became cluttered with scientific instruments, because this flight would not only set new speed records but also advance the art of scheduled flying. He chose his flight crew with great care, each man being able to perform at least two functions as an airman. Ed Lund would be his flight engineer, Harry Connor his copilot, Thomas Thurlow his navigator and Dick Stoddard, W6TSD, his radio operator.

Stoddard would work the amateur bands and the aeronautical frequencies as the situation demanded. Hughes was a strong believer in redundancy. He had Perrine build him a special light-weight transmitter of 100 watts output, which would cover a wide range of frequencies from 333 kc low band to 21,200 kc high band with 18 crystal-controlled frequencies. This would be backed up by a Bendix eight-channel transmitter. For reception, Stoddard had two Bendix super heterodyne receivers of the most modern design. Just to put the icing on the cake there were two direction finding sets and two trailing antennas adding to the fixed antennas.

In case of a forced landing Perrine had built a 15 watt transmitter with four crystal frequencies and a receiver covering the same range. The complete station, including a hand-driven generator was in a waterproof container measuring only 15 by 8 by 10 inches. A kite and a balloon would raise the antenna from the dinghy if it came to that. Ping-pong balls were stuffed in the wings and fuselage. Maybe *that* would make the aircraft float until some rescue craft appeared.

In addition to the registration letters of NX18973 (the X stood for experimental), the Lockheed was assigned a radio callsign by the FCC of KHBRC. Five-letter calls were assigned to aircraft while four-letter calls were assigned to ships at sea. Hughes wasn't happy with that rule. He wanted his personal letters of KHRH. After a little screaming his power in

Washington prevailed. As a radio man, that call allocation finally convinced me that money was power and could buy *anything*.

The ferry flight from California on 4 July gave the aircraft a good shake-down and there was plenty to do in the hangar at Floyd Bennett Field. Hughes's life was miserable as he dodged reporters who didn't believe his statement that he was only out to break the New York-Paris speed record. He might have taken refuge in Miss Katherine Hepburn's arms, as the leading actress was his latest love interest. Or more likely he personally oversaw the work on his precious aircraft. The Sperry automatic pilot had performed faultlessly and the huge 1,750 gallon gas tanks had not leaked, so two big items were signed off. The special heavy duty tyres Hughes had ordered from Goodyear had to be inspected, ply by ply. The Wright Cyclone engines had run like sewing machines, but for safety the spark plugs were changed and two cylinders with slight rust pits replaced. Approval for the flight finally arrived from Washington on 8 July, but still Hughes delayed, making sure his aircraft was in tip-top shape. There was also the weather factor. Rockefeller was looking for a combination of tail winds over the Atlantic and good landing conditions at Paris. The weather over the Atlantic was summery, which meant that the freezing level was a lovely six or seven thousand feet above the surface of the sea. Finally, on the morning of 10 July it looked like everything was in order and Hughes announced an estimated time of departure of 3 p.m.

But it wasn't to be. The starboard engine developed a faulty magneto. It was 6 p.m. before the aircraft was airworthy. Hughes the perfectionist had done all he could, yet he still took out heavy life insurance policies for his crew. Rockefeller finally said 'go' and Hughes scanned the latest weather map, tossed it into the plane and also said, 'Let's go.' Finally . . . but there was yet another delay.

Grover Whelan, New York's offical meeter and greeter, who was also president of the New York World's Fair, and New York City's Mayor Fiorello La Guardia each wanted to say several thousand words as they christened the aircraft 'New York World's Fair, 1939'. Finally the politicians had had their say and it was Hughes's turn. Much as he hated publicity, he stepped forward and in a high strained voice read from a paper he had prepared. His appearance contrasted markedly with that of the two pols who were dressed in the height of fashion. He wore his usual scuffed running shoes, wrinkled grey trousers, a white shirt open at the throat and a battered brown Fedora. Hughes's speech was short and to the point. He hoped that his flight would contribute to the friendship between nations and apologized to the reporters and photographers for his conduct the night before. For the first time the newsmen applauded.

Finally the time had come, and the crew climbed into the fuselage and scrambled over the long-range tanks. In addition to all the other equipment on board there was 150 gallons of oil for the engines. Who could tell what odd brand the Russians would serve up? So the all-up weight was almost 26,000 lb, a truly daunting overload. Fully loaded, the aircraft was actually a little 'sway-backed'. Not as bad as a dachschund, admittedly, but still visible to the naked eye. Airlines were restriced to 18,000 lb and in Ferry Command we took our Hudsons off with what was called 'War Emergency All-Up' weight of 22,000 lb, which presented quite a handful on take-off. So it was quite obvious that Hughes had no chance of staying aloft if one engine quit early in the flight unless he could dump one hell of a lot of gas in a big hurry, which I thought unlikely. No doubt Hughes had all the variables worked out in that methodical mind of his and had chosen to accept the risk.

Hughes had decided to take-off south on the short 3,500 foot runway, the wind being light. Besides, there was a hardpacked dirt overrun at the end. Ed Lund was in the copilot's seat as the silver aircraft taxied into position. Then there was another agonizing delay as Hughes completed his usual methodical run-up. Finally he opened the throttles and the engines roared a defiant note. The Lockheed began to move, but oh, so sluggishly! All overloaded aircraft take a long time to get up flying speed, and he was half-way down the runway before he got the tail up. Now he was fully committed. A loss of power and once again Hughes would be in the middle of a mess of twisted metal — hot metal being sprayed with volatile gasoline. On and on he ran, and there was a puff of dust as he ran off the end of the runway. The crowd held its breath until the aircraft appeared low on the horizon, already in a gentle turn. He had made it! The crowd cheered as the monoplane disappeared low over Jamaica Bay and started across Long Island. He dipped his wings over Katherine Hepburn's Old Saybrook home, then pointed his nose on the Great Circle course for Paris. What he didn't realize was that Mrs. Connor, the copilot's wife, had broken through the police cordon and stuck a wad of chewing gum on the aircraft's tail. 'For good luck', she had called to her husband. 'Be sure and bring it back safe for me! You, too!' You can't beat the Irish. And maybe Hughes wouldn't have removed it had he known. A bit of luck could help all the careful preparation.

Hughes had climbed slowly to conserve his fuel on the first part of his flight, and had reached 7,500 feet when he passed over Newfoundland, hopping-off place for many previous attempts by others and a continuing important link for aircraft deliveries to England. One of the trailing antennas had broken off but Stoddard had fixed the spare. At 10.30 p.m. Stoddard told the world that all was going smoothly. Hughes was busy and the sea below was covered with clouds.

Then, at 2.30 a.m., Hughes himself got on the radio to advise Odekirk about a problem. 'I hope we get to Paris before we run out of gas,' he said, his voice calm but with an undertone of urgency, 'but I am not sure. All I can do is to hope we will get there. I hope we will have enough gas to reach land. I am throttling back the engines as fast as the reducing load permits.' There was no joy in New York when the implications of that message sank in.

Newspaper editors prepared bulletins stating that Hughes was down at sea. But they were never printed, because Hughes had made a slight miscalculation in his fuel consumption figures. He had not realized how truly hungry is engines would be at maximum weight for the '14' not just to mush through the air. It was essential for the efficiency of his flight to stay 'on the step'. Then as the fuel rapidly burned off his weight decreased quickly and he was able to reduce his power settings while keeping his desired airspeed. He made no more pessimistic broadcasts, and he had a good fuel reserve when he landed at Le Bourget airport with the Eiffel Tower in sight just 16 hours and 38 minutes after the agonizingly long take-off at Floyd Bennett. The French were astonished. Their engineers were certain that no aircraft existed that could make the long flight non-stop in less than a full day of 24 hours. Indeed, Lindbergh's time of 33 hours and a few minutes, set eleven years before, had been cut in half by another pilot who had emulated his persistency in never leaving his cockpit.

The 'Fasten Seat Belt' sign flashed on, momentarily disrupting my line of thought. It was time to cinch up a little tighter, as I always flew with my seat belt fastened. Who could tell when we'd run into a hidden thunderhead or maybe have to take violent avoiding action to miss another aircraft? The Captain would be too busy saving our lives to bother to switch on the warning sign. Very soon we were bouncing around as dirty grey clouds streamed past my window. The stewardess was gamely tottering along the aisle hanging onto the tops of the seats as she made sure all her flock of passengers were safely tied down.

I began to compare Hughes's flight with my first Hudson delivery, just three years and nine months after his epic effort. On that day in 1942 Captain Louis Bisson, Captain George Evans and I had made the first flights from Goose Bay, Labrador, to Prestwick. We all had taken about eleven hours, which was excellent in-flight time for the route and the aircraft.

My flight had been uneventful, a marked contrast with my first flight from Goose to Greenland and Iceland then to Prestwick in a lumbering PBY5A just a week before. A more southerly flight path with no mountain of ice en route made the difference. I had acted as captain-navigator in Hudson Mk III FH342, aided by RNZAF Plt Off Lewis as copilot, although he had no flight controls. The RAF believed in single-pilot bombers, thinking that aircraft were easy to get, but pilots hard to train. Maybe they had a point but I was sure their thinking was short-sighted. We did have a Sperry autopilot, very reliable, which was good. Our Wright Cyclone engines were the same as Hughes's. They gave us confidence, just as they gave to Hughes's crew. So our Hudson was almost identical to his Model 14, except we didn't have quite as much fuel, as our flight was considerably shorter. My radio operator was Eric Rush, just as competent as any American. He kept in touch with the Ferry Command ground stations, so maybe we had an advantage there, as Hughes had to rely on amateurs and ships at sea for weather and other navigational information. The amateur radio operators were still helping, however, although their ham callsigns were silent. Many of them had joined the armed forces of various nations where their skills were of the greatest value.

In comparing meteorologists I put our Dr. Patrick McTaggart-Cowan up against the American Dr. William Rockefeller anytime for forecasting accuracy and knowledge of the North Atlantic.

However, Hughes had four compasses, while we got by on two. We had just one radio direction finder and one HF transmitting and receiving set-up. Redundancy? — Not in wartime, my friend. However we did have a feature that Hughes lacked. It was a Very High Frequency transmitter called IFF, which transmitted pulses that told the radar men on the ground whether we were indeed Friend or Foe. This made me realize that our welcoming committees differed substantially. While he was greeted by flag-waving Frenchmen we always had the thought that German Focke-Wulf four-engined raiders were out there somewhere. Their welcome would be a salvo of cannon or machine-gun fire. I guess I was lucky that I never did encounter one of the well-named 'scourges of the Atlantic', but they caused plenty of trouble to Allied aircraft and shipping.

The whole world relaxed when Hughes got his aircraft safely on the ground at the airport near Paris. But after he'd shut off his engines he found he had a serious problem. Really serious trouble. The bulkhead holding the tail wheel assembly in place had buckled, probably due to the overload and possibly when he'd taxied off the runway by mistake back in the USA. The damage was so extensive that one Gallic engineer shrugged his shoulders and said 'C'est fini!' But he had reckoned without the expertise of hard-bitten flight engineer Ed Lund. He and Hughes had inspected the damage, probably thanking the fates that the tailwheel did not retract, thus complicating their problem. The two men came up with a repair scheme like that used by the barnstormers in the 'baling-wire and chewing gum' school of engineering. Lund bolted angle iron onto the aluminium of the fuselage so as to carry the tailwheel stress to some undamaged bulkheads. The job took eight hours of heavy work in a cramped space. Meanwhile Stoddard, Thurlow and Connor grabbed some shut-eye, a sensible idea. But Hughes, possibly hoping to add moral support to Lund, just sat in a restaurant on the edge of the airport staring out of the plate-glass window, grimly watching the progress of the makeshift repair. Although he never mentioned his behaviour he would probably have said he was too tense to sleep in any case.

Finally Lund tightened up the last bolt and said the repair would hold. Hughes got his crew together and eagerly jumped into his aircraft. Although he'd lost eight precious hours he felt he could make up time and so meet his goal of a record flight around the world. By now the weather had changed; the ceiling was low and the visibility restricted. But Hughes took off anyway. The silver aircraft disappeared quickly into the grey ominous-looking overcast. Hughes welcomed the weather, because on their next leg they would be flying directly over Hitler's Germany towards Moscow. The Nazis, who wanted no strangers flying over their military installations, had not granted permission for the over-flight.

This attitude did not faze Hughes. Such was his determination that he would probably have pushed on no matter what the diplomats and the politicians said he should do. He figured that darkness would prevent the Germans from seeing him, and, anyway, no fighter could intercept him in the thick, all-enveloping cloud. And furthermore he doubted that the Germans would shoot him down in any case. A courageous decision in which he was proved right in the long run.

However, when they got over the Fatherland there was a lot of chatter in Stoddard's receiver, with the word 'Verboten' often repeated. In spite of the increased tension in the cockpit Hughes pressed on. It turned out that no one *did* shoot at them.

So a master gambler had once again beaten the odds.

They landed in Moscow at 11.15 the next morning to a rousing welcome. The Russians were determined to fête the crew, an attitude which was just as much a danger to would-be record-setters as bad weather or head winds. Mikhail Gromoff, who had made a record-setting flight of 62 hours' duration from Moscow to San Jacinto, California, the year before, understood. He helped shoo away the sightseers and press people. Hughes thanked him as he refused the parting gift of a huge jar of caviar. But he did take a case of mineral water, which was more to his taste. He forced his way back into the air after only a two-hour ground pause.

Airborne for Omsk in far-away Siberia Hughes for the first time stretched out on the metal floor for a rest. Just 20 minutes later he awoke refreshed and went forward to take over control again. The amateur radio network had been working faultlessly, passing weather to the aircraft and receiving position reports back. But now, on the other side of the world, signals began to become erratic. Back home the newspapers filled out the story of the flight with clips of Hughes's 'amatory prowess', and the longer the aircraft's silence lasted the more purple the prose became. Hughes was a hero, a movie producer of note, an ace pilot, an aircraft designer, a rich eccentric and an All-American playboy with limitless wealth. No wonder the readers in Canada and the USA hung on every word printed, true or false. It was the stuff that dreams are made of. Circulation figures soared.

But now things weren't going smoothly as the Lockheed drilled through thick driving rain in the blackest of nights. There could be no ground pinpointing or astro fixes. So it was all dead-reckoning navigation. Then, an hour away from Omsk, according to their flight plan, Stoddard picked up its weak radio beacon signal with his direction finding set. Saved once more by radio! But when they arrived over the beacon there was only a thin line of flickering red lights below them. Could this be the airport? It had to be! Hughes made a skilful landing aided only by the headlights of some cars parked along the perimeter of the grass pasture. Now there was another problem. The gas that Hughes had ordered at every stop was stored in 50-gallon metal drums which were scattered all over the field. The crew rounded up the drums and added tetra-ethyl to the low-grade Russian gas to make it more digestible for the high compression engines. But now another problem arose. The drums could very well be contaminated with water, which no self-respecting engine will accept. Where were the fuel filters, packed for just this very eventuality? They were 42 hours en route when Stoddard's Morse broke through to New York and their amateur station. Odekirk told them to look near the life rafts. For an aircraft parked on the ground this was a marvellous demonstration of efficient communication. Four hours later, greasy and stinking with gas, the crew climbed in. The take-off was through clouds of mud and water, and they barely staggered into the air from the perilous runway.

Now they headed across the steppes through yet another storm, bound for Yahutsk by way of Krasnoyarsk and Kansk. They outflew the storm and landed at Yakutsk just as dawn broke, after a rough flight of ten and a half hours. At the northern Siberian outpost their interpreter failed to meet them, but luckily a schoolteacher who spoke English came to their rescue. The tedious refuelling from drums was repeated. Lund said later that every take-off was a thrill but the one at Yakutsk was the hairiest. But now, at last they were bound for good old American soil at Fairbanks, Alaska. The fates had one last jolt for them. Their charts, supplied by the United States Hydrographic Survey, showed the range of mountains on course ahead as having a maximum height of 6,500 feet. But Hughes had to climb to 10,000 feet to clear the jagged peaks safely. He later remarked that if they hadn't had the unexpected delay at Paris he would have blundered right into the mountains in total darkness. I wondered how many of these lucky coincidences had kept airmen alive.

Now west coast station W6CUH was booming in across the Pacific with all the latest weather. It was 12 hours and 16 minutes after wiping the gumbo of Russian soil from their boots for the last time when they touched down at Fairbanks, Alaska. Good gas and plenty of help! It made the stop a pleasure. Wiley Post's widow was there to wish the flight Godspeed, in spite of the fact that it was her dead husband's record they were breaking. Hughes was bone-tired as he shook her hand and expressed admiration for Post's epic flight.

Since there were no more oceans to cross, the aircraft was stripped of its life rafts and survival equipment. A sack of ping-pong balls broke open on the runway and for a moment all work stopped as the Fairbanks people scrambled for the bouncing souvenirs. Hughes, tired and gaunt, turned away the inquisitive reporters. He said he must get back in the air. That was all that counted.

They had the fuel and the legs to overfly Edmonton, so I missed seeing them, damn it! It was right on to Minneapolis for a quick 34 minute pit stop. Then the weather gave them one more test, with hail as big as golf balls pounding them over Minnesota. Lund said they had to slow down before the plane shook itself to death. Finally, the active cold front was behind them, with Hughes staying obstinately at the controls. And there was New York's Floyd Bennett Field, with 25,000 people milling around to greet them. The crowd spilled onto the airport and Hughes was lucky to avoid hitting anyone. The flight of 14,798 miles was over in the astonishing time of 3 days, 19 hours and 8 minutes.

The reporters, photographers and radio men were there with their usual thrusting questions. Hughes had to face them, tired as he was, his dark mystical eyes sunken in his determined face. His slight stoop was a little more pronounced and he now had a four-day beard to go with his shabby clothes. His face had the look of utter emptiness, because in his brain he was still two miles high travelling at 200 miles per hour. But the insensitive reporters failed to realize his state, and one of the brassier members of the press surmised that he must be happy to have broken Wiley Post's record. Hughes snapped to attention and leaned forward. His words had a particular heartfelt emphasis as he said: 'Wiley Post's solo flight remains the most remarkable flight in history. It can never be duplicated. He did it alone. To make a trip like that is beyond comprehension. It's like pulling a rabbit out of the hat or sawing a woman in half.' A truly modest man.

That was the *second* reason I admired Howard Robard Hughes.

Chapter 14
The Hudson

The stewardess announced we were beginning our descent, so please fasten our safety belts. Far ahead I could see the sprawling outlines of Los Angeles and beyond that the limitless blue Pacific. We would be landing at Burbank airport which was to the north of the city proper. Mines Field was still in the process of being converted into a first-class international airport, which would become renowned around the world for its two, then three, parallel runways as LAX — Los Angeles International.

It was at Burbank that Lockheed had their main factory. They had had spectacular success with their wooden monoplanes and then moderate acceptance for their Models 10, 12 and 14. It was in April 1938 that the company really hit the big time. They had received only five days' notice that they would be visited by the British Purchasing Commission, who were seeking a replacement for the obsolete Avro Anson. Not everyone in England was blind to the threat that Hitler posed to the civilized world.

Lockheed engineers went to work with a will. They took the Model 14 and stuck a navigator's station in the nose, a radio operator's station in the cabin and provision for a Boulton & Paul upper turret. It was fortunate that the 14 was a mid-wing airplane, because that made it relatively simple to convert the belly into a bomb bay with wide-opening doors, which could hold 1,400 lb of bombs or depth charges. The Commission were impressed. So impressed that they expressed a keen interest in buying 200, which was a staggering order for any small aircraft manufacturer. They asked that their new aircraft be called the Hudson, after the English explorer who had left his name on Hudson's Bay in northern Canada.

Then the Britishers returned home to sell a rather reluctant RAF on their idea, not to mention strong opposition from English aircraft manufacturers. The English had the Handley-Page Hampden, the Bristol Blenheim, Armstrong-Whitworth Whitley and Vickers Wellington as their twin-engined bombers in production. But their factory output was insufficient for the demands of the upcoming war. As it turned out, three of the light bombers killed so many flight crew they had to be withdrawn from operations. Only the Wellington was able to continue the bombing of Germany throughout the long six years of war.

Lockheed followed up their initial advantage by sending a negotiating team who were very cooperative about any changes their customer could suggest. Not every factory could make that claim. So a contract was signed on 23 June 1938 for 200 Hudsons with an option for 50 more, provided they could be delivered by December 1939. The price for the aircraft was a staggering $25,000,000 and was by far the largest order placed with a single US aircraft factory at that time. It was in cash, as Lend-Lease was still in the future.

Only eight months after the initial mock-up inspection, the first Hudson made its test flight on 10 December 1938. Then Lockheed exploded as they added 7,000 people to their payroll by the middle of 1939, with two Hudsons a day rolling out. The 250th aircraft on the contract was delivered two months ahead of schedule. American know-how had shown the world what could be done for maximum production. Follow-on orders for the RAF, mainly Coastal Command, came in a steady stream as Britain fought with her back to the wall, or in her case, with her back to the sea. When production was finally terminated in May 1943, 2,940 Hudsons had been built, which was just 26 times more than the civil Model 14.

In the beginning the aircraft were tested in the air and then disassembled. With a thick covering of greasy 'cosmoline' to protect them from the salt spray they were shipped as deck cargo from either Los Angeles or an east coast American port. After a voyage across the stormy Atlantic, where German U-boats sank a high percentage of the cargo ships, they were off-loaded at Liverpool. Then, now menaced by the bombs of the Luftwaffe they were trucked to Speke airport where Lockheed reassembled them assisted by 'Kelly' Johnson, who thus saw the aircraft from just a gleam in a designer's eye through its birth pangs and finally to its ultimate destiny as a leading fighter for democracy and freedom.

And so it was that when the curtain went up, for what many people called 'the Big Show', the RAF's Nos. 233 and 224 Squadrons were ready to fight. In the early days of the war there was no comforting long-range fighter escort, so their losses were high, especially as the Boulton and Paul turrets were not fitted until early 1940. However the converted airliner had a unique honour when Wing Commander A. L. Womersly shot down the first German aircraft in the war on 9 October 1939. It was a Dornier 18 flying boat, and he used the Hudson's two nose-mounted .303 guns. Perhaps he was a frustrated Spitfire pilot!

Meanwhile, on land, the German army with their new Blitzkreig tactics of combining tanks and Stuka dive-bombers were everywhere successful. The British forces were thrown off the continent of Europe into the sea at Dunkirk in massive disarray. The fighters of the RAF had won a narrow victory in the Battle of Britain, which was the only bright spot in a black sky. At sea, Admiral Doenitz had his U-boats at their deadly work and their torpedo attacks were sinking hundreds of thousands of tons of shipping each month. And the deck cargo of Hudsons were among the material going to the bottom. This somewhat ironical development was a double loss, as those

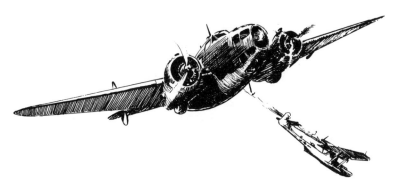

very precious operational Coastal Command squadrons could have protected the convoys in which they had been sunk.

Winston Churchill had maintained that of all the things he feared during the war, the worst nightmare was strangulation of supplies for the beleaguered island by U-boats.

The Atlantic had never been flown during the winter, but

desperate times call for desperate solutions. The British Government was prepared to accept losses of 30 per cent in order to get the desperately needed aircraft. Canadian Pacific Air Services, headed up by old-time fighter and bush pilot C. H. 'Punch' Dickins, was selected to plan the operation. He was assisted in the organization by a number of prominent businessmen. The Clayton Knight Committee found experienced pilots in the USA, while Imperial Airways loaned some of their most experienced flight crew. Canada supplied the majority of the radio operators from the Department of Transport and from Marconi. But there were few navigators to be had.

So, to the tunes of a military band, seven Hudsons took off from Gander, Newfoundland, on their long journey across the North Atlantic. They were crewed by six Canadians, nine Americans, six British and one Australian. The flight was led by the famous pilot/navigator D. C. T. Bennett, and the other six Hudsons were supposed to formate on him, as there was that critical lack of navigators. But the usual front-filled skies over the ocean forced them to split up. They eventually all arrived safely in Aldergrove due to the experience of the pilots who were aided by bearings obtained by their radio operators. Many people, including very possibly some of the Hudson flight crews, were both pleased and astonished. No losses! Incredible! There were two more mass flights with low losses and then the Air Ministry decided to switch the majority of the American aircraft production to air delivery. Thus the so-called 'Atlantic Bridge' began operating, now aided by a trickle of navigators as they graduated from the British Commonwealth Air Training Scheme.

More than 10,000 aircraft would be delivered world-wide by the flight crews who became RAF Ferry Command, and then 45 Group, RAF. As the war ground on, almost one man in five would die and thus never see the victory celebrations they had brought about. It was a heavy casualty rate.

When I joined the Ferry Command in November 1941 I discovered that the Hudson was the main training aircraft. One reason was that there were lots of Hudsons available, which was fortunate, because there were also plenty of training accidents due to the 'tail-dragger' being so short coupled. It was a tricky beast to handle on take-off and landing. Once you mastered the Hudson the Command figured you could handle any other of their delivery aircraft right.

However, the Hudson had some features which other combat aircraft lacked, such as rubber de-icing boots, *almost* enough carburettor heat and alcohol to back up the carb heat. The windshield also had wipers and alcohol. A lot of this improvement was due to Trans-Canada Air Lines who had flown the aircraft many hours in heavy ice conditions. This certainly was not the case in many of the other bombers we ferried across, such as the North American B-25, the Martin B-26, the Douglas A-20 and the de Havilland Mosquito. It also had a well-proven Sperry automatic pilot, just like the one Amelia Earhart and Howard Hughes had used. And if the Hudson had fully-feathering props, which most of the models did, there was a pretty good chance of not dropping into the drink if one engine failed. So the crews who drew a Hudson for delivery were happy — or as happy as any delivery crew could ever admit to — because deep down they trusted the Hudson to get them to the other side.

As one of the pilots lucky enough to survive, I suppose I should have been very happy. But somehow it didn't work out that way. There were occasions when I suffered a strong sense of guilt, wondering why so many others had been killed while I had been spared. I found out later I wasn't alone. The head shrinkers defined our cases as 'survivor's syndrome', a psychological hang-up. There was no known cure. In my case I reacted worst after too many Gibson martinis. So surely the cure was just fewer Gibsons, wasn't it Doc? Simplistic cures for simple people, maybe, but in the event only time, that reliable healer, cured most of us.

As I sat in the comfort of Lockheed's latest and best I reflected rather ruefully that no one had paid much attention to *my* pioneer flights. If accidents were the criterion, I'd had two; one a Norseman on skis in the Arctic and the other a Hudson at Churchill, Manitoba. If it was having an automatic pilot pack up, I'd had plenty of that with my Handley-Page Hampden flight, the first from UK over the Polar route to Western Canada. If getting lost was a qualification . . . better let that subject drop. I'd been lost my share of the time, but at least had always landed at the airport I'd flight planned. I hadn't had to fight mud, but maybe snow and ice were an acceptable substitute. Various members of my flight crew had done their best to kill us all, such as when my copilot had almost put us into the ocean in a Catalina on a long delivery flight from Bermuda to Scotland. And there were other instances . . . I decided to forget them.

However, there was one instance I just couldn't put out of my mind. A reporter from the *Edmonton Journal* had seen my aircraft at the airport and had tracked me down at the MacDonald Hotel. He wanted to know what I was doing. But the 'Crimson Route' I was surveying over the Arctic of Baffinland, Greenland and Iceland was top secret. So I kept my mouth shut. There's a war on, don't you know. Enemy ears and all that, so I'd turned away the reporters, who wanted to give a 'local boy' publicity, probably as much as Post or Hughes ever got in *their* home town.

Somehow it was bitterly ironical that the route my crews and I had pioneered was now being touted as the brand-new 'Polar route' by scheduled airlines such as SAS. The short way from North America to Europe. So thousands and thousands of passengers, would never learn that the time they saved on the shorter distance was due to the efforts of a Hampden or a Hudson aircraft.

Or of me either, for that matter.

We seemed to skim by the California mountains until the pilot put us on the ground with just a squeak of rubber in a perfect landing. It was time to forget history and the war, and maybe even Gibsons, and get on with my life.

Chapter 15
Loretta, where are you?

There was only a light haze in the California air when I stepped out of the Connie at Burbank airport, where Ron George was waiting for me. We dropped into Lockheed Aircraft's head office where he checked on the Connies he would be accepting for KLM, the Dutch national airline. Of course I made my pitch as a ferrying organization but it was no sale. Foreign buyers were sending their flight and ground crews to the factory for training and somehow the thought of four nice Wright engines made the over-water flight a lot less frightening for them than if there were only two.

That night we flew a few hundred thousand miles talking about our various exploits. Ron and I went a long way back. I had been in the control tower at Winnipeg when he had been operations manager for Trans Canada Air Lines just as the war was beginning. Then he had been my boss when he was in charge of operations for British West Indian Airways in Trinidad in the latter part of the war. He had made me Chief Pilot, a very responsible job in any airline. In fact I thought it was *the* toughest job; being the buffer between high-strung pilots and economy-minded management. Then he had gone off on his own to a freight operation in Central America after asking me to come with him. I often wondered what would have happened had I taken him up on his suggestion. Now we were together again and he had offered to help me qualify on the new Convair 240s that both KLM and Swissair had ordered to upgrade their postwar fleet. I had explained to him that the month-long course offered by American Airlines at their Texas training school would cost more money that I could hope to make for each delivery. He agreed that the ground courses in hydraulics, electrical system and the other

240 systems could be learned in a few full days of study, and he would see to it that I got to ride with him or his pilots on the new aircraft at every opportunity. We both agreed that any pilot with several hundred hours as captain on the heavy four-engined B24 Liberator made by the same company really didn't need much of a conversion course.

When we started off in his car for San Diego the next morning I was fully appreciative of the favour he was doing me. The drive down on the scenic Pacific highway was pleasant with the mountains on one side and the sparkling blue ocean on the other. George was positive that the KLM 240s were coming off the line as promised and that we would be flying in a couple of days. The Swissair 240s were well down the long production line, which was running some months behind the salesmen's promises. This delay was more the norm than unusual. Aviation sales people are by nature optimists.

We checked into Imig Manor, a picturesque, sprawling motel/hotel which George assured me most of the itinerant flying types made their headquarters while in San Diego. My cabin was alongside a swimming pool with palm trees, just like in the movies. And there were a few swimmers whose bodies rivalled those of real movie stars. It looked like a lot of fun.

But the factory soon spoiled my plans. Some unexpected delays had stalled the production line. There would be no test flying for at least a week. I grumbled that maybe we should expect unexpected delays. George laughed and told me to use the time to study up the aircraft's systems. Soon I was deep in the voluminous technical manuals. As usual the engineers had overdone the information needed by a pilot. They seemed to think it was important that flight crews should know how clever they had been when they had designed every nut and bolt. This impressed me not one bit. Like most pilots, I wanted to know just what could be done from the cockpit in case of an emergency. Like an in-flight fire, or a balky gear before a landing, or maybe an instant depressurization. At the factory I sat in the roomy cockpit for several days, memorizing the positions of the controls as I relaxed in the comfortable chair. Pressurization was new to me, as were auto-feathering propellers, which took the decision away from the captain of when to feather a balky engine. This was a feature that could cause trouble if an over-eager torque meter sent an improper signal to the feathering pump. I decided I probably wouldn't arm the system until all the inevitable bugs were ironed out. The propellers were of a new design and the blades looked like they'd been stolen from a Dutch windmill. They were reversible, a good feature which could save a lot of brake lining. The view from the cockpit was excellent through new electrically heated glass which should clear away the ice during that miserable approach to an elusive runway through moisture-laden clouds.

Then the novelty of the new aircraft faded away. Sitting in the cockpit without the engines running was a poor substitute for the real thrill of flight. The days dragged on. Even sitting in the dark, secluded hotel bar exchanging flying stories with other pilots started to bore me. The girls in the pool all seemed to be spoken for by the regular residents. A low pressure weather system fell over the land. A dank fog enveloped the swimming pool. My cabin started to resemble a Nissen hut in Iceland.

It was time for a change before I went off the deep end. So I got on the phone to Montreal and proceeded to tell Loretta I needed her. That is the most powerful verb for a case like mine. Although she wasn't too keen or thrilled with the idea of riding across the continent on a sked flight, which could take all night and part of the day, she finally agreed. I told her that she could be our tame stewardess on the 240 delivery flight from San Diego to New York City, which meant there was more than one reason for her visit. Just to make sure she didn't change her mind, an age-old feminine habit, I phoned our general manager Bill Baskerville and told him to purchase her ticket, give her some travelling money and shepherd her onto a Colonial Airlines DC3, which would connect with an American Airlines DC6 at La Guardia Field. The object of using American was that the important connection could be made close to head office, in case of trouble, rather than far from home in Los Angeles.

American had had a lot to do with designing the Douglas DC3 and making it work day and night under stringent scheduled airline conditions. They had decided to stick with Douglas products and the DC6 was an upgraded, pressurized and modernized version of the reliable DC4, which had done more than its share to win the war. When Loretta had actually left Montreal Baskerville phoned me and gave me the American flight number and estimated (or should that be scheduled?) time of arrival at Lindbergh Field. A good half-an hour before the appointed time I was pacing the rotunda impatiently.

But the DC6 wasn't on time. The ticket agent didn't seem very concerned, like most of his type. After I raised my voice a little he finally went back to his teletype and returned with the news that the flight was delayed because of a 'mechanical' — that all-encompassing term. The new estimated time of arrival would be just two hours from now. I left for a quick visit to the factory, muttering to myself.

When I returned an hour and a half later there was a new and even more insolent ticket agent on duty who haughtily informed me that the flight had landed and been cleared an hour ago. He sort of intimated that it was all my fault. And no, he didn't have a passenger list, and no, he couldn't be expected to remember each individual passenger, could he? I told him what I thought of American Airlines, which did nothing to solve the problem. Where was Loretta? As I looked around the dingy terminal the taxi line struck my eye. Taxi drivers always seemed to know what was going on. I took out a five-dollar bill and walked over, asking each man in turn if he'd taken an angry, beautiful brunette with a smashing figure to any local hotel. On the third man it worked! So I hopped in this fine, intelligent gentleman's cab and we whistled down to San Diego's foremost hotel. The desk clerk was also cooperative and very shortly thereafter I was pounding on the thin door that was now all that stood between myself and the solution to my problem.

It seemed like forever before I heard a familiar voice asking who was making all that row. I roared, 'Me', an identification I thought sufficient unto the moment. I hopped from one foot to the other until finally the door opened a crack. Loretta took off the heavy chain and I rushed in. There she stood, just as I had envisioned. All pink and warm and smelling heavenly from the bath she'd just stepped out of. She was wrapped in a thick white towel which failed to conceal her charms. But she was frowning. When advised that this wasn't the proper attitude she said that she was planning to go back home on the next flight because I didn't care for her, as proved by my not meeting the plane. This nonsense had to cease, so her voice gurgled to a stop as I held her tight and gave her a big kiss which expressed my longing far more positively than any words I could dream up. Then my clothes went flying and soon it was my turn to get warm, although I never did turn pink, I think.

She told me that the DC6 had thumped its way through plenty of bad weather across the southern United States and just near Tucson, Arizona, the captain had announced an unscheduled landing to check on one of the engines. That explained the estimated two-hour delay. But somehow the engine trouble had been cured in half an hour or so and they'd taken off again. That explained the new, unexpected arrival time. She said that the stewardess hadn't understood what she meant when she asked if they had a 'snag'. I laughed, because that term for a malfunction seemed to be unique to Ferry Command. I stopped laughing when she told me that the US Navy men on board had suggested she accompany them when I'd failed to show up. She insisted they were all very polite. I replied that they'd better be, or else. She smiled at her little triumph which proved I was still jealous, then leaned over and sealed my lips with a kiss. Sort of tit for tat.

We decided to check into Imig Manor, where we would be in the company of our own aviation types. The bellhop transferred my baggage from the Nissen hut to a warm room in the main hotel, thus lessening my chances of influenza. Ron George greeted her with open arms and after more than a few stiff, salty Margueritas bought us dinner. All I can remember of the momentous event was that he introduced us to Caesar's Salad. Things were back to normal at last.

Finally on 1 November, ten whole days after I'd left Montreal, I got my first flight with Bill Martin of KLM aboard a 240, PH-TEE. It was all I had dreamed of. The light aircraft leaped off the ground and climbed like the famous homesick angel. All the brand-new instruments glistened in the well laid out instrument panel and the welcome smell of new aircraft reminded me of other initial test flights. Once the delay on the

production line had been solved the test flights became a twice-daily occurrence. I spent perhaps 16 hours at the factory on the ground to get two hours a day in the air, but it was time well spent. I rode with Bill Eddy of Convair, George, and John Michie of KLM, an ex-Ferry Command buddy. Everyone wanted to help, but it wasn't until 5 November that George accepted PH-TEF. On the delivery flight he let me split the captain's duties and share in the flight planning and navigation. We landed at Tulsa, then Dayton for gas, then, after flying all night, because George was *the* original pusher, we arrived at newly commissioned Idlewild Airport, built to take the strain off La Guardia and Newark. Loretta had worked as hard as the cockpit crew. She had looked after no less than 26 'freebees' with coffee, sandwiches and orange juice. So when we climbed out at the new big airport we were well satisfied that after a rather rocky start everything had come up roses.

But even roses have thorns. Our particular thorn was that we couldn't get out of New York City. Colonial Airlines had an exclusive on the route from the big city to Montreal, in accordance with an ancient bilateral agreement between the two Federal Governments. As I finally gave up, most frustrated in my efforts to get on one of Colonial's rickety DC3s, I thought once again that Canadian bureaucrats who attempted to negotiate fair agreements with foreign governments must have been chosen for their stupidity. It seemed to me that we Canucks always came out of these deals sucking the hind tit, as Westerners described a poor settlement. TCA was to be shut out of the lucrative route until April 1950.

Fortunately we had the answer, which we had used before in cases such as this. A phone call to head office and dependable Alphonse Elie whipped down in Bonanza CF-FFK and took us back to the cold country. To me it looked good. Snow had to be better than sunburn. Loretta didn't agree with that attitude at all. But of course she'd never been in Trinidad where the humidity always seemed to be 110 percent and my elbow scab which the Yanks called 'tropical crud' had refused to heal until exposed to the cool dry air of Canada.

Chapter 16
'Our Trusty and Well Beloved Captain'

Back in Montreal Loretta and I were having an after-work drink in our little hideaway on MacKay Street, which was just a few blocks from World-Wide's headquarters on Drummond Street. I had convinced Bell Telephone to string a long extension so that the hideaway phone rang along with the one in headquarters. This meant that a lot of people got a good impression of how many hours I put in at the office sitting in my president's chair when in reality I was in a much more comfortable position flat on my back on our double bed. A pilot hungry for work was finally disposed of and I hung up. Then I fingered a letter which had arrived that afternoon, having finally decided to show it to her. The white envelope was embossed with the royal coat of arms and I said, 'Guess what I've got?' This surely must be one of the stupidest questions known to mankind. It often angers the person questioned, understandably.

But she was patient, sensing my mood. 'It looks like some kind of an invitation. What does it say?'

'Well, it appears that although I've been wearing my OBE ribbon since 1944, now His Excellency the Governor General of Canada wants to invest me with the medal. Here's what they sent me.' I handed over the two pages which comprised the invitation.

Government House
Ottawa
Office of the Secretary
to the Governor General   30th October, 1948.

Dear Sir,

His Excellency the Governor General will hold an Investiture at Government House, Ottawa, at 2.30 p.m. on Wednesday the 1st December when, if you find it convenient to be present, he will be pleased to present to you the Insignia of an Officer (Civil Division) of the Most Excellent Order of the British Empire.

Should you be unable to attend, your Decoration will be sent to you or arrangements made to present it to you on some future occasion.

If you are able to be present, the Governor General desires me to say that if you should care to bring not more than one of your relatives with you, Their Excellencies will be very glad to receive them. It is most important that I should be informed of the name of the relative accompanying you.

In order that there may be no misunderstanding, I have to inform you that I have received a ruling that no expenses in connection with the attendance of Recipients and their relatives at the Investiture will be defrayed by the Canadian Government.

DRESS:
(a) Civilians (gentlemen) — morning or business dress.
(b) Civilians (ladies) — afternoon dress with hat.

Any further instructions that may be necessary will be given you on arrival, which should not be later than 2.10 p.m. Will you please enter by the front entrance.

Please reply as soon as possible to the Secretary to the Governor General, Government House, Ottawa, repeating date and time.

Yours truly,

(H. F. G. Letson)
Major General.
Secretary to the Governor General.

Captain D. M. McVicar, O.B.E.,
1407 Drummond Street,
Montreal, Quebec.

MEMORANDUM FOR RECIPIENTS

1. The attached list contains your name. When that of the Recipient immediately preceding yours is announced, please move from your place to the centre aisle and stand facing the Throne.

2. When your name is called, advance to the foot of the Throne and bow (or curtsey) to the Governor-General. His Excellency will then invest you with your Insignia. You then bow (or curtsey) again to His Excellency and return to your seat.

3. The case for your Insignia will be handed to you before you leave Government House by the Administrative Officer. Please do not leave without it. Your Warrant of Appointment will be sent to you by mail.

4. At the same time, those to whom temporary brooches were given before the Investiture are asked to return them to the Administrative Officer.

5. At the conclusion of the ceremony and when leaving the Ballroom, guests are asked to allow the row ahead of them to file out first into the centre aisle and towards the back before they themselves proceed to do so. Guests are asked to refrain from engaging in conversation as they approach the exit from the Ballroom.

6. Following the Investiture, his Excellency will receive the guests in the Saloon, immediately adjoining the Ballroom. The order of presentation will be: the Recipient first, followed immediately behind by the relative or relatives accompanying the Recipient.

7. After being presented, the Recipients and relatives will proceed to the large room, or Tent Room beyond, where tea will be served.

Her concentration was intense as she read the measured phrases, then she looked up, her face eager. 'What are you going to do?'

'Let 'em mail it,' I blurted. 'You know how I hate crowds.'

'Oh, you can't do that, Don. You've just got to do it for your father, and your grandchildren.'

She had a good point. My father had put up with a lot of my mischief as I had grown up in Edmonton, and had never let me down. So I temporized. 'I'll tell you what, I'll go if you'll come with me.'

'I haven't a thing to wear,' she wailed, which I translated into her acceptance.

'We'll soon fix that up,' I said, 'but Jesus, I've never had a "morning suit" and my business outfit is a Harris tweed jacket and a pair of Daks slacks. I don't think the high mucky-mucks would like me dressed like that.'

'Why don't you wear your uniform?'

The more I thought of her idea the better I liked it. The dark navy-blue tunic sported our own wings, Canada shoulder flashes and four wide gold stripes of rank. And besides my OBE ribbon I was proud to wear a 39-45 Star, a North Atlantic Star and the Victory ribbon with an oak leaf showing I had been given a King's Commendation. A quick phone call to Government House in Ottawa and a cool voice said there would certainly be no objection.

Loretta was jumping around like a kid with a new toy. 'I'll bet you'll be the only civilian there in a uniform. And I'll bet you'll be the only person honoured for Valuable Services in the Air who gets his award wearing the uniform of his very own aviation company.'

This novel thought appealed to me. I responded, 'You're probably right. Maybe in the whole bloody British Empire, what's left of it.'

We flew down in one of our Beech Bonanzas to the nation's capital, a routine flight which was followed by a good deal more dangerous taxi ride to Rideau Hall. Government House was a sprawling building, located in spacious private grounds of cultivated woods and flower beds. It was built in the rather gloomy style of the Victorian era; massive grey granite as powerful and unyielding in appearance as the British Empire once was. Now a Labour Government over in London was busily engaged in throwing away those foreign conquests, so hard won by the blood of English and Scottish regiments and the Royal Navy. Some misguided politicians thought that was the proper thing to do. 'Free the natives, old boy. Splendid thought,' they said. There was a problem they hadn't considered. When British sovereignty was removed, then so was British justice and the spirit of fair play. It would not be very long before the 'liberated' people of those countries formerly coloured red on the maps of the world would be busily engaged in evening ancient scores and differences and killing each other by the thousand.

These thoughts were far from our minds as we were ushered through massive carved oaken doors into a vaulted reception area where we got rid of our overcoats and galoshes. Then we were guided into a large reception room and seated in chairs facing the throne. After a proper period as the noise of people settling themselves abated, we rose as the Governor General, Lord Alexander, Field Marshal The Right Honourable Viscount Alexander of Tunis KG, GCB, CSI, DSO, MC, LL.D., ADC, strode into the room. He was a man of medium height with square shoulders and a very military bearing. His three aides-de-camp followed him, then his private secretary. The contrasting uniforms of the Army, Navy and Air Force made a colourful spectacle. Immediately the Secretary began to call out the names of those who were receiving an accolade. With the number to be presented there had to be some fast action, and then the whole show would have to be repeated tomorrow. I followed instructions when my name was called and found myself on the raised dias. We were not wearing hats, which was a blessing as it meant no saluting was necessary. The Americans salute when bareheaded, but the British do not. We were taught that in reality we were not saluting the man opposite us, rather we were saluting the Crown affixed to his uniform.

Alexander fastened his keen gaze on my small row of ribbons, and there seemed to be an extra bit of enthusiasm in his voice as he pinned on the pale pink ribbon with the odd-looking Cross hanging below. I in turn looked at the blaze of colour on his chest, mute evidence of his bravery as a servant of the British Crown. His DSO and MC were the most impressive, in spite of the other honours given precedence. Because these two had been awarded to him for bravery in the field during World War I, when he had been wounded three times. Then in World War II he had whipped the British Eighth Army back into shape after Rommel had chased it to within 60 miles of Cairo in 1942. I had been at secret landing ground No. 224 near Cairo after delivering the first RAF B26 to the Middle East at the time. Churchill had put him in charge, with General Montgomery his General in the desert. Ferry Command had flown in almost 75,000 rounds of .75 artillery ammo with fourteen Libs which had helped the Eighth Army win the Battle of El Alamein. Churchill had called this episode the 'Hinge of Fate', and he certainly was the one to know. Then the Baltimores, B26s and other aircraft which we ferried over helped the Allies gain air superiority. Finally, Rommel was tossed out of Africa with hundreds of thousands of German and Italian troops surrendering at Tunis. When General Eisenhower had been made Supreme Commander Allied Expeditionary Force, Alexander had been named Supreme Commander of the Mediterranean. After a long drawn out, bloody campaign, in which Canadians suffered equally with Americans and English troops, he accepted the surrender of the Germans in Italy on 29 April 1945, just a few days before Hitler and his mob threw in their hand in Germany.

Now he was still serving his King as one of his Majesty's top diplomats. As I looked into his eyes I was attracted to him. He was far from the prototype English 'Colonel Blimps' I had tangled with during my wartime flights as a Colonial in an English outfit. I remembered that only the Colonel Blimp types were stupid enough to refer to Australians or Canadians as 'Colonials'. Maybe they only did it once.

The last person had finally been honoured and the Governor General and his staff left the Ballroom. As instructed, we kept our mouths shut until we were given the signal to proceed to the Saloon, which Loretta assured me was not what I hoped it would be. Their Excellencies and their staff did their duty as we passed down the line. I didn't envy them. Now Loretta's choice of clothes was apparently very popular. She had told me that the style of the moment was 'Monotone'. So she had a two-piece beige tailored wool suit with the pleated skirt cut just below her knee. White gloves, pearl earrings and a pearl necklace of course. Beige stockings, shoes and handbag complemented a saucy beige pillbox perched on her head.

In the Tent Room we were served tea and those little slivers of cucumber sandwiches reserved for high social gatherings. Their Excellencies did the 'Royal Walkabout', and I wished I had my Short Snorter Bill with me. Alexander would have been a great addition to my collection of signatures. People who had never met before and probably would never meet again were bowing and there might even have been a little scraping too.

I ran my finger around the neck of my spotless white shirt, which seemed to be shrinking. Loretta was perfectly at ease but that old phobia of mine, which appeared when I was confined or with a lot of people, was causing me to feel nervous and itchy. But my beautiful companion hung on my arm and gave me a warning glance when I had the temerity to suggest the weather might be getting worse and maybe we should start back. Maybe I'd trained her too well and so she believed that the Bonanza could conquer any type of weather.

So I tried to socialize. It appeared the brilliant red and white canvas of the Tent Room was to cover the rough finish of the walls when the room had been a tennis court. I was told that Official Guests, Royal Visitors, Heads of State and Commonwealth Prime Ministers normally stayed at Government House when they came to Ottawa. I reflected wryly that maybe I should try and enjoy my visit more because it sure as hell looked like I'd never be invited back.

I had my OBE certificate already and remembered the flowery language it used. It matched the Sunday-best behaviour of the guests and went like this.

GEORGE THE SIXTH

"By the Grace of God of Great Britain, Ireland and the British Dominions beyond the Seas, King Defender of the Faith, Emperor of Indian and Sovereign of the Most Excellent Order of the British Empire to our trusty and well beloved Donald Moore McVicar Esquire Captain of Aircraft North Atlantic Service.

GREETING
Whereas We have thought fit to nominate and appoint you to be an Additional Officer of the Civil Division of Our said Most Excellent Order We do by these presents grant unto you the Dignity of an Additional Officer of Our said Order and hereby authorize you to have hold and enjoy the said Dignity and Rank of an Additional Officer of Our aforesaid Order together with all and singular the privileges thereunto belonging or appertaining.

Given at Our Court at Saint James under Our Sign Manual and the Seal of Our said Order this Eighth day of June 1944 in the Eighth year of our Reign.
By the Sovereign's Command
(Illegible signature , "R")
Grand Master

Grant of the dignity of an Additional Officer of the Civil
Division of the Order of the British Empire to Captain Donald
Moore McVicar

So the dignified, archaic language of the certificate gave a
sense of importance to the award, which everyone seemed to
think only proper. Finally the signal was given. Their
Excellencies departed and we lesser luminaries began to file
out. As we left the deference-laden room I wondered just how
the dignitaries and the proud freshly minted members of the
Civil Division of George's Most Excellent Order of the British
Empire would have reacted if they'd seen the spoof award for
Superior Sexual Service I had designed for members worthy of
note according to *my* lights!

Chapter 17
Home is a Hamshack in a hangar

We were gradually getting settled into our new hangar at St. John's. It was a great improvement having a roof over our heads to work on aircraft. Ray Roy had taken a few loads of woodcutters from Matane, a small town just down-river from Rimouski, to Thessalon on the north shore of Lake Superior near Sault St. Marie. He had chartered and flown CF-FKZ on behalf of his life-long friend, woods contractor Gerry Joncas. Alf Elie had been his copilot and reported that the farmer's field could have been considered a shade short at about 2,000 feet, but it was smooth so that Roy fitted the big aircraft in with no trouble. But still, when I heard that I went out and walked around my last remaining Dak. There was no visible damage so it seemed only right that Roy should be allowed to take one of the Norseman, CF-GIA, on skis and set up an operation to supply the men in the bush. The Air Transport Board granted our application for a new base and Roy agreed that a fair deal would be that he would do all the work while I supplied the aircraft. After expenses we would split the revenue trip by trip. For a while the arrangement worked, but then in the spring communication between Thessalon and me seemed to shrivel away and finally dry up. That called for an inspection trip with a Bonanza, to work out the difficulties in a face-to-face discussion, by far the best way.

St. John's had seen the ceaseless activities of No. 9 Observers' School whose Avro Ansons had flown millions of miles, by day and by night, training navigators as their part of the British Commonwealth Air Training Scheme. The school was one of Canadian Pacific Air Lines', headed up by C. H. 'Punch' Dickins who had left RAF Ferry Command, which he had helped set up, to undertake this other important job in wartime Canada. Now some of the hangars had converted to civilian use. Wally Siple had one filled with an interesting collection of aircraft parts and engines he'd won on various bids to Crown Assets. The Babb Company had another filled temporarily with the Cornells we'd ferried from out west. The spaces along the three rather short runways were littered with Consolidated Cansos, Ansons, the odd Harvard and even the occasional Hudson Lodestar and Ventura. Although we didn't realize it at the time we had a real aircraft museum right in front of our eyes. Charlie Babb had hired none other than Howard Hughes's flight engineer Ed Lund to oversee his varied and widespread operations. They certainly handled a hell of a lot of airplanes.

The local Air Observers' School had been headed up by Peter Troup, assisted by a fiesty little red-headed man called Joe Lucas. Postwar, many of the members of No. 9 joined Air Industries of Canada who also were our neighbours. They specialized in converting wartime aircraft into civilian configuration and quickly built up a good reputation for skilful, careful work. Of personal interest to me was the fact that John Brown and Harry Harris, the crew of the Stranraer I'd met in Labrador when I was flying my Stinson on floats on my ill-fated fur-trading venture, were part of the Aircraft Industries crew. Fellow-ham Syd Walker VE2 was in charge of radio installations. He went right back to the earliest aircraft installations in the bush, where the set carried on board could only be operated from the ground in case of a forced landing. Better than nothing, of course, but not much. But year by year men like Walker improved airborne radio equipment until finally it was considered a necessity rather than a luxury by the pilots.

The airport manager was Tom Wrathall, an amiable man who had been a fighter pilot on Camels in World War I. He was assisted by his son Derek, who attempted to keep the runways, taxiways and our hangar apron clear of snow with the inadequate equipment furnished by the municipality. Tommy Colahan and his charming wife Gwen moved into the old airport guardhouse, which solved their transportation problems and made friendly neighbours. Most of the rest of our employees preferred to commute from the Big City of Montreal because St. John's was a good example of a company town. The largest employer was the Singer Sewing Machine

Company, who operated a large manufacturing plant. The American-owned company employed a large staff of underpaid Canadian labour. So it was that 'the natives' slaved for long hours over their machines for a pittance, much like other Canuck hewers of wood and carriers of water, to the ultimate benefit of some remote American stockholders. And were glad to have the job.

The double hangar we had rented was of standard British Commonwealth Air Training Scheme design, one of hundreds erected in a big hurry at the beginning of the war. It was constructed of wood with a flat roof, was about 150 feet deep and had two door openings of about 100 feet. Hanging metal doors slid on tracks which seemed to be forever filling with dust or ice, depending on the season. Along each side were single-storey flat-roofed additions called 'lean-tos'. They were divided into spaces according to the needs of the workers, with most of the rooms being about 20 feet square. We established our offices and workshops on the south side, which overlooked the airport. But only the northside had water and toilet facilities, which meant a long walk through a forest of props and aircraft antennas waiting to blacken your eye just to go the toilet. We installed oil space-heaters to prevent the water pipes from freezing as there was no heat available in the hangar proper. The rent was $400 per month, which didn't seem like much, except we had very few transient aircraft to share the load.

The hamshack was in the south lean-to, between the machine shop and the stores. Loretta had furnished it with a convertible couch, a strip of carpet, a two-burner electrical hot-plate, a phonograph, and, most importantly, filled a big fridge with food and beer. I furnished the radio equipment. The room might have seemed rather spartan to the average person, but for us — with a little love — it was perfect. For me, amateur radio had been an essential part of life, getting me my first job in aviation and then preparing me for my commercial licence which in turn had led to my position in the DOT control tower. During the war my radio knowledge had helped me a lot because some of the radio operators Ferry Command used were fresh out of training school. Often on a delivery flight I would be sitting in my pilot's seat with my intercom selector turned to 'Liaison', monitoring our frequency. More than once I had to wake up the operator when he missed our aircraft's call. For some reason this didn't seem to make me too popular with some of the radio ops, so I kept my knowledge private.

There are many specialities in the amateur radio field. Some people got a big feeling of importance through handling traffic, both during normal times and especially in case of emergency. Others experimented with Very High and Ultra High Frequency equipment. At that time no one ever dreamed that some day the amateurs would launch their own satellites into space for their own communications. I was interested in working far-away places, which meant my antennas had to be of the very best. There was a lot of scope for experimentation there. In ham lingo I was called a 'DX-Hound', DX for distance and hound for a hunter; not a bad description. As a further refinement, if it could be called that, I had taken a liking to participating in code (CW) contests where the VEs, us, and the Ws, the Americans, competed with one another to work the world. A signal report and an identifying number were exchanged when you contacted your foreign country, and you could work the same station on any of the five amateur bands to add to your points. Then there was a 'multiplier', which was the total of 'band-countries'. The final score was the result of total points multiplied by total multipliers. Some people went after a lot of contacts, but I always figured that getting a lot of multipliers was a better scheme. The radio organization sponsoring the contest awarded a rather nice engraved certificate to the winner of Quebec and other provinces and United States call districts. I collected quite a few, never having been beaten in Quebec in a CW contest. I really didn't care for the phone contests, which to me were just screaming sessions. When asked how much my certificates had cost I always told the story of the salmon fisherman who worked it out that his cost per pound was so much higher than if he had bought at a fishmonger's there was no point in discussing the matter. Especially if his wife happened to be in the audience.

I had built a final amplifier which featured two heavy-duty 813 vacuum tubes. It was set up for quick band-switching with an input of 500 watts. The power was suitable for punching through the competition, called 'QRM'. The band-switching feature saved precious time when changing bands, an important feature because every minute lost during the 48-

hour endurance test was lost forever. The contests started at midnight GMT on a Friday and I always warned Loretta in advance that I'd be out of circulation for the weekend. So at 7 p.m. local time I would be sure all my equipment was in first-class shape, because a breakdown would be fatal. Usually I started on 10 metres, the highest frequency band, looking for Australians, VKs, New Zealanders, ZLs, and other Pacific stations. Ten metres was pretty well a daylight-path band, just as 80 and 40 metres were night-time bands. Twenty metres was the real workhouse band and sometimes was open to some part of the world 24 hours a day. Of course, part of the thrill was switching bands to nail some rare station such as PK400 in Sumatra just as the band opened and before the opposition got in the act. I used my Dow-Key, a semi-automatic 'Bug' Key, which made dots automatically, thus preventing an attack of the feared CW-man's 'glass arm'. The station desiring a contact called CQ, but I rarely did, as I preferred to hunt for my own DX. A lot of other North American stations didn't see it that way and used code wheels to blast out endless CQs. I thought it was a waste of time and a way of hogging the frequency.

It took Loretta quite a while to accustom herself to seeing the back of my head adorned with earphones for hours at a time — if indeed she ever did. When the complaints got too loud I told her it was better than wondering where I was when I wasn't around. Like chasing a blonde maybe? This is known as attacking before you get attacked. I'm not sure it worked, but an awful lot of hams used the ploy. She finally became a convert when we visited hams in strange cities. A phone call, backed up with my personal visiting card called a QSL, and we entered many a perfect stranger's home to a warm welcome. In my estimation ham membership was a more powerful voice of friendship than any service club, or a secret society's password and special handgrip, or whatever.

There was another award I desperately wanted to win — to be the first VE2; to confirm 100 different countries worked and thus get a DXCC certificate issued by the American Radio Relay League. To do this my station had to be exceptional. A sensitive receiver with good selectivity was a necessity. It was well said that 'You can't work 'em if you can't hear 'em'. My National HRO receiver was as good as any. Then, to be the loudest signal in the foreigner's earphones was almost a must, because that would be the signal he would pay attention to. Of course there were other cunning ways of putting your signals where you thought he might be tuning, but 500 watts would still be a big help. Formerly I had used a modest 100 watts, but every time the power was doubled there was a three decibel increase in signal strength. And three decibels made you signal sound twice as loud, because ears operate logarithmically. Now the rest was up to the antenna.

Perhaps there was a little serendipity involved in moving to St. John's airport. The height above ground has a tremendous effect on the efficiency of any antenna. And St. John's lay over an ancient lake bed, which put the electrical ground almost 40 feet below the point where the grass grew. The hangar roof was about 30 feet above the surface so my antennas would be at the equivalent of 70 feet, a great advantage over hams in a city or over rocks such as the Laurentian Mountains to the north. To my mind, the bleak scenery was more than compensated for by the radio conditions. Loretta never did become quite convinced, however.

On the lower frequencies, such as 40 and 80 metres, the half-wave antennas just had to be long wires or possibly 'V' beams. Although the antenna handbooks gave them interesting decibel gain figures, they never proved out for me, and besides their directivity was blurred by spurious lobes in the radiation patterns. However, wire antennas were all I could use so I stuck up a couple, one along the hangar roof and the other to the convenient tail of a Canso just the right distance away.

But rotary directional arrays for 10 and 20 metres were feasible, even if a half-wave was a hefty 33 feet on 20 metres. A Japanese scientist called Dr. Yagi had discovered that if you put a piece of wire, called a director and about 5 per cent shorter than the driven element, about a tenth of a wavelength ahead of the current-carrying element there was a significant increase in signal strength. The same thing occurred when he installed a reflector 5 per cent longer. Now a new directional rotary using this theory had appeared on the market, working on both 10 and 20 metres. It was constructed of fluted steel elements coated with brass, as aluminium tubing of the right size was unobtainable. The specs made me drool. This I just had to have! A forward gain of no less than nine decibels was claimed. Imagine what *that* would do to VE2WW's signal in some far-away hamshack in Tibet! But, equally important from a contest man's point of view, this Mims 'Signal Squirter' would attenuate the signals from the rear by 30 decibels and from the sides by no less than 40 decibels.

I got the thing assembled and installed on a rotator on the roof with the directional indicator right at my operating position. At first the results were a little disappointing, but I tuned it up with a field-strength meter and it finally did all that Mims claimed for it.

Anyway, I got the first VE2 DXCC for a CW station — No. 479 dated 6 May 1949. I guess it must have been among the very first in all of Canada, too. The delay in issuance was because it took so long to get the 100 foreign QSL cards. I actually had 173 countries worked by the time I had 100 confirmed, which was just about average for the operation, I suppose. Some might call it a waste of time but it sure got my mind off the business of day-to-day aircraft and hangar operation . . .

Chapter 18
Swissair's Convairs

Out on the west coast the Consolidated factory was beginning to catch up with their over-optimistic delivery dates. It seemed that when the dam broke, so to speak, Swissair's four 240s would come off the line in a relatively short time. Of course the airline expected World-Wide to have four fully qualified crews standing by at all time, which from our economical point of view was very unrealistic. *Two* crews would do the job efficiently if we planned it properly. So on 14 December, after a call from Ron George, Chief Pilot Bill MacLaren and I flew in the Bonanza to La Guardia, then boarded a TWA Constellation for Los Angeles and then onwards to San Diego, once again.

I got MacLaren on several 240 test flights and gave him the guided tour of the factory, and then on 17 December we got away late in the afternoon with George on a KLM aircraft landed at Kansas City and then flew through the night to Idlewild. I let MacLaren act as copilot on one leg. Part of the type qualification accomplished. Once again there were no seats to Montreal on Colonial, but a phone call worked and soon Alf Elie was on the scene with Bonanza CF-FYE to take us back to Canada.

Christmas and New Year's celebrations were kept to a low roar as there didn't seem to be as much to celebrate as in previous postwar years. Or maybe we were getting older and wiser. No, impossible. That could never happen. Not to us.

The only way to defeat the factory delivery-date promises, which were always optimistic, was to establish a spy in the factory. I had met one of their pilots who had been with Ferry Command and each time I got a 'definite' delivery date from the factory the phone wires would get hot and then he'd tell me the truth. Thus it was that on 7 February MacLaren and I arrived at San Diego and got away in HB-IRP just four days later. Not bad. I did the first leg over the mountains at night to Wichita where there were friends if needed. The weather was quite foggy in the gloom of night as we left. It seemed that test flights always managed to use up all the daylight for their own purposes so that the delivery crews got into a fresh, possibly bug-filled aircraft under the worst conditions. We wanted the Swiss to be impressed with the first delivery so we pressed right on to Cleveland, cleared US customs and so to Dorval. There were some mechanical discrepancies we fixed up and I gave MacLaren a couple of landings. He handled the 240 with ease. It was a lovely aircraft to fly in any case, and I figured that anyone who had flown a de Havilland Mosquito like he had would have no trouble. The next day I crewed him up with Frank Staskow, copilot/flight engineer and Bud Birchall as radio operator/navigator, gave them all a hearty slap on the back and pointed them east to Goose, just like we did during the war. Then I took Alphonse Elie with me and we jumped on an airline back to the factory.

On 18 February we test-flew the second 240, HB-IRT, and came back with a small bagful of snags which the factory departure mechanics cleared up in a hurry. That night we landed at Amarillo, then Cleveland and so to Dorval. MacLaren took it away the next day with Alphonse Elie for copilot and my good friend Russ Holmes as radio op/nav. He had pulled a few strings to get back in time to Montreal, aided by our new Swiss friends. I hopped on the airline — God, was I getting tired of those transcontinental flights! This time I had a new pilot, 'Ollie' Olmstead, for copilot. He seemed like a very smooth pilot with a tour in Bomber Command on Lancs behind him. This time my spy apparently had begun to believe the stories from the factory, because it wasn't until 26 February we got a test flight on HB-IRS, then a short hop to Albuquerque. The weather to the east was pretty stinking so it seemed like a good time to catch up on something I'd been missing for the past few weeks, namely sleep. The next day we got into Wichita, but the Great Lakes region was all socked in, which gave me a really good excuse to go via Nashville to show off my new toy to Jesse Stallings. As usual the Southern hospitality was almost overwhelming, but the next day we tore ourselves away and got into Montreal on 1 March. Now it was time for a change of tactics. I wanted to deliver one of the 240s myself, of course, and the brass at Swissair were anxious to meet me. And with future business in mind I was anxious to meet them. This time the aircraft needed a lot of tuning-up. Why this should be I never could figure out, but in any case we never did get the pressurization fixed before we left for Goose on 8 March. Something to do with the compressor quill shaft, or something. This time I took Russ Holmes as copilot/radio op/nav and Tommy Colahan as flight engineer. The 240 only required a two-man crew but I had decided that to do a good job we should carry three, most of whom could perform two functions. I was using the Howard Hughes theory of redundancy.

It took 3 hours and 35 minutes of night flight to get to Goose, the idea being to make the flight up the fjord to Greenland's BW1 the next morning in daylight. This was my first North Atlantic flight since I'd brought back Dakota KG349 from Silloth in the fall of 1946. It felt just great, just like old times, to be in charge of a live, vibrating, smoking aircraft once again instead of flying the office desk. But it was also just like old times because the fjord into Bluie was plugged solid with ice-filled cloud. It reminded me a lot of my last delivery of a Boston with Ferry Command, when my Radio/Nav Johnsen and I had decided to fly over the bad weather direct to Iceland. But the Convair couldn't make it unless we went high, and with no cabin pressurization I was afraid I'd hurt Colahan. He had shown some alarming signs of anoxia when we had flown the Mosquito from Wichita en route to the Bendix cross-country race last year. Why the Convair had no oxygen I've often asked — maybe Swissair were going to put it in at Zurich? The crew sure would need it if the pressurization packed up while they were negotiating the Alps.

While I was hanging over the Goose weather map, as if wishing and studying would affect Greenland, the news came through that MacLaren had accepted the fourth and last 240, HB-IRV, at the factory. That good news almost made up for the delay we were now enduring. Goose Bay Labrador isn't exactly on a par with Dorval/Montreal for fun when the weather acts up. Also, Ferry Command had long vanished and with them the help we aircrews took for granted on the ground. The RCAF did a little, but then they had their own aircraft to worry about, although it made me feel, perhaps a little unfairly, that there was an awful lot of difference in attitude between people in the peacetime and the wartime air forces of the world.

It was during the second night of imprisonment that something happened to change my mind about direct flight to Keflavik. Ron George landed with another KLM 240, and as I watched him calmly and competently filling out his flight plan at 19,000 feet I decided to check *my* figures. I knew he hated the approach to Bluie, but that certainly wouldn't affect his judgement. The longer I observed him, the ultimate, cool, square-cut, superior pilot in my estimation, the more the thought of emulating his flight became paramount in my mind. I reworked my figures. If we stayed down at just 15,000 for Colahan the flight was possible. I looked at my burly flight engineer with an engaging grin. He read my mind and shrugged his shoulders. That was enough for me. So, shortly after, there were two Convair 240s in the air on direct flight plans from Goose to that cold little island up where the Arctic Circle warns aviators that any slight miscalculation could result in a dip in water that freezes the human body in a matter of minutes.

As the Convair climbed smartly away and we set course I thought how similar this flight was to the Boston of five long years ago. The flight plan was identical; the weather, with a deep low over central Greenland that gave us the necessary tail wind component, was a carbon copy; and I suppose I hadn't changed. But there the similarity ended. Instead of a crowded cockpit where I had sat in solitary if rather uncomfortable splendour there was now a roomy layout with my flight crew within easy reach. Instead of hand flying, there was a newly designed automatic pilot which put even the old reliable Mark III Sperry to shame. The Boston had had very elementary de-icing, but the Convair was fully equipped to handle itself in any condition except heavy clear ice. The engines were P & W Double Wasps, undoubtedly the best piston engines the factory would ever manufacture. The radio was up front where I could monitor it, rather than behind the bomb bay where the radio/nav had his equipment plus a set of elementary flight controls. I wondered if anyone had ever actually used them. The radio man couldn't see out, just for openers, and had no way of lowering the landing gear or the flaps. But maybe a

controlled crash was better than baling out. It would have been
an interesting choice.

Although we could have navigated the flight reasonably well
with just radio aids Holmes and I used our sextants to get some
star fixes. He was a very able radio man, having actually been
the R/O when Captain Bill Vanderkloot was flying Winston
Churchill to Moscow and other interesting places in Liberator
'Commando'. He had received an MBE for that. Then he had
qualified as a navigator, that qualification being necessary for
the many two-seat, two-crew de Havilland Mosquitoes that
Ferry Command had flown to the UK. Now he had a
commercial pilot's licence and I was happy to be able to help
him along his chosen career in commercial aviation. After all,
his path to the left-hand front seat in an aircraft was very much
like my own had been. Anyway, to use astro was a great
pleasure. The trans-oceanic airlines were beginning to phase
out navigators to save overheads. Soon they would phase out
radio men as well, because the advance in electronics would fill
the pilot's instrument panel to give all the information he
needed. Until the electrical system packed up, of course. But to
management, and their obsession with the famous 'bottom
line' of their financial statements, that was an acceptable risk.

Holmes was plotting our position lines, which showed our
ground speed was just about what we expected. Now the only
other factor was our fuel consumption. I had been watching
Colahan pretty closely and he seemed to be coping well at the
altitude. So there was no worry there. Anyway, I knew that the
only serious effect, called 'the bends', didn't occur until way up
there about 30,000 feet. So he was sitting up in front when the
left engine gave a frightening backfire. I slipped the mixture
control back into 'rich' and the engine smoothed out. Now we
set up the mixture control in the leanest mixture position
possible without damaging our precious engines. The cylinder
head temperatures were a good indication as to the health of
the engines and now we had a reasonably accurate fuel flow
indication with the two dials every aircraft should have had.
We were right on our 'howgozit' curve as we passed our Point
of No Return. We could hear the KLM aircraft making his
position reports, which gave us a rather nice feeling of
companionship in the pitch-black night. It's good to have a
friend along. If either one of us had caught fire or force-landed
the other would have circled while the Air Sea Rescue planes
got into the air.

The weather at Iceland was just flyable, which most pilots thought about the best you could expect. The runway was covered with slush, which is a mixture of not quite solidly frozen snow and water. Bad stuff for braking, but we made it. Prestwick was forecast to be zero-zero, so it was time for an overnight stop. Keflavik was a USAF base and we were treated like military personnel, which meant we were confined to the airport. Apparently there had been some sort of a dust-up between the soldier boys and the civilians in Reykjavik, the only city of importance. Our crew had all seen the non-existent delights of the Icelandic capital and really didn't think we were missing much.

Early the next morning Prestwick was forecast to improve. Not much, but enough to get us in the air. But as the wheels left the ground there was a hellish vibration in the airframe, so bad that the instrument panel became just a blur. For a moment, as I selected landing gear up, I thought that both engines had decided to act up at the same time. But then the vibration ceased and I decided to press on. Maybe the mechanics of Scottish Aviation at Prestwick could pinpoint the trouble. Now the engines ran perfectly, which was just as well as we were in cloud with a lot of turbulence all the way to Scotland. We never glimpsed storied places like Stornaway or any other island airport. At Prestwick I got on the Instrument Landing System which took me down the glide path to the end of the runway. It was an excellent aid, with just two instrument needles to keep crossed by the rudder and the rate of descent. Then, just to put sauce on the haggis, the radar scanners of the airport's Ground Control Approach System chimed in to reassure me I was doing the let-down properly. It was time to get the aircraft into landing configuration. But when I lowered the landing gear that hellish vibration came right back. For a split second the thought of pulling up and going around crossed my mind, to be instantly rejected. I was well down the approach and going around would really not solve the problem. In fact it would only prolong the agony. Still, it seemed like forever before the outline of the grey runway in the grey 'Scotch mist' appeared and I slid the easy-to-land tricycle-geared aircraft on the runway. Once again the vibration disappeared as we taxied in. I looked over my shoulder at Colahan and once again he shrugged his shoulders. I was beginning to wonder if that gesture might not be his best act.

That was an unworthy thought, because he spent all the next day with me while we ran up the engines with a Swissair representative on board. When we proposed a test flight he respectfully declined, which made the intrepid flight crew of HB-IRS grin.

While we were screwing around with our problems MacLaren had caught up with us in HB-IRV. So on the 13th we took off and flew to Zurich together. There was no vibration! The weather was overcast, which for us meant an undercast, until we crossed the southern coast of England where the English Channel joins the North Sea. As the outlines of Europe's coast loomed ahead through a light sea fog I was reminded of the title of Bomber Command's crack pilot and Victoria Cross holder Guy Gibson's book *Enemy Coast Ahead*. He had given his life so people like us could go on what was really a scenic tour, compared to the flak and Luftwaffe fighters he had endured. The huge port of Antwerp was off to port, which reminded me of the many Canadian casualties suffered when our army had liberated Holland. A brave and difficult operation. What we wouldn't know for a long time was the search of many, many Dutch children for their missing Canadian Army fathers. Then we were over Luxembourg where the 'Battle of the Bulge' had taken place. Historians would spin millions of words about that one. The ground was gradually rising, with mountains to about 5,000 feet, as I spotted Zurich at the north end of its private icy-blue lake. To the south the Alps towered into the clear air, making me rather pleased our long ferry flight was over without any more oxygen problems.

The other Convair landed just behind us and when we taxied up to the Swissair ramp there was a group of friendly faces to greet us. Their precious modern aircraft, the first of the post-war crop, were now ready to go into service to replace the venerable, slow and reliable Douglas DC3s on their domestic flights. They would continue to use the venerable, slow and reliable four-engined DC4s on their overseas flights for some time to come, however. At the cocktail reception our hosts threw for us I learned that Swissair had been an early user of American aircraft. They had replaced their single-engined Fokkers with Lockheed Orions in the early '30s because the new aircraft were no less than 60 mph faster, always a Lockheed trademark. Then, realizing that there was no future in single-engined passenger flight, they had ordered Douglas DC2s, followed by DC3s. I told them it was too bad World-Wide wasn't in the ferrying business then, because shipment of disassembled aircraft by sea was slow, with a good chance of damage en route. They smiled politely.

A couple of drinks later I tried again and told them about the Trans Australian Airlines' 240 sitting at the side of the airport at Keflavik with the nose gear collapsed and a couple of badly bent props. They thought it odd that the Australians had chosen the long way around the world to ferry their aircraft, rather than fitting long-range gas tanks for the flight from North America to Hawaii and beyond. I agreed, then rather cruelly told them that the Australians would have been a lot better off it they'd used World-Wide to do their ferrying, because the reason for the accident was that the pilot had reversed the props with a light coating of fluffy snow on the runway. He had created his own blizzard and had run off the runway in zero visibility. Of course, northern pilots like ours would never make *that* mistake, in case they had more aircraft to ferry.

They smiled politely.

Maybe having so many numbered savings accounts made the whole nation close-mouthed. While the rest of our flight crew took the train to Geneva, where the international airlines landed, I stayed in Zurich trying to be the master salesman. They never said no, but in the long run we never did get another Swissair aircraft to ferry. No doubt their own pilots liked the California weather and prevailed. So then one of their executives did a ferry job on me in a Messerschmitt 108, HB-IKE, and flew me down the winding valleys to Geneva. The little four-seater reminded me of my Bonanza, and was my only connection ever with any model of Messerschmitt, which

was fine with me as the Me 109 had shot down many an Allied airman.

A British Airways Viking, a derivative of the Wellington bomber, took me to London. It was just like stepping back in time after the Convair. The English were also working on a monster aircraft called the Brabazon. By the time they got all the bugs sorted out it was too slow and obsolete. Bad luck, don't you know.

The real pioneer of the North Atlantic ferry operation, Don Bennett, after a brilliant wartime career as King of the Pathfinders was now heading up an outfit called British South American Airways with a mid-Atlantic route through Bermuda to the west coast of South America. He had operated converted Lancaster bombers called Lancastrians, just as Trans-Canada Air Lines had done when nothing else was available. My rides in them had convinced me I'd become permanently deaf if I kept it up. Good for bombs and freight but horrible for passengers. Then Bennett had operated some Yorks, which really were just a Lancaster wing with a big, clumsy fuselage added. They didn't last either. Then he'd started to operate Tudors, England's ugly abortions in reply to the sleek American four-engined long-range aircraft. He had lost one just last January and was to lose another a year later. The mystery of their disappearance was never solved and Bennett finally threw in the towel.

On the other hand, Vickers had come up with a real winner with the four-engined Viscount, mainly because it sported four new Rolls-Royce turbine Darts. It was fast and comfortable, flying swiftly well above where the people thought the bad weather topped out.

De Havilland also had a potential winner. They had used the name of their famous two-engined racers once more in their Comet aircraft. It had four pure jet Ghost engines, which took it up to over 40,000 feet for near-sonic, smooth flight. It was far ahead, engineering-wise, of any other aircraft in the world and for a short time destroyed every point-to-point speed record. But the de Hav engineers had come too far, too fast. Every facet of their engineering design had been perfect except one: the premature ageing of metal under incessant pressurization and depressurization. After a series of tragic accidents the futuristic aircraft was grounded and de Havilland never really recovered from the setback. Boeing and Douglas brought their aircraft on the market years later, aided by de Havilland's experiments.

In London I took time out to visit my old boss Taffy Powell, who was deep in getting his company Silver City Airways into a really innovative scheme of flying people's automobiles from England to the Continent. He had decided to use a Bristol Freighter for the job. The ugly but useful aircraft was ideal for loading cars because the whole nose opened up, which allowed the smaller English cars to taxi right into the capacious freight hold of no less than 34 feet in length. For his assistants he had a selection of old Ferry Command types including a large, ever-cheerful man named Bill Franklin. I remembered him as an operations type who tended to let the Captain make his own decisions on a ferry flight.

Now it was time to select an airline for the flight home. Trans-Canada were now using their new North Stars, which were DC4s with pressure and four Rolls-Royce Merlins on the wings, as turned out by Canadair Ltd. The noise in the cabin was just as anyone would expect from an in-line engine, with exhaust stacks barking straight against the drum-like metal fuselage. The cooling radiators set up a real wall of resistance so that the aircraft's performance was not as good as it could have been if reliable Pratt & Whitney round engines had been installed inside their streamlined cowlings. No doubt the top brass had their reasons but I never heard a really satisfactory explanation of the decision to use the Merlins, which were perfect only for fighters and bombers with short bursts of power. Over the long haul of day-in and day-out scheduled flying they were a great source of trouble with frequent cylinder bank changes and other bugs which only show up when an airline really puts equipment to work. Rolls-Royce even admitted they only learned about their famous Merlin after TCA and BOAC in their Argonauts started to hammer the hell out of the engine.

But it didn't make any difference to me, because TCA had no seats. So it was on to a DC6 of American Overseas Airlines, a late arrival in the American transatlantic scheduled scene. After landings at Shannon, Gander and New York I was more than happy to stagger off Colonial's DC3 at Dorval. Maybe the Ferry Command types had it right when they said we were paid for the flight back, not the delivery over.

Chapter 19
The Dollard des Hormones Cocktail

After the tension of the Convair deliveries the months seemed to drag by. In March I'd visited Ray Roy at Thessalon where he was flying Norseman CF-GJN on skis, supplying the woodcutters and doing a fine job of it all by himself without an engineer to hold his hand. I'd landed FZC on a farmer's snow-covered field and got away with it. Roy promised to be more serious about sending me my share of the charter money. We had made an arrangement that after expenses for gas and repairs he'd take his share for the first flight, and I'd take my share from the second flight, and so on. But it seemed as if that share for 'Don, de boss' was getting overlooked more and more. But I trusted him. What else could I do, after all? In the long run he did return my Norseman to me. Then he went into a partnership with his friend Joncas, who controlled the woodchoppers. They bought a Stinson Reliant on floats and one evening, coming in late, Roy hooked the top of a jack pine and spun the thing into the water. Everyone got out, but when Roy pulled himself up on the wreckage he refused to try to reach the shore. It turned out that after all his years in the bush, he'd never learned to swim. And so a bright light on the Canadian bush-flying scene lost his life — through drowning in the very waters he, of all people, knew so well.

April was one of those months when nothing seemed to happen, with few charters and no deliveries or sales.

In early May I took the other Norseman, GIA, up to Lac la Tortue where Art Jarvis would install the floats so necessary for any type of flying into the bush. He was a dark, rugged Englishman with a rather sardonic sense of humour. He ran his repair shop almost single-handed, and was one of Canada's top engine overhaul men. However, his landing strip of sand was short, with the lake on one end and a set of towering high-tension lines on the other. He kept the surface in about the same shape as the bunkers on a golf course. When I complained about the danger of snapping the nosewheel off a Bonanza or flipping a Norseman over he just smiled sort of evilly and said that he had no intention of improving the surface of his landing strip. After all, he said, his face very serious, he was in the repair business, wasn't he? Then he'd invite you into his house and prove to be a marvellous host, so that he never got the proper answer to his ridiculous proposition. And thus kept his customers happy.

So perhaps it was inevitable that 24 May would be the day when we just had to have a little fun. I'd declared a holiday, remembering the old school children's rhyme:
'The twenty-fourth of May is the Queen's Birthday,
and if we don't get us a holiday, we'll all run away.'
The party got under way slowly. We always believed that the naval types had the right idea when they said that there should be no drinking before the sun was over the yard-arm. I'd solved that problem by having a movable yard-arm attached to the hangar. We had a player piano with three whole rolls of ancient music, and Derek Wrathall had built me a fine wooden bar. It had VE2WW and an intriguing flash of lightning painted on the front of it. Even had a brass rail. Now that's class! Various people drifted by, some of them because they could sniff out a party at ten miles, and some others because they naturally came to the airport on their day off. We had some deck chairs, a couple of benches and an assortment of chairs removed from various aircraft for the visitors. In case of loss of balance all the aircraft chairs still had their safety belts attached.

In addition to our player piano we had a phonograph with a rather catholic selection of records which included 'Pistol-Packin' Momma', 'A Gordon For Me', 'The Massed Pipe Bands of the Scottish Regiments,' and that ever-popular favourite, 'Life Gets Tejus, Don't It?' Beer was the drink of the day, and we had a generous supply of Quebec quarts of various brands such as Molson's, Black Horse, Dawe's and Dow.

One of our part-time helpers wandered in, obviously wondering what in the world was going on. He was a French-Canadian lad who said he'd never heard of Queen Victoria. We immediately improved his knowledge of history, whereupon he informed us that 24 May had another significance. He said that a French fur-trader had saved Montreal by killing a couple of dozen of Iroquois Indians somewhere on the Ottawa river away back when. The hero's name was Dollard des Ormeaux. We drank to him, and that seemed to spark another line of mischief. I decided we'd concoct a special cocktail in his honour.

A few were already drinking Winnipeg Red-Eye, which is about a quarter of a glass of tomato juice mixed with beer. Sort of a poor man's Bloody Mary. But this had no proper French connection, so I decided that the proper thing to do was add a couple of dollops of pea soup, and all present hastened to mix this cocktail which was promptly christened 'Dollard des Hormones', because it obviously contained a lot of life-giving calories, hormones and what-not. The lumpy mixture was just a tad hard to swallow, and the purplish colour didn't help. Nobody refused, however. Then, as more guests arrived, the cocktail got more interesting. When they asked to try our invention we dropped a raw egg in their mix. When they got to the bottom — it was by rule a chug-a-lug operation — some of them turned as green as the pea soup and for a moment or two it looked like they were about to toss their cookies. They swore we were savages. However, when a new customer appeared I noticed they were the first to talk the sucker into trying this marvellous new drink.

As parties are wont to do, this one progressed, and we could feel ourselves loosening up as the May sun beat down to such an extent we could actually feel the difference from the weak, yellow winter rays. Even the hard-packed snow which had turned to black-flecked ice on the north side of the hangar began to run off as it reluctantly melted away. Then someone pointed out that fireworks were necessary to celebrate properly the great Queen's birthday in style.

The problem was that we had no fireworks, not even a sparkler or a string of tiny Chinese fire-crackers. Then I had an idea. I had a couple of Very pistols on hand, and a fair number of the large coloured cartridges which were part of an aircraft's equipment during wartime. The brightly burning flares were fired in accordance with instructions as to which colour was the 'colour of the day', on that particular day at that particular time. I never used them, as I felt that those trigger-happy gunners would just think I was shooting at them. Of course, if you were bobbing around in a dinghy the sight of a small flare just might attract a rescue aircraft, or maybe even a rescue vessel. The burning cordite or whatever it was, would arc gracefully through the air up to perhaps a hundred feet or so.

So why don't we pick up sides and have a war?

The sun slid below the hangars to the west while we made our preparations. The flares must be divided evenly. That was the first rule. We had a Jeep for hauling aircraft around and Frank Staskow and Derek Wrathall thought they'd like to drive it. I thought a roof over my head was more important than quick mobility so I took my Dodge. Tommy Colahan was the driver. As an old de Havilland Mosquito flight crew we just had to stick together. When it got really dark we drove out on the airport, which had no lights of any description. The three runways were laid out in the classic triangle of a typical British Commonwealth Air Training Plan station. There were also wide concrete parking areas, so Tommy and I decided to keep to the hard surface as the frost was barely out of the ground and the grass in-field was soft and muddy. Whoever got stuck would be just like a sitting duck to a hunter.

We had also decided that the first vehicle to catch on fire, or the first combatant to need a doctor's attention for burns, would be the losers. Maybe those D.D.H. cocktails were more powerful than we thought!

When the combat commenced we both discovered that the flare would only carry a hundred feet or so in a straight line, but that a shot fired in the air would carry well and cause the enemy to try to scurry away. If the driver was quick with the steering wheel and the gas pedal he could make sure the flare didn't make a direct hit. While we circled around, the airport looked like a German squadron was bombing, but neither side scored any hits. It looked like a stand-off. But I had a secret weapon, just like the Yanks had their atom bombs. It was a photographer's magnesium flare. I looped it over the dark outline of the Jeep and it burst in the air with a blinding white flash and the frightened faces of our enemy were revealed in stark relief. 'We surrender,' they shouted, although I could foresee many a quart of beer down the hatch before the legality of my photographer's flare was established.

Just then the rotating red light of a police car showed up on the highway leading from the town to the western entrance. It had a mile or so to go. It was time for a mass retreat. 'War's over,' I shouted. 'Let's get the hell back inside the hangar.'

We raced back to our cheering fans and drove right into the hangar, then slid the big doors shut. Soon we heard the cops drive past. Our girls were giggling so loudly that I thought they'd give the game away. Somebody had phoned the airport manager's office and he'd called the police. Perhaps it was just as well for Derek that we weren't caught. His father *was* the airport manager, after all.

Chapter 20
Barnstorming

We had been visiting town fairs, air shows and farmers' fields with our wheeled aircraft, carrying out sightseeing flights. Now that we had a Norseman on floats available it was possible the blasé riders who were looking for a new thrill would take a short hop off the water. Besides, there were nine seats in the bush aircraft, so with a full load the rewards were a lot better than a Bonanza with just four seats, or our Luscombe with only two seats. So I checked out MacLaren, Olmstead and Holmes on floats.

On wheels it was possible to refuel quickly at the nearest airport, or if the occasion was an air show the oil company would have a truck conveniently available. But it was a different operation on floats. First there was the necessity of making sure the water was clear of rocks and other debris. Then a dock was necessary to load the passengers, which never was a problem. But refuelling *was* a problem, and that big P & W 550 hp engine gulped down a lot of fuel during take-off and climb. We loaded our truck with two or three 45 gallon drums and had one of our ground crew drive to the lake or river. There he would also act as helper to load the passengers and catch the float or wing strut when the pilot was making his return. I remember spending a day on Lake Champlain, where an ex-RCAF man had a hotel. It was on the extreme northerly part of the lake and there was just enough space to take off from his place on the west shore of a small inlet across the narrow neck. We found that just after Mass on Sunday was the best time to get the sightseers. Their consciences were clear and a lot of them were lowering the level of a bottle of de Kuyper's Gin . . .

Of course, we had to have promotion on the ground, so

Loretta and MacLaren's girl friend, Jackie La Pointe acted as our sales persons — in both French and English. After a day's sightseeing everyone was exhausted. It was a tough way to make a buck, but somehow when we got back to the hangar and dumped out our dollar bills and silver the pile looked a lot more impressive than a piece of paper called a cheque.

We used our Anson and the Dak at Dorval for taking people up, but somehow it was the little airports where most made their first flight. But there was an exception, when the boosters of Granby, a small industrial city about 80 miles from Montreal, invited us to their air show, and please, please bring the Dak. The grass field was just right for a light aircraft but it was mighty tight for a Dak. There was a barbed-wire fence at one end and a railroad embankment at the other, with a line of telegraph wires as an added attraction. However, with a light load of gas I was able to get off reasonably well. The landing was another matter. It had to be a perfect three-pointer every time. But with twenty-odd pax at a crack the money was good. On the other hand we soon exhausted the supply of people who could spare five dollars. That was when Albert Lamoureux, our ace hydraulic man, had a good idea. He was a persuasive talker and so we arranged for a short walk through the fuselage up into the cockpit at fifty cents for an adult and a quarter for a child. In the long run his idea made more money than my sweaty flying.

Early one morning I got a phone call. An American voice was trying to pierce the fading and the static of a long-distance call. Somehow I knew this would be different from the usual probing, brain-picking conversation. And when I found the call was from Hong Kong I was sure. The voice wanted to know if I was the owner of the Mosquito advertised for sale in *Trade-a-Plane,* which was a yellow sheet that came out twice a month with column upon column of aircraft of all types for sale. There was also a 'wanted' column or so, and it was said that a smart operator could make a living by matching up the two sides of a deal.

When I said I was the real legal owner the voice wasted no time. 'What will you take for it?' he said through the crackle. I thought of the blown engine and blurted, 'Five thousand, as is where is.'

'Where can I get it fixed?' the voice wanted to know.

I thought of my friend Jesse Stallings and the hangar he ran at Berry Field near Nashville. He certainly had got a lot of experience with the Mosquito I'd sold him last year, so I recommended him. The voice said he'd call me back. I hung up, thinking that the whole episode had been just another futile exercise so common in the sales side of aviation. But this time it wasn't.

The voice did call back and asked if my price was firm. I said it was and he said he'd cable me the five thou immediately. I thought I should have started good and high and let him wear me down. Maybe answering the phone in the early morning before your brain is in gear isn't the right idea. But when the bank phoned to say the money had arrived I didn't waste any time in getting it into my account, and then it was that I found that the new and lucky owner was an airline pilot named Don Bussart who had been flying in the Orient for a long time. He wanted to win the Bendix, just like I had, and was determined to do it with a pair of new, more powerful engines. I wished him all the luck in the world, because I knew he'd need it.

Still, it made we wonder about the barnstorming and charter business. On just one phone call I'd cleared more than six months' revenue from World-Wide's flying activities.

The next charter was as different from the ambulance flight as could be imagined. When I arrived in Newport, Rhode Island on a bit of a mystery flight all I knew was that two Americans wanted to go to the hotel at Murray Bay, a luxurious resort for the rich folk a couple of hundred miles down the St. Lawrence. When I loaded them into FZC I recognized them from the wide news coverage they were getting. One was Brenda Fraser, one of those "poor little rich girls" who had inherited a bundle of millions. She was quite attractive with a slim figure and dark hair surrounding a piquant face. Her companion was her new husband, a massive man who had been a professional football player, named "Shipwreck" Kelly. The publicity generated by this unlikely match, because professional football players were not considered socially acceptable, had forced the couple to try and hide from the press. They felt that by taking a private aircraft to a Canadian hotel they might gain a bit of privacy, which had been noticeably lacking on their honeymoon.

When we landed at Quebec City to clear Canadian Immigration and Customs I encountered a problem common to all executive pilots. As the owner and proud pilot I didn't really feel much like toting their heavy and numerous bags inside the terminal building. Kelly solved the problem by grabbing a couple, and I took the rest, while the beautiful socialite took her jewel case.

The next problem was more serious. The closest I could get to the hotel, which had no airport, was a short strip on a farmer's field close to the river at a small village called Baie St. Paul. There was a brisk wind right down the strip and I got in with no trouble. Then we all piled in a taxi the hotel had sent and took the scenic road alongside the wide river to the sprawling old-fashioned buildings of the resort.

That night I had super with them but slipped away before the drinking got heavy and the nightly dance began. The next morning they got their particular show on the road with a couple of rounds of "Bloody Marys", which I cleverly declined to partake. We took the taxi back to the strip and loaded ourselves and the baggage into the suddenly-small Bonanza. I gave the engine a good run-up and turned onto the strip which sort of decayed into a rough patch of pasture before ending at the river. The wind was almost calm and already the day was heating up. I poured on full throttle and discovered we were accelerating slowly. The blue water of the river got closer and closer with the airspeed still under the stall. For a moment I was tempted to horse the ground-hugger off, and try and hang on the prop. But the Bonanza was a high performance aircraft and couldn't handle such shenanigans like my old Norseman could. So I cut the power and could almost feel the drop in tension in the cockpit. Kelly was sitting beside me and his normally florid face was a chalky white.

"I'm sorry, I just can't make it," I said.

"Don't apologize, Mac. I can see you know what you're doing. I'll take Brenda and the baggage and use the taxi to get to the airport at Quebec City."

"Well," I replied slowly, "If you don't mind."

"Mind, hell," he shouted, relief evident in his voice, "But will you be able to get off by yourself?"

"Certainly," I replied, and then shut off the engine and soon the heavy luggage and the valuable passengers were in the taxi.

With a smooth application of power the airspeed flicked up to a reasonable speed and I lifted off and selected gear up, then flew back across the barn which marked the end of the strip. I was a bit surprised but pleased to find both my passengers had waited to see how I made out and were waving frantically, both with big smiles.

As I set course I though philosophically that if we'd gone in the river and survived at least I'd have gained some publicity.

The hard way.

When we were all together again there was no problem taking off from the long hardsurfaced runway at Ancienne Lorette. They had decided they wanted to return to Bangor, Maine. The afternoon was perfect and it was a scenic trip across the dark green forests and blue lakes on the direct flight. When we got on the ground it was apparent the press had been following our flight plan. After they disembarked and thanked me very sincerely I saw them both take a deep breath as they faced the endless and somewhat stupid questions the reporters had dreamed up.

On the way back to Montreal that night with the stars twinkling above and my Continental engine running as smooth as a kitten in the cool air which had not a tremor in it I thought that maybe being just an ordinary pilot had a lot to recommend it.

Back at the ranch, which was a rather apt description of the St. John's airport things were moving along at their usual placid pace. Sightseeing took up some of our time, but even with Anson GDZ at Dorval with Loretta for stewardess we weren't making any money. I put ads in the local newspapers that we were offering night flights over Montreal, but even that failed to stir up much business. There were some charters for various lawyers such as Ivan Saborin, a local legal beagle who represented the Johns Manville asbestos people, but not enough to justify keeping a hangar and maintenance staff going.

If we wanted to be successful in the bush we had to fly on floats. But Seven Islands was being serviced by my old rivals Northern Wings and there was a ring of bases north of Montreal. Tom Wheeler had a good service from Lac Ouimet about 70 miles to the northwest, and there was a couple of operators near Lac a La Tortue about 90 miles to the northeast. It was a good place for changing from floats to skis and vice versa, run by a taciturn engineer called Art Jervis.

That left an opportunity to the north, and I managed to fit

the Bonanza into a small field next to the Catholic church at a place called St. Michele des Saints. There was a large lake nearby, suitable for a Norseman and a chance for some charters when the moose hunting season started. The manager of the local hunting lodge which controlled a lot of lakes and preserves to the north was, unusually, a woman. She was a tiny bundle of energy named Carmel Daury who had been known to act as a guide when her customers desired it. Her lodge was well built, situated on a small rise near the village, and was named "Kanamouche". I understood this Indian name to mean "black fly", which meant the name was rather unsuitable, considering what the black flies did to the tender white skins of pilots and hunters. In any case she said she'd welcome a Norseman all for herself sitting on the lake when the moose hunters arrived.

Back in the hangar at St. John's I reviewed what had happened on the aviation scene in Canada, and the more I thought about it the more I became unhappy about being out of the so-called "Main stream".

Canadair was just about out of the DC3 conversion business, which meant we were out of the DC3 ferrying business. They were deep into their North Star programme with deliveries to Trans-Canada Airlines. BOAC had given up on the Avro Tudor and had ordered 20 of the four-engined craft. I was pleased to see that two stalwarts from The Ferry Command, Captain Al Lilly and Flight Engineer "Smokey" Harris were prominent in the demonstrational and instructional work, mainly in CF-TEN-X.

The RCAF had taken their share, including the non-pressurized versions. I guess you're supposed to be deaf already if you are in the service. Then Canadian Pacific's dynamic president Grant McConachie had made Minister Clarence "Dictator" Howe change his "chosen instrument" policy and let CPA fly the Pacific. The price was that CPA had to use Canadian-built aircraft, and so they purchased four North Stars. I had grown up in Edmonton in McConachie's shadow. He was six years older than I, which is a hell of a difference when you're young. I'd handled many messages when he was hauling fish from Peter Pond Lake to Cheecham for the McInnis Fish Company. The roster of pilots assigned to the run made me drool. Maybe I should have gone with the airline after the war after all. There was North Sawle as Chief

Pilot. We'd gone to the University of Alberta together. J. K. "Bud" Potter, Ralph Oakes, R. Leslie, Cec McNeal, Don Patry and a host of copilots I had checked out on Douglas Dakotas or North American B-25s, or both. Maybe I could even earned a super-low seniority number with my service with Mackenzie Air Service and No. 2 AOS (Canadian Airways Training) added together.

But for me the Pacific would always remain an unfulfilled dream.

The most noteworthy event on the 1949 aviation scene in Canada was undoubtedly the flight at Malton airport on 10 August of the Avro C-102 CF-EJD-X "Jetliner". The sleek, speedy four-engined jet had been beaten in its quest to be first passenger jet in the sky by a very slim margin when the de Havilland Comet made its initial flight at Hatfield, on 27 July. Canada was well in the lead in North America as the

Americans had nothing on their drawing boards to compete. Once again Ferry Command types were to the fore with test pilot Don Rogers and Flight Engineer A. W. "Bill" Baker (*my* favourite engineer) at the controls. The future for Avro and Canadian aviation looked bright.

There was one cloud on the horizon a good deal larger than a man's hand. The logical customer, Trans-Canada Airlines, had decided not to honour their commitment to buy a goodly number. They had decided that the substitution of four Rolls-Royce "Derwent" engines in place of the initially-planned two Rolls AJ 65 "Avon" engines made the aircraft uneconomical. It was the British government who pulled the rug out from under Avro when they decided not to release the Avon for civil use.

But both American and European airlines continued to express keen interest for their scheduled routes. Avro went on to demonstrate the use of the aircraft with a series of inter-city flights where the jet cut the times of pro-driven aircraft just about in half. Everyone who flew expressed amazement at the lack of noise and vibration, and for a couple of years the "Jetliner" continued to set records. The Canadian government withdrew its backing and insisted Avro build an all-weather fighter, the CF100. Although 692 CF100s were built they never fired a rocket in anger, and the Jetliner never flew commercially, so in effect they both tied for last place, thanks to political interference.

Avro's famous bomber, the "Lancaster" had been built at Malton during the war under Victory Aircraft Co in the same hangars that saw the construction of the Jetliner and the CF-100. Ferry Command delivered 422 of the world's best bomber to England with zero losses. Naturally all the flight crews were pleased to be assigned a "Lanc" to deliver.

The same couldn't be said of the de Havilland Mosquito, built right next door. There were 1134 of the little "wooden wonders" built and Ferry Command delivered 646, losing no less than 28 aircraft in the process.

We suffered various percentage of losses for the Consolidated Liberators and Catalinas, the Lockheed Lodestars, Hudsons and Ventura/PV1s, the Boeing Flying Fortresses, the North American Mitchells, the Douglas Dakotas and Bostons, the Martin Marauders and Baltimores, and the Handley Page Hampdens we ferried. I suppose the Mosquitoes and the Marauders had the worst record, but only the Lanc was perfect.

Dreams of glories both past and might-have-been drifted away as I realized World-Wide needed other projects to stay out of the red. So I bought various offerings from Crown Assets and then took over all of Wally Siple's stock when he vacated his hangar near mine in order to let Continental Can take over. Siple's biggest unit was the complete fuselage of a DC3, which was mechanically sound, but had all the electrical and hydraulic guts stripped out. It would be a challenge to rebuild it. In fact some people said it was impossible. I didn't agree. If Donald Douglas could do it, why then Donald McVicar could do it too. Besides I now had a good stock of flight surfaces and instruments, so that after a few thousand man-hours of labour it would fly once again. I put out of my mind the thought that after all the expenditure on labour and parts it would *have* to fly. Or I would be dead broke.

The fuselage already owned a rather colourful history. The RCAF had declared it to be scrap, and Siple had towed it from a junk dealer's yard in Ottawa to our airport. On the main highways with a police escort there was no problem, but when they had to use the narrow country roads built for a horse and buggy they encountered plenty of trouble. Many trees had to be trimmed back to allow the eighteen feet centre section free passage. That was a simple saw and axe job, but the narrow iron bridges presented a more formidable problem. Siple's boys solved it by taking a cutting torch and temporarily opening up the steel supporting structure.

It was a typical example of Wally Siple's drive to get things done. They'd stuck the pieces back together with a tack weld. I admired their spirit while at the same time I couldn't help thinking they were lucky to have left their police escort behind.

I had accumulated a good stock of Pratt & Whitney engines, such as the 1830-90Cs which had the supercharger still attached. They would be good for Daks with the heavy gearbox replaced to make them into 1830-92s, and a lot lighter and more trouble-free to boot. In addition the smaller 450 horsepower 985s were appearing by the thousands as light trainers such as the Anson were scrapped out. The going price for one in reasonable shape with logbooks was a mere fifty bucks. They had cost the government at least one hundred times that amount.

So, in my own way, and against my own inclinations I was becoming a parts dealer. Loretta thought it was a great idea, but I still had my heart set on operating some kind of a scheduled airline.

On the other hand, if real junk men get rich by buying stuff by the ton and selling it by the ounce . . .

Chapter 21
Off to the Races Again

The first Monday in September is Labor Day. To some it signals the end of summer, but to Loretta and I it meant the National Air Races were on again. We wouldn't have missed the event for the world as it gave us a chance to meet all our aviation friends. As we flew along the south shore of Lake Erie we could hear the control tower at Cleveland coping with the rush of visitors. And as we got closer we could see the swarm of aircraft looking like bees seeking the honey of their hive. I took FZC into the circuit behind a string of assorted aircraft, got a late landing clearance and finally found a place to park amongst the other thousands of thrill-seekers.

Our main reason for attending the airshow was to see my old Mosquito CF-FZG win the cross-country speed dash of the Bendix, even if it was racing under American colours as N37878 with China National Airlines pilot Don Bussart at the controls. I had put Bussart in touch with Jesse Stallings outfit, Capitol Airways, at Berry Field in Nashville and was anxious to hear how they had installed new engines and additional gas tanks. Over a few "Old Grandads" and branch water Stallings told me the story of how Beech Aircraft at Wichita had made a new engine mount and changed the cowlings on the right side to replace the engine I'd blown when I'd made my shot at the Bendix the year before.

Then his operations manager Mack Rowe had ferried the bird with two dissimilar engines to Nashville. It was apparent that both Rowe brothers had been born natural pilots, as his brother Gene had proven a good pilot with the RAF Ferry Command before he'd lost his life by sticking with a Martin Baltimore with two sick engines so his crew could bale out. I had always thought Gene Rowe should have received an award for his bravery, but civilian pilots didn't get their just deserts in the RAF.

Capitol had installed two standard de Havilland wooden drop tanks on the wings and a huge 550 US gallon bomb bay tank. Now there was plenty of fuel to stay in the air for many hours pulling high power, although the bulged belly made the aircraft look slightly pregnant. It looked much like those which carried the 4,000 pound bombs to keep Hitler and the people of Berlin awake night after night in the latter stage of World War II. There were instances when the same Mosquito made *two* trips to Berlin during one period of darkness. No other aircraft could have done it.

Both engines were now Packard Rolls V1650-7 of 2000+ horsepower, the same as the North American P-51s used. I was a little upset to learn my beautiful paint job of Diana Cream and Stinson Green had been covered over with a coating of dark blue with cream trim. The name "Wooden Wonder" had been painted on the nose, which seemed quite appropriate. When Stallings finished the installation and the modifications to the cowlings he phoned Bussart in Hong Kong to hurry over to test his new speed bird as quickly as he could as time was getting tight. And then the fun began.

Bussart had never flown a Mosquito before, but he climbed in with all the assurance of a very experienced pilot with many thousands of hours. First, on the ground, he found with the props set at 3100, which was 100 RPM, higher then recommended by Rolls, he could pull an inspiring 105 inches of boost on the chocks, although his Wooden Wonder wanted to fly away right then.

A swift climb, which astonished and pleased him, and he was at 30,000 ready for his speed run. When he opened his throttles to full bore he found his true airspeed was just over 510 mph. Surely enough reserve to beat those pesky P-51s! But three minutes into the run he had to throttle back in a hurry as the

Zues fasteners on the right engine were letting the cowling separate from the mount, and even more frightening, the exhaust stacks were burning off. As Stallings told me this I swirled my bourbon around, thinking that if I'd had the same problem at just 68 inches of boost it was no wonder the Mossie had been shedding stacks.

When he landed under reduced power a phone call to de Havilland in Toronto advised him that there wasn't a stack made for the Mosquito which would take that power. So Capitol welders got to work and used my old flanges with heavily beefed up barrels. But they weren't able to duplicate the curve of the Mosquito stacks which took the hot exhaust down and out from the engine's manifold. This was to cause plenty of trouble later. In addition a 12 mph speed advantage was lost, as the factory said the proper stacks gave with a "jet" effect below the wing. But there was no time for further experiments, so Bussart took off for Rosamund Dry Lake bed where he would engage in a "race-horse" start. En route he stopped at St. Louis and Las Vegas to give potential backers in his proposed round-the-world speed attempt a look at his exceptional aircraft.

Stallings looked at his watch and suggested we'd better get up in the grandstand to witness "our" Mosquito zooming across the finish line in first place. The loudspeakers boomed the message that all six entrants had taken off safely, which brought a cheer from the crowd. Then we watched other events, such as an American pilot named Bevo Howard doing acrobatic things with a Bonanza which made me nervous. I'd always believed the aircraft manual specifically prohibited loops and rolls and other things which put a big strain on the airframe. But Howard was a skilled pilot with a delicate touch, so the wings and the airframe of the little V-tailed gem stayed together.

But later Howard put a heavy strain on *my* airframe at a 203R gathering in the Beech hospitality suite. I had left Loretta alone and the handsome blond pilot made a pass at her by telling her she was the most beautiful woman he'd ever seen. He had disappeared by the time I rejoined her, and I became quite irritated when she told me what the smooth Southern gentleman had said. Howard had put me in an uncomfortable box. If I agreed with him Loretta would surely ask me why I hadn't told her *before*, and if I didn't, I was a typical Canadian lout.

At the grandstand the next news about the Bendix racers was that some had passed over Pueblo, Colorado with the Mosquito in the lead. This brought a murmur from the crowd and wide smiles to our faces. Then an hour or so later there was another announcement that some unidentified racers had passed over North Platte, which meant they were only an hour or so away. Instinctively, just as when I was looking for Iceland or some other evasive target, I edged forward on the edge of my hard wooden bench. The race-horse start might have been dangerous but at least the crowd knew that the first aircraft across the finish line was the real winner. When the Mossie flashed across the finish line we'd bask in a bit of reflected glory, which isn't quite up to the real thing, but surely better than no glory at all.

But it wasn't to be. The first aircraft over was a P-51 flown by Joe deBono, the same pilot who had run out of gas almost within sight of the finish line the year before. This year he'd figured his wet-wing fuel load just right and had averaged an impressive 470.136 mph over the 2008 mile course. Eleven minutes later another P-51 showed up in Paul Mantz' red colours with Stanley Reaver at the controls. He was followed closely by another red P-51 flown by "Fish" Salmon who'd decided he'd like a Bendix trophy to add to his collection of closed-course collection.

It seemed like forever before the blue Mosquito appeared. But . . . could it be? The right prop was FEATHERED. Shades of 1948! Stallings and I looked at each other. What had gone wrong? We followed the aircraft around the circuit and were relieved to see the prop unfeather, and soon Bussart was on the ground and safely taxiing to the parking area. It was a disappointing anti-climax, but at least the Mosquito *had* finished, which was more than Lee Cameron in his Martin B26C Marauder and Vince Perron in a Republic AT-12 could say.

When Bussart climbed out of the Mosquito's tiny belly door we made an arrangement to see him later when the heat was off and find out what had happened to him.

"Well," he said, as he hunched his powerful shoulders over a healthy shot of Scotch, very necessary to untighten nerves and lubricate tongues, "it was a race-horse start all right and I was in a 50 foot lane like the rest of the boys. The desert has smooth sand, so we could have started a couple of dozen easily. I was

third to break ground just behind deBono and the Republic."
He rubbed his forehead, "and furthermore I had a slight
hangover."

"No kidding?" I said, thinking of how many delivery flights
I'd commenced early in the morning after a night at the Mount
Royal hotel's Piccadilly Club.

"Yeah, I felt like a sort of farm boy in the middle of all the
high-powered racing guys. We had gathered near the Edwards
Air Force Base at "Pancho" Barnes' Happy Bottom Riding
Club. She was a retired racing pilot herself who loved flying
and the people who did it, and had started this bar on her
ranch. I didn't have any backers like deBono did. Actor Jimmy
Stewart owned his Mustang and he had plenty of clout. I even
heard that an American Airlines DC6 had gone on a high
cruise to find the best winds. Naturally I had to try and pick up
the clear dope like that."

"And naturally you couldn't do that with an empty glass," I
said with a mixture of envy and sarcasm, which I instantly
regretted.

Bussart disregarded my remark, which was what it deserved,
and rushed on as he began to unwind. "When I pulled the
Mossie's gear up not much seemed to be happening and I saw
deBono's gear flick up like he had a CO2 bottle helping out, or
something."

"I remember when I started my Mossie almost got away
from me, and when I finally did get off that gear took about 19
seconds," Stallings said.

"Seemed like longer," Bussart replied, "anyway, there was
deBono climbing out at about 45 degrees, and when I got the
gear tucked away I began to catch up with him. I sure didn't
want to lose him because my compass was acting up and
furthermore he had an ADF, which *I* sure as hell didn't have."
I felt Bussart's eyes boring into mine.

"Well, Jesus, don't blame me," I spluttered. "I took out that
big old heavy military ADF to save weight." I hesitated, as
another thought struck me. "But surely you replaced that
stupid little lowpowered Motorola transceiver I left in the
aircraft?"

"No, I damn well didn't. Not enough time and *I* was trying
to save weight too. I figured to follow deBono at least until I
crossed the Mississippi river, and then I'd just map-read my
way in. I know every inch of that ground like the back of my
hand."

I had nothing to say to this outrageous suggestion, as it was exactly what I'd planned to do the year before. Stallings, always the gentleman nodded and said, "then what happened in the climb?"

"I was in a good position to formate on deBono who had a blue P-51, not red like the other two, when at about 12,000 feet my right engine gave a big belch and coughed up a cloud of greasy-looking black smoke. I pulled off some power and it smoothed out, and I finally got to 30,000 feet, but by that time I'd lost deBono in a deck of cloud."

"I hope my oxygen system worked," I said meekly.

"Well, *no* it didn't. I had to use my jump bottle for a while while I got it all sorted out. Meanwhile the right engine was in and out, coughing and farting, although I was still getting a good true airspeed."

"The announcer said you were ahead at Pueblo," Stallings offered.

"I was," he paused and added "I think we must have had at least a 50 mile tail wind component. That left engine at full bore never even hiccupped. It purred like a kitten. Here's to it." He raised his glass and we followed suit.

I had a sudden thought. "You know that the right engine on our Mossie put us *both* out of the race, but the left one didn't let us down."

"True. Well, my right engine was running out of oil and finally the temperature needle pegged and the pressure gauge went to zero, so I feathered it while I still had a chance. I was just over Burlington, Iowa when I did it, less than an hour out. But when I got here the oil had cooled down so I was able to unfeather."

"I'd say you made a damn good effort," I said, and Stallings nodded. We'd both previously agreed that one Bendix in one Mosquito in one lifetime was sufficient for us.

The next few days the races proceeded at their usual frenetic pace, and I saw the only other Canadian registered aircraft to compete. It was a Spitfire with its distinctive elliptical wing, raced by Flight Lieutenant J. H. G. McArthur as CF-GMZ. He had a big Griffon Rolls engine, but still only placed a disappointing third in the Timmerman closed-course race.

There were closed-course races with everything from the Kendall, my favourite oil company because they'd donated the oil for FZG, to the Sohio which was won by Bill Odum in a P51, the dark green beautiful "Beguine", which I had seen when it was being converted in Houston by J. D. Reed. The musical notes on its side were unique. Meanwhile the military was doing its share. Five Republic USAF F-84E, Thunderjets had flown their version of the Bendix with four finishing after a fuel stop with averages of well over 500 mph. The fifth unlucky fellow had run out of fuel but managed to land safely at Peoria, Ill. The USAF also had their own jet Thompson race with three F-86 Sabres hitting very close to the speed of sound as they flashed around a fifteen mile circular course. The United States Navy flew their own unique race with four McDonnell F2H-1 Banshees racing to Cleveland from the aircraft Carrier *Midway* out in the Atlantic Ocean near New York. Lieutenant Laird beat his shipmates with a speed of 549 mph, more correctly expressed as about 484 knots for naval people.

The prestige race was the Thompson with no limitations on the horses the engines could produce. Odum was there in the P-51, now owned by Jackie Cochrane. Some said he shouldn't have been there, because although he was an excellent pilot with long-distance records such as his 5,000 mile flight in a Bonanza from Hawaii to Teterboro, New Jersey, and his round-the-world record of 73 hours five minutes in a Douglas

A-26, he'd had little experience in closed-course racing. In racing circles it was a generally held opinion that a throttle-bending pylon-shaver should have aerobatic ability, and to have been a fighter jock as well.

Cook Cleland an ex-USN fighter pilot, was there with his heavy but powerful Goodyear F2G-1 *Corsair* and its Pratt & Whitney R-4360 engine which he intended to push to more than 4,000 horsepower. He'd clipped no less than four more feet off his wings to bring down the span to almost the same as my Bonanza's of just 33 feet, and had added wing tip plates guaranteed to increase roll rate and reduce vortex. This year he had his own secret high-octane fuel, still claiming that the reason he'd lost the '48 Thompson when his engine had blown up was due to Shell's high-octane fuel. There were two other Corsairs, a lone Bell King Cobra and five more Mustangs who all took off in a thrilling race-horse start. They all flew very low to avoid missing a pylon which would have disqualified the unfortunate pilot. Odum, who had been seventh to break ground had soon advanced to third place in his speedy craft. Then he over-turned No 2 pylon, and as he turned back he got into a high-speed stall and flipped over on his back. He failed to recover and hit the ground and exploded in a ball of fire, taking a woman and her baby with him to a fiery death. And so it was that the doubters were proven right.

The race announcer made no mention of the accident, but Loretta and I were sitting with Walter Beech, and we all saw the pyre of black smoke. We were horrified. Beech just put his head down without saying anything. After all, he'd been in many an air race himself. Later, he said with great feeling, that a fatal accident to a well-known pilot like Odum would cast a pall over the whole racing scene. It turned out he was right! Although the Corsairs finished 1, 2, 3, there would be no more air races at Cleveland, although they made a comeback at other locations with less habitation on their pylon-studded courses.

Our flight back to our isolated hangar at St. John's was a big let-down, an anti-climax, after Cleveland. It looked like a long, cold winter with not much money coming in. I'd already figured out the money Bussart had paid me for my Mosquito had just about brought me even with my race expenses, and most of *that* money had gone in wages and hangar rent. So

Russ Holmes, VE3KT, and I were overhauling my ham antennas before the snows came. It looked as if amateur contacts would be a big feature in breaking the monotony until spring. I had checked Holmes out on floats on one of our Norseman, CF-GIA. He'd done extremely well, but it looked as if charters for him would be few and far between. I reflected that it was a shame his proven ability as a radio-navigator wouldn't be put to proper use. After all, a man who'd flown with Captain Bill Vanderkloot in the famous black Liberator *Commando* when they'd taken Winston Churchill to Moscow among other places should have found a better future in aviation. He had a marvellous personality, always cheery, and wore his rare Member of the British Empire ribbon with pride. But he was now too old for the airlines to consider. They were getting rid of their own radio operators and navigators anyway as fast as they could when new navigational aids came into use.

Later I had found out that Bussart had flown the Mosquito to St. Louis, his home town, where he now hoped to start his attempt to beat Odum's round-the-world speed record. He'd originally planned to flash across the finish line at Cleveland and then continue on to New York thus gaining a new transcontinental speed record. His red-hot right engine had squelched *that* plan, but he was still determined to make his try. He would install new exhaust stacks which wouldn't pour super-heated exhaust fumes into his oil coolers. He'd figured out that the reason the left engine was running cool while the right one was burning up was due to the rotation of the propellers. The right prop drove hot exhaust directly into the right oil cooler, and it was especially critical at the high power he was pulling.

He told the press that although he was looking for a sponsor he'd fund the attempt by himself if he had to. Then he jumped on an airline and two short days later was back on his flying job in the Orient.

But when Brayton Flying Service did their inspection they found quite a few things wrong with the aircraft. The most serious was the fact that two of the bolts which attached the empennage to the fuselage had pulled loose. When I heard this I remembered that numerous Mossies had disappeared without a trace while being ferried by the Ferry Command. The Brayton mechanics thought it might have been due to the strain of high-speed dashes or possibly vibration from the right engine. I had my own theory. Captain King Parker had been a test pilot on the Mosquitoes at London, and he'd told me that a lot of fuselages had been stored outside one winter until other components caught up with their production line. And further that they hadn't been very well protected from the weather. Result could have been rotten wood. I gulped as I remembered *my* high-speed 465 mph dash across Dorval. Maybe Bussart and I now knew we were a lot luckier than we would ever have realized without that teardown.

Late one afternoon when the frost was on the pumpkin Holmes and I were just climbing down from the hangar roof where we'd overhauled my beam, a "Signal Squirter" with good gain had made a lot of long distance DX contacts possible, when the phone rang. The operator asked for the person in charge and I said gaily that I was the guilty one. Then I wished I hadn't been quite such a smart-ass.

Because the cool voice at the other end of the landline was obviously very sincere. How much did we want to ferry a DC3 with photographic gear and long-range tanks from Philadelphia to jolly old England? Being a confirmed optimist I had the mileage and price at my fingertips, and the voice warmed up and accepted my firm price. Please pick up the aircraft ASAP. Half payment before departure and remainder on delivery. I was smiling as I hung up. What a break!

Holmes was now wearing a grin which split his face and could have caused permanent disfigurement, especially when he learned he would be part of the crew. I liked to have him aboard, one reason being he didn't smoke, and I hated the stink of burning tobacco. Another good reason was that he only drank cokes, an advantage in case I over-indulged in some dingy bar in some far-away hostile country.

He rubbed his hands in anticipation and said: "I'll dust off my Mark IX sextant, get the maps, and the Air Almanac and AN tables." He trotted off, humming happily. I knew I wouldn't have to remind him to check the new transatlantic radio frequencies.

I felt just as happy as he. *Oh Boy!* I said to myself, a Dakota of all things . . . Money for old rope as they used to say in the RAF.

Of course the delivery flight didn't work out quite as smoothly as I'd hoped, but that's another story.